A Pelican Book

The Struggle for the Middle East

Walter Laqueur is Director of the Institute of Contemporary
History and of the Wiener Library, London. He is Professor
of Politics and the History of Ideas at Brandeis University,
and a Professor in the University of Reading. His previous
publications include *Communism and Nationalism in the
Middle East*, *The Middle East in Transition*, *The Soviet
Union and the Middle East* and *The Road to War*, 1967–8.

The Struggle
for the
Middle East

The Soviet Union and the
Middle East 1958–70

Walter Laqueur

Penguin Books

Penguin Books Ltd, Harmondsworth,
Middlesex, England
Penguin Books Inc., 7110 Ambassador Road,
Baltimore, Maryland 21207, U.S.A.
Penguin Books Australia Ltd, Ringwood,
Victoria, Australia

First published in the U.S.A. by Macmillan 1969
Revised edition published in Pelican Books 1972
Copyright © Routledge & Kegan Paul, 1969, 1972

Made and printed in Great Britain by
Hazell Watson & Viney Ltd,
Aylesbury, Bucks
Set in Monotype Times

Contents

Preface to the Pelican Edition

Some fifteen years ago *Communism and Nationalism in the Middle East* and *The Soviet Union and the Middle East* were published; I am only too aware now of the shortcomings of these books, the facts I should have known but didn't, the development I misjudged, the undue emphasis I put on certain movements which appear quite insignificant in retrospect and the fact that I neglected others which were to be of far greater importance. My basic thesis I think was right, namely that the Soviet Union was bound to play a much more important role in the Middle East in the years to come. This sounds now trite, but, strangely enough, it was widely disputed at the time.

The other day I reread the reviews published at the time. The reviewer of the (London) *Times* said I was quite mistaken in assuming that great changes were likely to happen in the Middle East; there was always a great deal of sound and fury in the Arab world, but in the last resort 'they moved seldom far from their moorings'. I had expressed in my books doubts about the future of the Hashemites and Nuri Said in Iraq, which provoked immediate contradiction both on the left and on the right. Sir David Kelly, a distinguished former British diplomat and an oracle of the Conservatives, wrote in the *Sunday Times* that there was an atmosphere of 'confidence and realism' in Iraq, while Richard Crossman, the future Labour minister, wrote in the *New Statesman* in the same context that Mr Laqueur's 'cocksure predictions are unconvincing'. Two years later the mutilated bodies of Nuri Said and Abdulillah were dragged through the streets of Baghdad. Walter Lippman, the most prestigious American political commentator of his time, wrote that the lesson to be learned from my book was that the West should establish closer cultural relations with the Arab intellectuals. The reaction of the Soviet and the Egyptian press was curious: a Mr Vasiliev wrote in *Literaturnaia Gasetta* that it was a deliberate calumny to argue that the Soviet Union was bound to get politically, let alone militarily, involved in Egypt; its interest was purely platonic: it sympathized with the Arab national movement and that was all there was to it. The Egyptian newspapers maintained that it was ridiculous to assume that relations between Egypt and the Soviet Union could conceivably lead to anything beyond normal economic and political relation between sovereign states.

I mention all this not to show how wrong these critics were, all of them seasoned political observers. One-upmanship is not much fun fifteen years after the event. I quoted them to show that it is exceedingly difficult to form a correct opinion of political trends without the benefit of hindsight. The present study (*The Struggle for the Middle East*) was written in late 1968 and during the first half of 1969; only two years have passed since then, and yet how much has occurred, and what further changes are likely to have happened by the time this book reaches the reader! To write a new preface in these conditions is, to put it cautiously, a risky business. As these lines are written, the Jordan civil war has entered a subacute phase, which reminds me that I did not pay sufficient attention to the role played by the Palestinians in the Middle East imbroglio. I did not believe then, and I do not assume now, that the Fatah, Dr Habbash's, and Naif Hawatme's groups are likely to be a factor of decisive military importance as far as Israel is concerned. But it should have been clear already in 1968–9 that in view of the unstable political situation inside Jordan and perhaps elsewhere too these groups and their activities might well affect domestic politics in certain Arab countries. I did say 'There is growing bitterness and frustration, and as the destruction of Israel does not seem near, [they] are likely to turn sooner or later against the Arab governments of the day which have been unable to fulfil most of their promises'. There is some similarity, as far as their historical function is concerned, between the Palestinian para-military organizations and the terrorist groups which existed on the Balkan before and after the First World War. IMRO, the movement for Macedonian independence, did not attain its aim but it certainly caused a great deal of trouble in Bulgarian politics; and the shots in Sarajevo in 1914 of Gavrilo Prinkip, the young Serbian nationalist, triggered off the First World War.

It has been the great achievement of the Arab guerrilla movement (still internally divided) to give fresh hope to the Palestinian refugees at a time when all seemed lost. It has made an impact, albeit short-lived, on world public opinion through its spectacular exploits such as the hijacking of civilian planes belonging to third nations. But militarily it has been a failure: neither the hijacking nor the hit-and-run raids across the borders have made any impression on Israel. Another in-built weakness is the absence of a clear and consistent programme. They try not to repeat Shukairy's mistakes: 'Throw the Jews into the sea.' (Poor Shukairy has to serve as a scapegoat for what, after all, everyone was saying at the time.) But old habits die hard and some apparently persist for ever. They still insist on the destruction of the Zionist state and society and they demand the establishment of a democratic, secular Palestinian state. They are willing to accord to the Jewish citizens of such a state cultural and religious rights: the Jews will be permitted to pray in their synagogues and to be buried in their own cemeteries. But since in their view the Israelis are not a people or a nation they should not be given equal national rights. The character of the future Palestinian state as they envisage it would be therefore Arab, not bi-national. Such a prospect is unlikely to appeal even to those Israelis who think that the Palestinians have been wronged and that amends should be made to them.

During the last two years Turkey has been shaken by internal ferment, and a dangerous polarization between left and right has taken place. The Ba'ath dictatorships in Damascus and Baghdad are still in power and they are still not overly fond of each other. Their survival shows that military regimes have little to fear from their civilian opponents as long as the majors and colonels stick together. But they never stick together for long; there have been important changes in both capitals and there will be more to come. Egypt has recovered more quickly and more fully from the defeat than anyone would have expected in June 1967. Its position has been strengthened by the emergence of regimes in Sudan and Libya which are in sympathy with the present Egyptian leadership. New efforts have been made to achieve a greater degree of Arab unity, but whether this well extend to sharing Libya's oil revenues is not yet certain.

Egypt owes its recovery to the massive military and economic help provided by the Soviet Union. The number of Soviet experts and military personnel has trebled or quadrupled; Soviet pilots are reported to fly operational missions and Soviet missiles have been deployed along the Suez Canal as well as in other parts of Egypt. Nasser's sudden death was a heavy blow; the whole Arab world, even his critics and enemies, had somehow become accustomed to his presence. But again, the recovery from the shock was quicker than anticipated, even though Egypt will not easily regain its predominant role in the Arab world. The 'collective leadership' which inherited Nasser has not lasted long but decisive changes in Egypt's domestic and foreign policy seem unlikely for the time being.

The Soviet Union has decided to become involved in the Arab-Israeli conflict to a much larger degree than generally anticipated even two years ago. What are its aims and to what limits are the Soviet leaders willing to go? Some observers have expressed the view that the Soviet Union has a vital interest in reopening the Suez Canal; as the Russian fleet in the Indian Ocean is strengthened and as new naval bases have been acquired in this area the lines of communication between these units and the Black Sea ports, as well as the Soviet fleet in the Mediterranean, are of considerable strategic importance. But this interest, real as it is, is hardly sufficient to explain Soviet military involvement in Egypt, which can be understood only against the background of the wider Soviet political interests in the Middle East. There is no particular urgency to reopen the canal from the Soviet point of view; the over-riding aim is to strengthen the Soviet presence to make the area a sphere of Soviet influence. Military and naval bases, spheres of influence – all this sounds very old-fashioned, very much in the nineteenth-century imperialist tradition. But Soviet foreign policy is old-fashioned. It does not think in terms of 'proletarian revolution'; it knows that even political forces ideologically much nearer to Soviet Communism than the present military rulers of Egypt, Syria and Iraq cannot be wholly trusted. It was perhaps my main mistake in 1955 to attribute too much significance to ideological factors. I assumed that Soviet ideology would exert powerful influence on the radical intelligentsia and the military in the Arab world. Fifteen years later we are all wiser men. The Communist bloc is no longer monolithic; at a time when Soviet industry is in danger of being overtaken by the Japanese, the Soviet Union is no longer even a model for underdeveloped countries in the process of rapid industrialization. Politically it has ceased to be a centre of attraction; in as much as radical movements of the left are emerging in the world they are looking for their inspiration elsewhere. They may still want Soviet loans and Soviet arms but they are not particularly interested in Soviet ideology.

But the Soviet Union is still one of the two super-powers, and geographically nearer to the Middle East than the United States is. During the last years it has caught up with America as far as intercontinental ballistic missiles (ICBM) and the means of delivery are concerned. In some respects it may have overtaken America, not that it greatly matters once the stage of 'overkill' has been reached. As a result, the Soviet leaders, as I predicted, are showing signs of willingness to take bigger risks than before. Their basic aim remains to remove the Americans from Western Europe and the Middle East: the 'Finlandization' of the area. This policy is less likely to succeed in Western Europe than in the Middle East, not only in view of the intrinsic strength of countries such as Britain, France and West Germany, but mainly because these countries agree at least in principle on the necessity of a common defence system. The Middle East, intrinsically weak, is moreover torn by internal conflict and it seems, therefore, that it is precisely in this region that the Soviet leadership will take bigger risks than anywhere else. So far, since the end of the war, the countries of the Middle East owe their independence to the global balance of power. If the balance of power should be radically upset the area is likely to become a Soviet sphere of influence with all that this implies. The Arab governments continue to act as if they were totally unaware of the danger to their independence, as if the Israeli menace was more formidable than the dangers of domination by a super-power. Anyway, they argue, 'we have no alternative . . .' The situation reminds one of Eastern Europe between the two world wars with its disputes, and the readiness to fight to the end over such vital issues as Teschen, Vilna, Transylvania or Macedonia. Once the Germans, and later the Russians, had established their rule in Eastern Europe, no one cared any more how the frontiers were running: it no longer mattered greatly whether one lived on one side of the border or the other. The Arab governments in all probability still take the global balance of power for granted; if so there will be a rude awakening one day and it may be too late to do anything about it. For while the American administration does not want the Middle East to become a Soviet sphere of influence, there is a growing number of Americans who believe that their country is overcommitted in world politics and who wish to concentrate their efforts on the domestic front.

This trend towards neo-isolationism has been a source of encouragement to the Soviet Union; it used to underrate it in the past and seems to exaggerate its extent now. There are obvious limits to Soviet risk taking: it is difficult at one and the same time to call a European security conference and to become engaged in a Middle Eastern war. Moscow cannot hope to induce the Americans to reduce armaments while simultaneously escalating the Arab-Israeli conflict. It can try, but the attempt is likely to fail. The Soviet leaders know that even if America is at present undergoing a crisis it is still very strong militarily. They are aware that American action and reaction is not always predictable and that if they push the Americans too hard they may find themselves in a direct confrontation they did not want to provoke – at least not yet. The Soviet leaders, in other words, will go on probing American weaknesses, ready to beat a partial retreat if the risks should be too high. The Soviet Union wants controlled tension all the time in the Middle East: not too little and not too much of it. But it is not easy to control the situation since so many factors are involved over which neither the Russians nor the Americans have control. Hence the Soviet acceptance of the Rogers plan and simultaneously the deployment of many further missiles on Egyptian territory. American diplomacy has tried hard to induce the Soviet leadership to help to defuse a dangerous situation, to find some common ground, to limit arms shipments if it was impossible to agree on positive steps. These efforts were, of course, bound to fail since they were based on unrealistic assumptions such as the belief that Russia was more interested in peace in the Middle East than in strengthening its own position.

Israel has entered a period fraught with grave dangers. Future historians will no doubt devote much attention to the question to what extent Israel helped to bring about the new stage in Soviet military involvement by the decision in early 1970 to raid military installations inside Egypt. My own feeling is that the decision was mistaken from the Israeli point of view but that Soviet involvement would probably have reached this stage anyhow at some later date. But this is speculation; there may never be a conclusive answer. The euphoria prevailing in Israel after the Six Day War was followed by a long period of inaction and then, in April–May 1970, by a period of sudden and occasionally even exaggerated alarm. If the optimism of 1967–69 was unwarranted there was no reason for undue pessimism in 1971.

During the two years since this study was written the situation of Jews in the Soviet Union and Eastern Europe has deteriorated. This development may well have been inevitable in as much as the general trend in the Communist world is away from 'proletarian internationalism' to a nationalist brand of socialism. It seems to provide a belated justification of the Zionist case, for if, as the Communists argued, antisemitism was bound to disappear with the capitalist order, how are we to explain the expulsion of Jews from Poland? It is doubtful whether ten years ago, given the chance to emigrate, a significant part of Soviet Jewry would have opted for Israel. There are indications that the situation has now changed: the Soviet leadership by engaging in a policy of 'Antizionism' had made all Soviet Jews suspect and thus given Zionism a new and unexpected lease of life.

Some of the critics of the present book maintain that I tended to belittle the intrinsic significance of the Middle East in world affairs. A discussion on these lines would be more than a little academic. I readily agree that it is futile to consider the Middle East as it were in in isolation from world politics. I simply wanted to stress that the Soviet advance now gives it a significance it would not otherwise have. This is not to belittle the dangers: Sarajevo was not exactly the centre of the world in 1914, nor was Danzig in 1939. But even so events in these distant places triggered off two world wars. If Soviet involvement in the Middle East should gather further momentum it is difficult to see how a showdown with the United States can be prevented.

But it would be against human nature as well as against some of the evidence to conclude this preface on a note of unmitigated gloom. There have been some encouraging developments in the Arab world and in Israel. The Palestinians are gradually realizing that they cannot in the last resort rely on the Arab governments all of whom pursue political aims of their own which are by no means identical with the Palestinian Arab cause. They are a little more willing than before to accept the existence of Israel and inside the Jewish state the conviction has been growing that far-reaching concessions could and should be made in a peace settlement. Once the Israelis and the Palestinians begin to talk, the Arab governments will not stand in their way – the Palestinian issue has preoccupied them for too long and sapped too much of their resources. It may well be that the climate is not yet ripe and that more death and destruction will be needed to create that minimum of psychological readiness necessary for a compromise. Eventually, of course there is bound to be a compromise for the only alternative to coexistence is mutual extinction.

London, 1971

1
Introduction

The present study is devoted to a review of Soviet policy in the Middle East during the last decade and to an analysis of its future prospects. It also deals with developments inside the various Middle East countries in so far as they may influence the outcome of the struggle for the Middle East. It is in some ways a sequel to *Communism and Nationalism in the Middle East* (1956), and *The Soviet Union and the Middle East* (1959). The shortcomings of these earlier books were, and are, obvious to the author. They were written at a time when little source material was available, and when it was just beginning to be realized that the topic itself was a legitimate subject of study. The general outlines of Soviet policy in the Middle East could be only dimly recognized at the time. Since then the situation has changed radically; as far as source material is concerned, the danger now is not of drought, but of drowning, and many new problems have appeared. In the nineteen-fifties Soviet relations with Iran and Turkey were much less complex than they are today; Soviet interest in Middle East oil barely existed, and there was virtually no Soviet interest in Cyprus, Sudan, Algeria, South Arabia, and a great many other places. There was no Soviet fleet in the Mediterranean and, on a different level, hardly any Soviet writings on the Middle East; but as the area assumed growing importance in Soviet policy, so has the volume of literature expanded. I was tempted at times to bring my two earlier books up to date, but refrained for a number of good reasons. They summarized the early stages (the 'prehistory') of the Soviet drive towards the Middle East. It was not simply a question of continuing the historical narrative and adding fresh material; the whole perspective has changed. I believe that the basic assumption of these two earlier books was correct: the Soviet drive towards the Middle East was gathering momentum in the fifties; given the weakness of the area as a whole and the domestic situation in the Arab world, the Soviet Union had an excellent chance greatly to strengthen its position in the Middle East and perhaps even to become the dominant power there. These assumptions were by no means generally shared fifteen or even ten years ago. Soviet pre-occupation with Europe was taken too much for granted, while the prospects of Nasserist Pan-Arabism as an independent political force were overrated.

It was difficult to foresee in the middle fifties exactly what form the radicalization in the Middle East would take in the years to come. The communist camp was still united; no rival centres had arisen to shake the monolithic bloc. We are much wiser now. During this past decade the importance of communist parties has on the whole decreased; there has been a far-reaching *rapprochement* between a number of Middle East countries and the Soviet Union, but it has largely by-passed the official communist parties in the area. Military dictators and new political groups (such as the neo-Ba'th) have been of far greater significance in this context. Even in the nineteen-fifties there were reasons to doubt the relevance of the doctrinal discussions in Soviet writings as a key to the understanding of Soviet policy in the Middle East. These books and articles were of some interest because they helped to explain shifts in policy; occasionally they reflected internal dissension. Today I feel even more sceptical about their relevance, for they shed very little light on the real mainsprings of Soviet policy. The interests of Russia as a great power have played a role in Soviet foreign policy from its earliest days, and this was, of course, inevitable. As the years passed their specific weight has steadily increased and that of Leninist ideology has steadily declined. It has declined, but not altogether disappeared. Official Soviet doctrine still survives almost in its pristine state, but the discrepancy between theory and practice is still growing, and it is now very difficult to ascertain to what extent even those making the doctrinal pronouncements believe in them. The Soviet political and military leaders are, of course, communists, and any attempt to explain their foreign-policy decisions solely on the basis of traditional power politics is ultimately futile. But what does it mean to be a leading communist in the Soviet Union today? The writings of Marx and Lenin alone are unlikely to provide a satisfactory answer. For this reason I have dealt with doctrinal disputations in this book only in passing; it is still a legitimate subject of study, though no longer a very important one. I have had to neglect some other aspects of Soviet policies in the Middle East, and of Middle East reactions, in order to concentrate on the central issues. To treat the issues touched upon fully and exhaustively, each chapter would have to be expanded into a separate monograph.

Key sections of this book were written during the Czechoslovak crisis of 1968. All history is contemporary history, and even Western historians of ancient Rome and Greece are known to have been influenced by the impact of Hitler, Mussolini, and Stalin. There was an almost overwhelming temptation to deal with the prospects of the Middle East in the light of the Czech crisis, a temptation which had to be resisted. The historian knows from his own and others' experience that the danger of distortion is greatest at a time of crisis; that events which loom very large at the moment of writing may appear in a different perspective a few years later. He knows about the cunning of reason: a great triumph may be the prelude to disaster and a defeat may eventually turn into victory. Lastly, he knows that the future is *a priori* unpredictable, that there is no inevitability about it, and that even highly probable events may never come to pass. Nevertheless, with all these reservations, a major crisis such as the invasion of Czechoslovakia has its advantages for the historian: all the quasi-problems suddenly disappear and his perception of the essential issues is sharpened. An event of this kind furnishes a sudden and usually brutal test: it clears away the cobwebs of wishful thinking, of irrelevant theories and spurious explanations. It shows that at a time of decision it is power that matters and the firm resolve to use it.

The Soviet leaders have frequently stressed that the area adjacent to their southern borders is of vital concern to them. They regard it as their legitimate sphere of influence. But the Middle East is not Eastern Europe, and the Soviet capacity to intervene there will probably be limited for a number of years to come.

Soviet ties, even with Egypt and Syria, are not nearly so close as those with Poland and East Germany, but Moscow has no intention of giving up the bridgehead established in the Middle East at great cost and with great patience over many years. On the contrary, it will try to consolidate and extend it, and for this reason the critical years are still ahead. The Middle East is not intrinsically one of the most important areas in world affairs. It has long ceased to be a crossroads, its military bases are no longer needed, it has no important natural resources other than oil, but there is no lack of oil elsewhere in the world. And yet, in view of the delicate balance of global power, the Soviet Union attributes great importance to the Middle East, and its presence there may have far-reaching political effects in Europe as well as Africa and Asia. From the Soviet point of view, the area has a great attraction, both because of its nearness to its southern frontier and because of its internal instability. Among Soviet foreign political priorities the Middle East now takes a high place, not because it is intrinsically important, but because it is so weak. In many ways it seems to present the line of least resistance: in the Far East there is the growing threat of China; in Europe any advance beyond the 'red line' would mean a clash with NATO and the Americans. But the place of the Middle East in the contest between the powers has never been clearly defined, and it is therefore likely to remain one of the main danger zones in world politics in the years to come.

I have received assistance and advice from many institutions and individuals. I am greatly indebted to Dr David Abshire and Professor Alvin Cottrell of the Centre for Strategic and International Studies of Georgetown University, who first suggested this study to me and made it possible for me to write it. I owe much to Mr Zeev Ben Shlomo, who helped me in my research, to Miss Diana Langton, my secretary, and to Mrs C. Wichmann and Mr E. Kahn of the Middle East Documents section at the Institute of Contemporary History (Wiener Library) in London, who within a short period have made this a collection of great help to the student of contemporary history.

London/Boston, Mass.
June 1969

2
Prelude: 1945–58

Russian interest in the Ottoman Empire, its involvement in what was then the Eastern Question, antedates the revolutions of 1917 by about 150 years. In Tsarist foreign policy, throughout the nineteenth century, in the ideology of Slavophils and Panslavists the question of Constantinople and the Straits played a central, almost mystical, role. Turkey was about to disintegrate, the Hagia Sofia was at last to return to its rightful owners. The Russian mission in the Near East was the dynamic centre of Russian history; there its manifest destiny would be fulfilled. But the first world war brought not only the demise of the Ottoman Empire, it also caused the downfall of the Romanovs. With the Bolshevik revolution such imperialist ambitions were solemnly forsworn: communist Russia, the pioneer of world revolution, was to be also the friend and ally of all national liberation movements. The industrialized countries of Central and Western Europe were expected to play the leading role in the coming stage of the world revolution; the hopes of Marx and Engels had been centred in the West, and the eyes of Lenin and Trotsky were turned there too, although they did not entirely neglect Asia and the East. About a decade before the revolution they had begun to realize that there was a revolutionary potential in the East, that the colonies and the semi-colonial countries of Asia would not forever remain quiescent. Bolshevism tried to assist them in their fight; the Congress of Baku, calling on the toilers of the East to rise against foreign imperialists as well as against native capitalists and landlords, was the first important milestone in this struggle. The Soviet leaders followed with a great deal of sympathy the fight of the Turks under Kemal and the national movements in

Persia and Afghanistan. Not much attention was paid at that time to events in the Arab world. By the standards of those days, the Arabs were a faraway people; most of their countries were not yet even semi-independent. Nor was there a great deal of interest in Zionism, which at that time had just acquired a Jewish national home. Zionism, in the communist view, was an anachronistic, reactionary movement. The salvation of the downtrodden Jewish masses in the east-European ghettos would come with the victory of world revolution. The Jewish question could not be solved in a distant country under the protection of British bayonets. Moscow and the Communist International also attacked the pan-movements of the day – Panislamism, Panarabism, Panturkism; these too were condemned as reactionary in character. Support for 'progressive' movements in the Near East involved Soviet Russia from the beginning in political and doctrinal contradictions, since they could not be expected to embrace Bolshevik ideology and practice lock, stock and barrel. Islam, for instance, still had deep roots in the East, and a frontal attack against it was obviously out of the question, despite communism's unalterable opposition to religion in general.

The existence of Communist parties outside Russia was for the Soviets, needless to say, a matter of gratification, and in theory their interests could never collide with those of the Soviet state. In practice, alas, clashes occurred all too frequently from the very outset. The policies of Kemal Atatürk, the champion of the Turkish struggle for independence, were warmly supported in Russia, and close relations were established between Ankara and Moscow. But the political and military alliance with Russia did not prevent Kemal from suppressing the Turkish communists and from having their leaders assassinated, once they had challenged his rule. Their fate was deeply deplored in Moscow, but support for Kemal was not discontinued. Russia could not afford to be particular in its choice of allies, nor could it ignore the immediate interests of the Soviet state. This kind of dilemma was to recur many times.

With the ebbing of the first revolutionary wave after the first world war, conditions in Europe and Asia became more stable and the hopes for an early victory of the national liberation movements, let alone of the Communist parties, evaporated. Soviet relations with Turkey and Persia remained fairly close; there were no other independent states in the Near East at the time with whom Moscow could directly deal. Stalin prevailed in the struggle for power in the Kremlin; the construction of 'socialism in one country' got under way, and foreign policy was relegated to second place. Revolution, it was announced, was not for export. The Comintern underwent strange contortions. After 1928, in response to a new world crisis, it preached an ultra-revolutionary course of action, refusing to cooperate even with the left-wing leaders of the national movements in the East. 'National reformism' was now anathema; Kemalism was re-examined and found wanting. Only the Communist parties could be relied upon, but they, too, had to be severely purged before becoming truly Bolshevik in character. Followed to its logical conclusion, such a policy would have brought about a complete rupture between the Soviet Union and the national movements in the East. But extreme radicalism did not prevail for very long; by the middle nineteen-thirties the orientation was again towards a united front of all anti-imperialist forces. There was less warmth now in the relations with Turkey and Persia than in the early years after the revolution, but this was by no means the fault of the Russians alone, for with the changes on the international scene Turkey and Persia needed Russia less than in the early twenties. The Soviet Union, on the other hand, was deeply absorbed in its domestic problems, while in its foreign policy Europe all but monopolized its attention as both a promise and a danger.

During the first two decades after the revolution and almost up to the end of the second world war, the Near East, once a central preoccupation of Russian statesmen, did not figure high on the list of Soviet priorities. Seen in retrospect, it does not appear that the Soviet Union missed many chances in this part of the world. Of course, the narrow, sectarian approach of the Communist International towards potential allies was not very promising. It was unlikely that anti-religious slogans, with heavy emphasis on the class struggle and on the leading role of the industrial proletariat, would go down well in Turkey, Persia, and the Arab world. But it is doubtful whether Russia would have made much more headway even if Soviet policy had been more flexible and Comintern slogans less sectarian. A revolutionary situation did not yet exist in the Middle East; Britain and France, though facing some unrest, were still firmly in the saddle. Radical Arabs, Turks, and Persians riding the wave of the future were far more likely to opt for Nazi Germany and fascist Italy than for Soviet communism.

From time to time the Middle East cropped up in diplomatic negotiations. When Molotov, then Soviet Foreign Minister, saw Hitler and Ribbentrop in Berlin in November 1940, the 'general direction of the Persian Gulf' was mentioned as one of the obvious spheres of Soviet interest to be discussed at some future stage. But Hitler had different plans; during the first two years of fighting on the Eastern front the survival of the Soviet state was at stake, and Russia's Middle East interests were not energetically pursued. In cooperation with the Western allies, Soviet troops occupied part of Iran, and at the end of the war showed great reluctance to withdraw. But Iran had been occupied primarily to prevent a pro-Axis coup, as had happened earlier in Iraq, and to safeguard the delivery of Allied lend-lease supplies at a time when many other routes had been cut. Turkey was neutral during the war, but as the tide turned the Soviet Union became more and more critical of Turkish policy. Towards the end of the war the demand was pressed both for control over the Straits and for the surrender of certain Turkish provinces. While Russia's main concerns were still focused on Europe, and while the political and military problems of absorbing Eastern Europe preoccupied Soviet leaders, interest in the Middle East also reawakened. The claim for a Soviet mandate over Tripolitania made at the Potsdam Conference was perhaps not meant very seriously and was not pressed strongly when it encountered resistance. But it was indicative of the growing awareness in Moscow that the Soviet Union was now a global power and that there were many new opportunities to strengthen its position in various parts of the world.

The Palestine issue came to the fore as the war ended. Almost six million Jews had been killed in Nazi-occupied Europe, and the struggle of the Jewish community in Palestine for national independence came to preoccupy first the powers, and later the United Nations. Soviet policy, which had been violently hostile to Zionism, was modified and favoured the establishment of a Jewish as well as an Arab state in Palestine. This pro-Israeli phase in Soviet policy did not endure, but while it lasted it was an important factor in the creation of the Jewish state.

Soon after the war the Arab world entered a period of prolonged crisis. Syria and Lebanon attained independence, and anti-British feeling in Egypt and Iraq became far more intense than ever before. With the downfall of the Axis, many erstwhile supporters of fascism came to regard the Soviet Union as a potential ally in the struggle against the West. They were not necessarily willing to embrace the basic tenets of Marxist-Leninist doctrine, but there was considerable sympathy for an ideology favouring radical change – quite apart from the growing prestige of the Soviet Union as the main champion of anti-Westernism. As the war ended there was in the Middle East a growing reservoir of goodwill towards the Soviet Union. At first, Soviet policy made little use of these new opportunities. The intransigence of the Communist parties at the height of the cold war made it all but impossible for them to collaborate with other parties. Soviet political thinking contemplated a sharpening of the global conflict; the independence achieved by many Asian and African countries after the second world war was 'sham', not real, the leaders of these countries, the 'petty-*bourgeois* nationalists', were potential traitors – if they had not already betrayed the national interest. Stalin was firmly convinced that in between the Soviet bloc and the camp headed by the United States there was no middle ground; the slogans of positive neutralism, of a 'zone of peace', let alone of peaceful coexistence, were still in the future. In the view of the Soviet leaders communism could make decisive progress only in countries under the direct control of the Soviet army.

There were a few signs of a shift from this rigid position even before Stalin's death, but only after 1953 was there a basic reorientation of policy. Now Turkey was told that Soviet territorial claims had been dropped, and the attitude towards the Arab national movement became much more friendly. The colonels who

had overthrown King Farouk, and who had at first been denounced as fascist reactionaries, were now reappraised and upgraded. Syria became of considerable interest to Moscow in view
of the growing influence of the extreme left in that country. The
idea that only an industrial proletariat could lead a national
revolution was tacitly dropped, and the progressive character of
'military socialism' was discovered. There was even a certain
improvement in Soviet-Israeli relations. At the height of the anti-
semitic purge, during Stalin's last year, diplomatic relations had
been severed by Moscow. They were renewed some months after
his death, but relations never again became really close, for in the
Arab-Israeli dispute the Soviet Union gave increasing support to
the Arabs. The discovery of the revolutionary potential of the
Arab world was the great turning-point in Soviet Middle East
policy in the post-Stalin period. The great breakthrough came in
1955 – the year of the Bandung Conference, when Bulganin and
Khrushchev visited India, and when, perhaps most significantly,
the arms deal with Egypt was signed. The initiative for this deal
came at least as much from Egypt as from the Soviet Union.
Colonel Nasser was committed to Arab unity under Egyptian
leadership, yet the Baghdad Pact, the defensive alliance then
sponsored by the Western powers, was splitting the Arab camp
and jeopardizing his plans. Arms were needed by Egypt for all
too obvious reasons; Nasser wanted to reassert Egypt's strength,
to forge an Arab bloc which under his leadership would be a real
power in world affairs. He realized that economic development,
however urgent, would not give quick results; given the backwardness of the Arab world, it would be at best a long-drawn-out
process. The mood both among leaders and the public was not
one of patient waiting. Building up Arab military power seemed a
short-cut, and the Soviet Union offered arms in much greater
quantities and on far more advantageous terms than the West. At
this stage the Soviet Union probably wanted to keep out of
Middle East internal conflicts; the arms deal, it was asserted, had
nothing to do with the Arab-Israeli conflict. For the Russians
this was a side issue; their main purpose was, of course, anti-
Western. But the arms shipments directly affected the political
situation throughout the area; tension continued to grow and the

Soviet Union gradually became involved in the Arab-Israeli confrontation as well as in other local conflicts. The Suez crisis of 1956 helped to cement the Soviet-Egyptian alliance. On 5 November, 1956, Bulganin sent notes to Britain, France, and Israel announcing that the Soviet Union was firmly resolved to use force to destroy the aggressors and restore peace in the Middle East; the possibility of attacking these countries with ballistic missiles was mentioned. As for Israel, the note stated that its very existence had been put in question. Whether these threats really stopped the war is more than doubtful; they came only after American pressure on Britain and France had made it virtually certain that the 'expedition' would be a failure. But little credit was given to Mr Dulles in the Arab world, whereas the Soviet Union got all the praise for assisting Egypt in the hour of peril.

The Eisenhower doctrine which was made public several weeks after Suez caused further resentment in the Arab world; the reference to the vacuum that now existed in the Middle East, indirectly stressing Arab military weakness, was bound to cause great offence in the Arab capitals and to make them more inclined than ever to move towards a *rapprochement* with the Soviet Union. What had begun as a 'purely commercial transaction' to break the Western arms monopoly became the starting-point of a political and even ideological reorientation from 'positive neutralism' to 'scientific socialism'. In Egypt this was a more or less orderly process, the licensed infiltration by pro-Soviet elements of a nationalist one-party regime and the gradual change of its character. But the stormy developments in Syria and Iraq threatened to upset for a while the newly established alliance with Arab nationalism. The growth of communist influence in Syria frightened the radical nationalist leaders of the Ba'th and drove them into union with Egypt. In Iraq the overthrow of Nuri Said and Hashemite rule propelled the communists suddenly into a commanding position from which they threatened the pro-Nasserist forces. This challenge could not fail to alarm President Nasser, who sounded the tocsin during the last week of 1958. The communists in the Arab world were separatists, he declared, opposed to Arab unity – an assertion hotly denied by Khrushchev at the Twenty-first Congress of the Soviet Communist party. But

Nasser was not easily mollified, and Egypt's communists were again arrested for having deserted the national cause. Although relations with the Soviet Union became for a while markedly cooler, Egypt could not afford an open break. It insisted that the quarrel between the communists and Arab radical nationalism was a purely domestic affair which did not in the least affect Arab admiration for Khrushchev, Mao, Gomulka, and Tito. An Egyptian periodical argued that the Soviet Union would not sacrifice for the sake of the Arab communists the trust and respect it had won from the Arabs as a whole: 'The road to Moscow does not lead via the Syrian and Iraqi Communist parties.' This prediction proved to be surprisingly correct; Soviet policy in the Middle East was not to be deflected from its long-term aims by the temporary suppression of the Communist parties. Soviet patience paid dividends. The United Arab Republic broke up a few years later as suddenly as it had come into existence, and independent Syria again became the most trusted ally of the Soviet Union in the Middle East. The further radicalization of the Egyptian regime, the sharpening of the Arab-Israeli conflict, the end of the struggle in Algeria, and the war in Yemen offered fresh opportunities for consolidating Soviet influence in the Arab world.

The successes of the Soviet Union in the Middle East during the nineteen-fifties cannot be ascribed to any single cause; they certainly cannot be explained by the magic of such words as 'Israel' or 'Algeria' or 'Arab oil'. They cannot be interpreted solely in terms of foreign policies. Russia was not physically involved in the Middle East and thus could refrain from action on occasions and in regions where the West could hardly avoid it. In the Arab world Russia was not tarred with the brush of imperialism. For forty years it had been absent from the area, whereas the Western ('colonial') powers had been very much in evidence. The Western powers sought to 'organize' the Arab world, and established sundry defensive strongholds there, whereas Russia could advocate a neutrality which coincided with the desires of the Arab *élites*. The West, or to be precise Western Europe, was largely dependent on Middle East oil, and believed that its loss would be a catastrophe, whereas the Soviet Union could very well do without it. While Western interests clashed everywhere with the rising tide of radical Arab nationalism, Russia appeared to be a disinterested and benevolent onlooker. Both the Russians and the Nasserists had a vital interest in weakening and ultimately destroying Western positions in the Middle East. At the same time radical nationalists in the Arab world became more receptive to communist ideological influences. The Soviet Union evoked dazzling dreams of speedy modernization and industrialization. The general mood was anti-capitalist and the radical Arab one-party regimes, having decided to nationalize industry, foreign trade, and banking, and having greatly strengthened the State sector, seemed to be moving steadily towards a society that resembled communism in some important aspects.

There was no Soviet advance in other parts of the Middle East in the nineteen-fifties comparable with the dramatic breakthrough in the Arab world. Soviet friendship with Egypt and Syria precluded any closer ties with Israel. Relations with Turkey and Iran remained normal but cool. Ankara and Teheran noted with satisfaction that Soviet territorial claims had been dropped and that Moscow was showing interest in promoting commercial exchanges. But suspicions based on long experience with the powerful neighbour to the north lingered on. In Moscow, on the other hand, Turkey's membership in NATO and Persia's involvement in Western-sponsored defence pacts constituted a major obstacle to any real *rapprochement*.

During the decade between, roughly, 1948 and 1958, between the struggle for Palestine and the creation of the UAR and the revolution in Iraq, the Middle East stood high among the global danger zones. Every year brought new crises, military conflicts, revolutions, and *coups d'état*; at times the Middle East all but monopolized the world's attention, overshadowing events in other parts of the globe – such as the Far East – which were of equal if not greater importance. After 1959 the Middle East figured less frequently in the headlines of the world's press. Internal tensions did not abate by any means, nor was there any dramatic decline in Soviet interest in the area. But the strategic importance of the region was no longer regarded in the West with the same urgent concern, there was an abundance of oil from other sources, and, above all, the Middle East's near monopoly as an area of permanent unrest was broken. Crises in Africa, the Far East, and the Caribbean preoccupied both foreign ministries and newspaper offices to the detriment of the Middle East. This period of relative calm lasted for about seven or eight years, terminating in a new crisis. This lull before the storm is a convenient starting-point for the present study.

3
The Neutralization of the Northern Tier

Turkey

Adnan Menderes' Democratic party, which had ruled Turkey for a decade, was overthrown by a *coup* on 27 May 1960. His regime had alienated a great part of the country's *élite*, especially the urban middle class, many army officers, and the younger intellectuals, who by and large supported the Republican party. Many of the promises made in 1950, when Menderes came to power, had not been kept: political life had not been liberalized, and the government had retreated from secularism, one of the basic principles of the modern Turkish State. The Democratic party had strong roots in the countryside, for the peasants had on the whole benefited from the regime; but ill-considered economic policies had caused galloping inflation and led eventually to an unofficial devaluation which severely affected the urban population. Following widespread student riots, troops were called in by Menderes to restore order, but the army command refused to use force against the demonstrators; instead, a group of officers under General Gürsel, whose declared aim was to restore democracy, arrested Menderes and his closest collaborators and seized power. The new men were politically by no means a homogeneous body; some of them advocated a fully fledged military dictatorship on a Nasserist (or left-wing fascist) pattern. But in the tug-of-war that ensued, the upper hand was gained by those who stood for a compromise with the civilian establishment and for eventul reconciliation with the erstwhile supporters of Menderes. Conditions soon returned to normal; the elections of October 1961 were won by the Republican People's party, whose leader, Ismet Inönü, one of Atatürk's closest collaborators, became once again prime minister.[1]*

* The notes appear at the end of the book, pp. 228–45.

Under Menderes Turkey had collaborated closely with the Western powers; having joined NATO in 1952, it was one of the original signatories of the Baghdad Pact (subsequently CENTO). As the second world war ended, Turkey found itself under great pressure from the Soviet Union, which had demonstratively revoked the 1925 Soviet-Turkish treaty of neutrality and non-aggression; Moscow also demanded a revision of the Montreux Convention governing the Straits and claimed the Turkish provinces of Kars and Ardahan. After Stalin's death the Soviet leaders decided to revise their attitude towards Turkey. The governments of the Georgian and Armenian Soviet Republics renounced their territorial claims and Khrushchev admitted in a speech in the Supreme Soviet that 'we cannot say that this [the deterioration in relations between the two countries] occurred solely because of Turkey's fault . . .'[2]

No radical changes took place, however, in Turkey's foreign political orientation in the following years, and Soviet attacks on Turkey continued as the Menderes government showed little readiness to renounce its treaty engagements with the West. When the United States decided to send troops to Lebanon in 1958, following a request by the Lebanese government, the expedition started from the NATO base near Adana. At the time of the *coup* against Nuri Said, Menderes at one stage planned military intervention in Iraq; he desisted only after he had been warned by the Americans that the Soviet threats and troop concentrations should not be taken lightly. Towards the end of the Menderes regime relations with Moscow began to improve: the Turkish minister of health visited the Soviet capital, and in early 1960 an exchange of visits was agreed upon in principle between Menderes and Khrushchev.

The *coup* of 1960 was followed in Moscow with much attention and a great deal of sympathy. Though General Gürsel had made it clear from the beginning that there would be no substantial change in Turkey's foreign policy, Soviet observers knew that not all members of the junta shared his views. Inönü, who became prime minister the following year, had always advocated closer relations with the Soviet Union, and Selim Sarper, the new foreign minister, was thought to tend towards neutralism. In the following months there was a good deal of diplomatic activity. Sarper and the Soviet ambassador in Turkey, Ryshov, declared that a marked improvement had taken place in the relations between the two countries. Admiral Korutürk, the Turkish ambassador in Moscow, made soundings on his own initiative about the Russian attitude towards a new Balkan-Near East pact extending from Belgrade to Cairo. Turkish newspapers, especially those close to Inönü and his party, published favourable articles about the Soviet Union; all this was a far cry from the days of the cold war. Several new political and cultural associations came into being advocating left-wing policies at home and a *rapprochement* with the Soviet Union (the periodical *Yon*, the Peasants Institute, etc.). This ferment on the left produced a reaction on the right;[3] the Turkish public was traditionally suspicious of pro-Soviet activities, a label freely bandied about and often fatal in the domestic struggle for political power.

The diplomatic negotiations had no immediate tangible results, though a few minor economic agreements were concluded, and there was disappointment in Moscow that relations between the two countries did not improve faster and that NATO manoeuvres were still taking place in Turkey. Marshal Malinovsky again warned the Turks.[4] Sarper was replaced in 1962 by the pro-Western Erkin. The reaction of Soviet commentators was unfriendly; 'Our Radio', a communist broadcasting station beamed to Turkey from East Germany, asserted that since the progressive elements had been removed from the junta, reactionary policies were again being pursued.

The repercussions of the Cuban crisis in autumn 1962 were felt in the Near East too. When the Americn government decided to remove its Jupiter missile bases from Turkey, it was generally assumed in Ankara that this was part of a secret deal between Washington and Moscow. If the American government put its own security above the interests of its allies (it was reasoned in Ankara), Turkey, too, should put its national interest first and regain some freedom of manoeuvre. Several members of Inönü's cabinet and some senators suggested that Turkey should contribute towards the new climate of coexistence by a gradual reduction of its military and political obligations towards the West and

by a neutralist foreign policy.[5] They referred to the friendly
relations with Russia which had prevailed in the twenties and
thirties, a state of affairs that had changed as a result of Stalin's
aggressive demands and threats. Inönü was often quoted at the
time to the effect that Turkey had to find its place in the new
world that was being born.

Tension between the left and right became more acute throughout 1963. Parliamentary debates and discussions in the press gave
the impression that communism had suddenly become a burning
issue.[6] Various popular and national front organizations were
established, and the right wing reacted by creating associations to
combat the spread of communism. Between these claims and
counterclaims, it was not easy to form a realistic appraisal about
the real power of communism in Turkey. The illegal Turkish
Communist party had only a few thousand members, but there
were in addition a great many intellectual fellow-travellers in
public life, some of them in prominent positions in the mass
media. Their doings attracted much attention, the more so since
up to 1960 all pro-communist activity had been strictly illegal.
The Turkish right prepared new laws to ban communist activities,
but in the changed climate of 1963 these encountered strong
opposition. The right could not even prevent communists (appear-
ing on behalf of the Turkish Labour party) being permitted for
the first time in Turkey's history to broadcast on the occasion of
the municipal elections in November 1963. Representatives of
twenty-four left-wing organizations, including the Socialist
Cultural Society, the Village Teachers Association, and others, in
May 1964 established an executive committee to combat Pan-
turanianism, fascism, and religious reaction. Many regarded this
as another attempt to establish a pro-communist 'national front'
on a broad basis.[7]

The left-wing advocates of Turkish-Soviet *rapprochement* were
heavily handicapped in their efforts by the Cyprus problem. The
Soviet Union openly supported Makarios, and in September 1964
signed an agreement to supply arms to Cyprus. The Turkish
government was firmly resolved to assist the Turkish minority, by
military intervention if necessary, but it gained little encouragement for such action among its Western allies. In a letter to

Inönü in June 1964 President Johnson gave the Turkish government to understand that it could not count on automatic American support if by its actions it provoked Moscow to intervene. Turkey felt betrayed by its allies and some influential voices suggested that the country should either reduce its NATO obligations or leave the Treaty Organization altogether.[8] Erkin, the foreign minister, went to Moscow in October 1964, and though he talked to his hosts mainly about the promotion of trade between the two countries, the intention was clearly to 'clear up old misunderstandings' and to create a better atmosphere between the two countries.[9] It appeared highly doubtful whether these or other Turkish overtures (such as negotiations with Bulgaria) would induce Moscow to change its policy on Cyprus. Since Inönü could not point to any tangible achievements or even any specific promise, the government's foreign policy was attacked by many critics who felt that it might leave the country during a crisis without any allies at all.[10] The Justice party was among the critics of a comprehensive reorientation towards the East, so were leading army circles, and Erkin advocated a more cautious line than the prime minister.

In 1965 the initiative again passed to the diplomats, with Podgorny's and Gromyko's visits to Turkey and Urgüplü's trip to Moscow; but again there were few tangible results. Inönü's domestic position had progressively weakened; after a defeat in parliament in February 1965, he resigned. Urgüplü was made head of an interim government and after the great electoral victory of the Justice party in October 1965, Demirel became the new prime minister. After the fall of Khrushchev, Soviet Near East policy, too, was re-examined. Obviously it was not a suitable moment for any far-reaching new departures in Soviet-Turkish relations.

Inönü's policy towards the Soviet Union had been motivated not by any ideological sympathy with communism, but by his interpretation of Turkish national self-interest. The Kemalist tradition had played a great part, and the example set by de Gaulle also had a certain impact. Inönü was firmly convinced that if Turkey was too closely connected with the Western powers it would find it difficult to pursue its own national interests; in addition, there was always the danger of a deal between the two super-powers in which Turkish interests would be sacrificed. Demirel, a much younger man than Inönü and more modern in his outlook, was more sceptical about the prospects of Soviet-Turkish *rapprochement* and the political benefits that Turkey could derive from it. He did not in principle oppose closer relations, but the main purpose of such moves was, in his view, to bring pressure on Washington. His attitude began to change only after Moscow reversed its Cyprus policy.

Demirel's great electoral victory came as a surprise to Moscow. Soviet observers expected that Inönü would continue in office or that the army would again intervene to prevent the accession to power of a party which, in some respects, was in the Menderes tradition. This was, however, a misreading of the Turkish situation: Inönü's position had been precarious even before the acute crisis developed, Demirel was not a new Menderes, and the army seemed perfectly willing to work with him.

With the establishment of the Demirel government and the resulting reshuffle, many left-wingers and fellow-travellers lost their position in the public service. Demirel announced that the country would stay in NATO; his government refused to ratify the cultural agreement with the Soviet Union which had been prepared under Inönü. (This did not prevent a steady stream of cultural exchanges; Soviet literary delegations came to Ankara and Istanbul, the Soviet Union bought several Turkish movies, and an agreement on the promotion of tourism was reached.) Demirel's lack of enthusiasm did not exactly endear him to Moscow, even though the Soviet government preferred not to engage in polemics. But the Turkish communists stepped up their propaganda campaign against the new government: the Justice party, they claimed, was hostile to all the domestic progressive forces; it was enlisting all the extreme reactionary forces; it was an American puppet brought to power by the American imperialists; it did not want good neighbourly relations with the Soviet Union.[11] It was accused of having killed Gürsel with the help of the Americans in a most horrible way, for its members regarded him as an obstacle to their plans; did he not return a living corpse from the American hospital where he was to have been cured? Then they had placed Sunay, who agreed to cede new bases to the Americans and to make other concessions, in the presidential mansion, while Tuval, a 'reactionary with fascist views, opposed to the principles of Atatürk', was made chief of the general staff.[12] While the Demirel government denied that there were any new military bases in Turkey, a new base had in fact been established at Sogauli.[13] In an official statement the Turkish CP asserted that Demirel was about to establish fascism and an open military dictatorship in Turkey; it was stirring up anti-communist hysteria which threatened everyone; it had made the country into an American and NATO base for military aggression against both the socialist camp and the freedom-loving peoples of the Middle East – all this despite the fact, freely and cynically admitted by the Western imperialists, that in the event of a nuclear war Turkey would be the first country to be obliterated from the face of the earth.[14] Under Demirel the nation was facing economic and political ruin, as well as military disaster; fully implementing the American cold war policy, it was engaging in aggressive military manoeuvres directed against the Soviet Union.[15]

The propaganda campaign was extremely violent and it could have created the mistaken impression that Soviet-Turkish relations had reached an all-time low. But there was, as so often, a division of labour; Moscow acted as if the Turkish communists did not exist. There was a definite improvement in relations in 1966, Turkish trade with the communist bloc (about which more below) expanded, and several high-level meetings took place. Demirel and Caglayangil, the new foreign minister, had stated soon after their party came to power that, while they did not feel too sanguine about the prospects of Turkish-Soviet relations, they would do nothing to antagonize Moscow, but would work for a *détente*. By December 1966, on the eve of the Kosygin visit to Ankara, there had already been a definite change for the better; official Soviet spokesmen noted that 'favourable conditions existed for a radical improvement in Soviet-Turkish relations', while the Turks likewise commented on the 'positive changes that evoke satisfaction'.[16]

The gradual reversal of the Soviet position on Cyprus had

much to do with this change. In 1964, after the Soviet decision to send arms and equipment to Makarios, the Turkish foreign minister had given warning that open Soviet support for the Greeks would bring the improvement in Soviet-Turkish relations to a standstill.[17] Ryshov, the Soviet ambassador, tried to explain that Ankara was interpreting the Soviet position wrongly. Why would it not trust Moscow as a mediator in the conflict? There were in fact certain straws in the wind that suggested a Soviet retreat from its extreme position; Cyprus was not important enough in Soviet eyes to sacrifice good relations with Turkey. Gromyko had declared as early as January 1965 that the USSR would support an arrangement that would permit Cyprus to continue as an independent state, in which the rights of both the Greek and Turkish communities to live in peace would be observed.[18] This was not incompatible with the Turkish position on Cyprus (independence plus federation). The Cyprus communists noted with regret that the Soviet Union was talking increasingly about 'two communities' in Cyprus, that it was no longer giving all-out support to AKEL – that, in brief, it was moving towards a neutral line, a shift which became even more obvious after the right-wing *coup* in Greece in April 1967.

In Turkey national passions had been running high in connection with the fate of the Turkish minority in Cyprus, and there was deep disappointment when it was realized that Ankara could not muster international support for its position. The Western countries were not sympathetic, while of the Muslim countries only Iran and Pakistan (no Arab country) had voted with Turkey in the UN General Assembly. The signs of a change in the Soviet position were therefore all the more welcome, and there was increasing belief in Ankara that the key to a desirable solution of the Cyprus problem was to be sought in Moscow, not in the West. The Soviet press, in contrast to the propaganda of the Turkish communists, had noted soon after Demirel had taken over that the new regime intended to work 'for the establishment and development of good neighbourly relations',[19] and, as a first sign of goodwill, a Soviet Armenian party secretary was removed from his post in May 1966 for having permitted anti-Turkish demonstrations in a border district. Soviet spokesmen, in preparation for Kosygin's visit to Ankara in December 1966, stressed that the Soviet leaders had no ulterior motives in their desire for good neighbourliness and that their policy was based solely on the principles of 'equality, respect for territorial integrity, sovereignty, and non-interference. In return for friendship the Soviet Union had not interfered with Turkish relations with other countries, had not burdened the country with unbearable military expenditure, and had not asked for immunity for its citizens on Turkish soil so that they could behave arrogantly and insult the national dignity of the Turks.'[20] *Sapienti sat.* Kosygin's visit to Ankara was the first ever by a Soviet prime minister. There were a great many Turkish and some Soviet flags at the airport, and banners reading '*Hoş Geldiniz*' (Cordially welcome); there was much curiosity and traditional hospitality, neither much hate nor much love. Traditional friendship was invoked incessantly in the after-dinner speeches, but observers noted that the general atmosphere, though polite and dignified, was on the whole quite cool.[21] The Turkish opposition did not exploit the occasion for partisan manoeuvres, while Kosygin was exceedingly cautious in his speeches, which were for the most part devoted to the need to expand economic relations. He stressed time and again that there were no longer any questions in dispute between the two countries; statements by Turkish leaders that they were striving for a further improvement in relations had been received with trust in Moscow. Kosygin also emphasized repeatedly that 'we do not consider that such a development should happen at the expense of a worsening of Turkey's relations with any other state'.[22] His trip to Turkey, he said, was not an isolated episode out of context with what had already happened and without continuation in the future; it was part of a consistent political line which would not be subject to fluctuations: 'The Soviet Union was prepared to take definite steps in order to assure and consolidate this feeling of confidence in our peoples.'[23] It was not quite clear what definite steps he had in mind, unless he meant the non-aggression pact he had suggested in an interview the year before.[24] Views were exchanged about the Cyprus situation, and Kosygin seems to have expressed regret about an arms shipment to Nicosia made shortly before by the Czechs. In the final communiqué reference was made to the Middle East ('both sides expressed the desire that the Near and Middle East should become a zone of peace and security'), as well as to disarmament and European security.[25] Most of the formulations were vague, but the inclusion of a reference to the war in Vietnam was interpreted by some as a Soviet diplomatic victory. However, Kosygin's main intention was not to discuss detailed questions with a view to reaching full agreement, nor would the trade negotiations have made his presence necessary. Above all he wanted to reassure the Turks and to create a climate of confidence, and in this, to a certain extent, he succeeded. One week (some Turkish observers noted) was too short to eradicate the memories of several centuries, but it helped to establish the basis for further agreements paving the way for a general *rapprochement*.

The Soviet leaders did not, of course, expect that Kosygin's visit would solve all problems and prevent future tension altogether. In connection with President Sunay's visit to Washington in 1967, Moscow revived the old issue of American bases. The Soviet press gave a great deal of publicity to appeals by groups of Turkish intellectuals to remove these bases; *Pravda* seemed willing to put the main blame on the Americans 'seeking to keep, by hook or by crook, their rights and privileges'.[26] The Turkish communists, as usual far more outspoken, attacked the 'Demirel-Sunay clique' for accepting the Acheson plan (for establishing new American bases in Cyprus):

> During the first phase Cyprus's independence will be destroyed and during the second phase America will establish . . . radar stations, nuclear stockpiles, rocket-launching pads and air and naval bases. . . . The Demirel-Sunay group, which has betrayed the Turkish people and its territorial integrity, is diligently helping the imperialists in the Cyprus question, too.[27]

Official Soviet statements did not, of course, put it so crudely. On the contrary, they went to great lengths to make a success of Demirel's visit to the Soviet Union in September 1967. The communiqué published after the meetings in Moscow mentioned 'positive results brought about by a constructive approach to problems of bilateral relations'.[28] In an interview after his return, the Turkish premier said that his visit had 'eliminated the last traces of hostility from Soviet-Turkish relations'.[29] In 1966, when Kosygin and Demirel had met in Ankara, there had been 'exchanges' on Cyprus; less than a year later, following the deterioration in the relations between Moscow and Athens, the communiqué was more positive. 'The Soviet view on Cyprus is fairly close to ours', Demirel said in his interview.[30] The discussions on disarmament and European security still seemed somewhat academic at the time; but when the Turkish foreign minister again visited Moscow in July 1968 he took with him more specific proposals; moreover, he was also speaking on behalf of his NATO colleagues, who (at their meeting in Reykjavik) had just decided on a common approach to the Soviet Union. Turkey was not willing to accept the Soviet denunciation of Israel as the aggressor in the Middle East crisis, but supported Moscow's call for Israel's withdrawal from the occupied territories. Demirel said that if there were several ways to preserve peace it was irresponsible of the Israelis to insist on one of them. This was a step in the right direction as far as the Soviet Union was concerned, and it was favourably received in Moscow.[31]

Demirel's mission to Moscow and his declarations after his return surprised the opposition at home. The right began to refer to him as 'Comrade Demirel', whereas the opposite camp claimed that his comments on Russia's technical and social achievements were not really consistent with his former style. The man who had once considered closer relations with Russia dangerous and a sign of enmity towards the West had mellowed. After his Moscow trip he had become fair-minded and realistic in his outlook. 'His enthusiastic praise of Russia boosted even Russian pride.'[32] The left was no doubt concerned that Demirel's policy would take much of the wind out of their sails, and the results of the elections of June 1968 seemed to confirm their fears. The Justice party scored minor gains; the People's Republican party, which under Bulent Ecevit had moved to the left, was split: in protest against this trend some fifty of its deputies and senators had broken away from the party in 1967 and established a new group, the Reliance party. The Turkish Labour party, which for practical purposes represented communist interests in the country, had a sizable following among intellectuals, students, and some trade unions, but with its fifteen seats in the 450-member National Assembly it did not constitute a major political force.

What mainly mattered in the elections from the Soviet point of view was Turkey's attitude to NATO; wide publicity was given to demonstrations, appeals, and newspaper comments in Turkey calling for a withdrawal from NATO.[33] Since the NATO treaty was up for renewal in 1969, this had become a topical issue. The Soviet approach seemed to ignore the obvious fact that while there was concern in Turkey about restrictions imposed by the Western alliance and the presence of foreign bases, most Turks were more worried about the growing Soviet presence in the eastern Mediterranean. Military ties with America had been under review since 1965, and while many of the American bases were likely to be evacuated in the near future, the Soviet Union, to quote a highly-placed Turkish commentator, had worked diligently and methodically to eliminate the potential for US military interference, and was successfully filling the vacuum left in the Middle East by the West:

We used to be certain that the walls built by NATO and CENTO would keep Russia in the north. Recently, however, the Soviet Union has with great ease climbed over the walls to the other side. Today we do not feel the threat of her presence. The Soviets are particularly careful not to let Iran, Turkey, and Greece feel such a threat . . . leading countries in the West, possibly to avoid additional political and military obligations, look the other way, pretend they are not aware of a threat, and furthermore, try to convince others that there is no threat.[34]

Previously, Turkish leaders had been mainly concerned with the Straits and possible Soviet pressure for a modification of the Montreux Convention. But the provisions of the Convention made it perfectly legal for the Soviet Black Sea Fleet to enter the Mediterranean, whereas it restricted the entrance of ships of third powers into the Black Sea. In the circumstances there was no urgent need from the Soviet point of view to demand a revision of the *status quo*. There were occasional Soviet complaints about alleged violations of the Convention following the visits of American warships in the Black Sea,[35] but the Soviet Black Sea Fleet had meanwhile been built up to such an extent that Moscow could not plausibly argue that the visit of an American frigate endangered the security of the Soviet Union. The reason for Soviet restraint was, as a Turkish commentator noted, that the Straits had lost much of their original importance in the age of ICBMs and nuclear parity.[36]

They had certainly not lost *all* their importance, as the events of 1967 were to show: a record number of Soviet warships passed through the Bosporus and the Dardanelles that year, 167 to be precise, of which roughly two thirds went through the Straits after the Arab-Israeli war. There was a great deal of sudden concern about the successful Soviet attempt to by-pass Turkey. The pro-government *Son Havadis* asked: 'What are those Soviet vessels looking for in a sea where they have no coast? We should be vigilant and understand once again the importance of the Western alliance against which our leftists are conducting a fierce campaign.'[37] The non-communist left opposition also expressed misgivings: the presence of the Soviet Mediterranean fleet was not a development to be welcomed by Turkey, which preferred the previous balance of naval forces. But there was nothing Turkey could do about it; it had to get used to the idea of coexisting with the Russians in the Mediterranean.

To many Turks, the continuing economic and social backwardness of their country, in a world in which so much depended on technology and productivity, was an even greater menace than the Soviet army or navy. Three out of four Turks were still employed in agriculture, and almost a million citizens were unemployed or under-employed. If Russia had a certain appeal among some sections of the intelligentsia, it was as a once-backward country which had been transformed into a modern power.

The Turkish economy, after many false starts and a great deal of mismanagement, could point to substantial advance in the sixties. The average yearly growth of the GNP in the first five-year plan (which began in 1963) had been 6·4 per cent; in 1966 it reached almost 9 per cent. OECD, in its yearly report, called it a 'good year for the Turkish economy, with fast growth and a high rate of investment'.[38] But it was also a period of major problems: foreign exchange reserves fell to a very low level, capital inflow was reduced, and imports higher than had been envisaged. Optimists argued, not without reason, that if the same level of economic expansion was sustained for a number of years, Turkey would soon attain medium-power status. But fast and orderly economic expansion was threatened by the country's weak financial position. The second five-year plan envisaged investment at a level of 120 million Turkish pounds a year; the country faced an uphill struggle in attracting investors from abroad, and the capacity of the State Bank to finance the expansion of the public sector was also limited. Turkey was already heavily in debt; up to 40 per cent of its exports were needed to cover interest and capital repayments. Severe cuts in imports would have helped to remedy the situation, but would at the same time have caused a substantial decline in economic growth.

In these difficult circumstances the expansion of economic relations with the Soviet Union seemed an obvious way to eliminate or reduce the trade deficit. Negotiations started in 1964 and concerned several major projects, such as the building of an oil refinery south of Izmir with a yearly capacity of 3 million tons, and an aluminium plant near Seydişehir with an output of about 60,000 tons per year. Other projects included plants for manufacturing sulphuric acid, fibre-board, glass strip, and an engraved glass factory. Soviet geologists were to help in the search for Turkish oil, and an iron and steel mill was also under consideration. These talks lasted for more than two years and there was hard bargaining. The final offer made by the Soviet Union in this package deal was considerably below the figures quoted originally. Turkey received a credit of $200 million for a period of fifteen years at a 2·5 per cent interest rate to pay for these projects. Most important, the agreement provided for payment in Turkish surplus agricultural products, such as tobacco, raisins, fruit, olive oil, nuts, and cotton, for which it had been difficult to find markets in the West. At the same time Turkey also intensified its trade with the other Soviet bloc countries; this roughly doubled between 1963 and 1967. Seen in a wider context, however, it seemed unlikely that the Soviet Union and East Europe would replace the West in the foreseeable future as Turkey's main source of credit and its chief trading partners. The Soviet credits of $200 million over fifteen years compared with $350 million of loans provided yearly by Western states and private firms. The Soviet Union figured in 1967 only sixth among Turkey's trade partners.[39]

Soviet-Turkish relations during the nineteen-sixties reflected the changing world situation: at the height of the cold war and up to the early sixties Turkey felt directly threatened by Russia and regarded the Western alliance as its main shield against pressure from the north. With the *détente* in West-East relations, the American military presence became much weaker, while the practical value of CENTO in an emergency was more than doubtful. American economic aid, which had totalled $1·9 billion over nearly two decades, was cut to $59 million in 1968 and was to be phased out in 1972.[40] In these circumstances Soviet influence was bound to increase; the fact that Moscow had stopped threatening the Turks, combined with the feeling that the Western alliance no longer sufficed to safeguard Turkish national security, let alone guarantee Turkish interests elsewhere, such as in Cyprus, made for a switch towards neutralism in Turkish policy. Turkey's internal stability made such a reorientation appear less than risky. Close collaboration with the Soviet Union was unlikely to subvert the Justice party and to make it communist in character; even the Republican People's party further to the left and ideologically committed to a form of neutralism, could not compete with the attractions offered to Soviet foreign policy by regimes such as Nasser's, not to mention the Syrian Neo-Ba'th. The influence of communism in Turkey was small, nor was it always certain what kind of Marxism was preached by its adherents; in the age of Mao and Castro, the Soviet Union had suffered painful experiences with many revolutionary groups in the third world. The realization that communism was basically weak in Turkey and that its future was uncertain no doubt contributed greatly to the Soviet decision that wooing Turkey was preferable to using the frontal-attack approach advocated by the Turkish communists. Friendly relations with a 'reactionary' regime might gravely embarrass communists in Turkey (as well as in Iran and many other countries), but that was the price that had to be paid, in view of the higher interests of proletarian internationalism.

Many Turks were flattered by the attention given to their country by the Russians, and the economic help extended by the Soviets was gratefully acknowledged. Yet there remained a great deal of uneasiness and even fear, which was reinforced by the events in Czechoslovakia in 1968. The Soviet Union had solemnly declared that it would strictly adhere to the principle of non-interference, yet it was not clear whether the Soviet and the Turkish definitions of non-interference were identical. Did it mean that any criticism of things Soviet and of communism was ruled out, and that at some future stage only pro-Soviet politicians would be acceptable to Moscow? The Finnish experience was not encouraging, and Finland was so far the Soviet model of non-interference. What if Turkey should be sucked even more firmly into a new 'southern tier', a Soviet sphere of influence? Would Soviet benevolence still last, or would there be pressure for political change inside Turkey? The Soviet Union had legitimate interests in connection with the security of its southern flank, but how could Turkish independence be maintained against the much more powerful neighbour to the north without support from other quarters? Between the necessity to accommodate itself within reasonable limits to Soviet interests and the strong desire to stay independent, Turkey faced a future fraught with grave dangers. The balance of power in the area and in the world at large had guaranteed its independence in the past. Any shift in the balance was bound to imperil it.

Iran

Almost unnoticed at first, important changes in Iran's foreign and domestic policies were taking place in the nineteen-sixties. After many decades of stagnation the country had entered a phase of accelerated economic growth and social change unprecedented in its recent history. Soviet-Iranian ties became closer than ever before; the *rapprochement* began earlier and was more gradual than that between Russia and Turkey. Official Soviet relations with Persia had never deteriorated as they had with Turkey, and this although Kemalism had always been socially and politically more advanced in Soviet eyes than monarchical Persia. The overthrow of the Mossadeq government and the suppression of the Tudeh party in 1953–4 was deeply regretted in Moscow, but it did not prevent the Soviet Union from discussing with the government of the day outstanding issues, such as border revisions, fishing rights in the Caspian Sea, the problem of Persian gold retained in the USSR, and the Iran Sovneft Oil Company.[41] Persia's defence pacts with Turkey and Pakistan, and above all with the West, were viewed in Moscow with extreme disfavour. In an official note of protest, and unofficially on many other occasions, Persia was reminded that according to the treaties of 1921 and 1927 it did not have the right to join any 'anti-Soviet' pact.[42] The discovery of the big Tudeh conspiracy in the Persian army and air force in 1954 (in which the Soviet military attaché was implicated) did not improve matters. Despite mutual recriminations, the impression remained that Moscow believed Tehran more open to friendly persuasion or pressure than Ankara. The Shah went to the Soviet capital in 1956 for a state visit, a three-year commercial agreement was signed, and the Soviet Union became again one of Iran's best customers; in 1957, 21 per cent of Iran's exports went to the Soviet Union.

The year 1959 brought a crisis in Soviet-Iranian relations. The Soviet government had proposed a treaty of friendship and non-aggression, but this was rejected by the Shah and his government, who soon after, in March 1959, signed a bilateral defence agreement with Washington. This provoked bitter Soviet attacks: Iran had been drawn into the camp opposing the Soviet Union; it was being pushed into war and was being made to pay for the aggressive acts of the Americans. At the time of the U2 crisis the Iranian government was accused by the Soviet press of dragging the country down into an abyss and the Shah was personally attacked as a despised puppet, a traitor to Islam, and the oil monopolists' lackey. The Iranian communist broadcasting station based in East Germany summoned 'all true Muslims to follow in the steps of the sons of Ali and to remove the rotten regime'. The emphasis on religious themes was in the circumstances a little surprising; it may not have been unconnected with the conflict between Tehran and Cairo. In 1960 Iran broke off relations with the UAR following a massive and violent anti-Persian propaganda campaign that had been launched by Egypt, and it also extended diplomatic recognition to Israel. Soviet broadcasts warned Tehran that rockets might be used against the take-off bases of aircraft violating Soviet airspace. The execution of five Iranian communists added to Moscow's displeasure.

It seemed while it lasted a dangerous conflict, but towards the end of August 1960 there were the first indications of a lessening of tension. Eghbal, Moscow's *bête noire*, who had signed the treaty with the Americans, was replaced by Sharif Emani. An exchange of messages – six in all – took place between the Shah and Khrushchev in which both parties expressed their desire for a *détente*. The Shah said that Iran wanted friendly relations with the Soviet Union, but this would have to be based on mutual respect.[43] Iran had already proved her goodwill in various ways. Should not the past be forgotten and a fresh start made? The Soviet government in its answer stressed its belief in the principles of peaceful coexistence; but how could there be an improvement unless Iran ceased to be a spring-board for the US and other imperialist governments? The Soviet leaders must have realized soon after these first exchanges that their demand was unrealistic; Tehran would hardly give up its defence alliances simply because the Soviet Union objected to them. In a further note they retreated slightly from their earlier stand: the Iranian government was given to understand that a *rapprochement* was possible even without the abandonment of Iran's Western alliances if it made a real step in the right direction.[44] Tehran decided to compromise, and announced in 1962 that it would not permit the stationing of nuclear missiles on its territory.[45] This was surely a step in the right direction. Soviet commentators writing in later years all agreed that it had been the turning-point in Soviet-Iranian relations.[46] When Brezhnev made a state visit to Tehran in November 1963, relations between the two countries had improved to such an extent that he declared they could be an example to all powers. Transit and border agreements were ratified on this occasion, and an economic and technical co-operation agreement concluded for the joint use of the resources of the border rivers Atrak and Aras, and for the joint construction of a dam on the Aras. Other joint economic projects were discussed and the Soviet Union promised a credit of about $30 million. A Soviet-Iranian Cultural Relations Society based in Moscow was set up; the parallel Iranian branch of this society was headed by General Djahanbani, a member of the Iranian Senate. The countries of East Europe followed Moscow's lead: Poland and Czechoslovakia, Rumania and Hungary extended credits to Iran and there was a steady flow of delegations between their respective capitals.

This improvement in the relations between the two countries between 1960 and 1963 should be viewed against the background of developments inside Persia. These were years of deep internal crisis; at the same time the decision was taken to carry out far-reaching reforms in Persian society. The elections of 1960 had been a disappointment; the *Majlis* was suspended in May 1961 and not reconvened until October 1963. During the interval the country was ruled by decree; there was not even the pretence of democracy. When Dr Amini took over from Sharif Emani as prime minister in May 1961, he found himself faced with a grave financial crisis and drastic steps had to be adopted to overcome it. Years later he was accused of having quite unnecessarily declared the country bankrupt and thus having played into the hands of the oil companies. With the benefit of hindsight the events of 1961 may appear in a less serious light; at the time it certainly seemed to be a real crisis. On Amini's advice, the Shah promulgated reform proposals to eradicate corruption, improve tax-collection and justice in general, and confer more administrative authority on provincial governors. Above all, land distribution became a firm reality with the Shah's signature on a revised Land Reform Bill.[47] This was the beginning of the 'white revolution'.

The land reform aimed at breaking the domination of the great landowners. It was applied first in north-west Persia, where unrest was rife among the local peasants. During the first stage of the reform, land in almost 15,000 villages was bought up and distributed among more than 600,000 peasants. This land was valued at 13,000 million reals, but the owners were paid only 2,300 million, receiving the rest in the form of shares in State or mixed enterprises. The first stage lasted until the end of 1967, but even before it was concluded the second and third stages got under way: middle and small landowners were instructed to sell or lease their holdings above 30–200 hectares, depending on the fertility of the land and the part of the country. Cooperatives were established and agriculture modernized in every way. These agrarian reforms amounted to a break-up of the traditional social structure in the countryside, the end of the share-cropping system, and the emergence of a new class of small landowners. The redistribution of landownership had far-reaching social and political effects; it had undoubtedly been the original purpose of the Shah and his advisers to gain the support of the peasant majority against the power of the big landowners. In a referendum, there was an overwhelming majority (about thirteen to one) for the royal decree. These figures do not, however, provide a clear picture of the intensity of opposition which the reform schemes provoked. When Amini told the big landowners in 1961 that they had to give up some of their land, for the only alternative facing them was eventually to lose it all as well as their lives, they were not easily convinced. They had the support of the *mullahs*, the champions of Muslim orthodoxy, who claimed that redistribution of land was contrary to the principles of Islam. Some of the tribes, such as the Qashgai, rebelled, and the Arab separatists in Khuzistan used the opportunity to stage an insurrection. The merchants, who had been affected by the new austerity decrees (involving higher customs duties), turned against the government. The intelligentsia was alienated, anyway, and Iranian students abroad protested against decrees which cut off their allowances unless their examination results were satisfactory. This they regarded as a gross interference in their human rights, and it contributed to the spread of radicalism among Persian students abroad. The Tudeh party had not yet recovered from its defeats in 1953 and 1955; it had merged with the Azerbaidjani communists in 1960, but riddled by internal splits, it did not represent a serious internal challenge to the regime. More serious was the opposition of the members of the National Front, the party headed at one time by Dr Mossadeq, who, often from within the lower echelons of the civil service, sabotaged the reforms. Riots against the modernization decrees took place in June 1963 in various districts, and the *mullahs* became even more restive when women received the vote; there was growing disaffection among the army command and in the upper reaches of the civil service as the anti-corruption drive culminated in the arrest of several high officials. There was a curious alliance of all the opponents of the reform: big landowners and left-wing students, fanatical *mullahs*, merchants, and separatist tribes. It was a dangerous period, and the assassination of Ali Mansur, the prime minister, in January 1964 was a manifestation of the strong opposition which the reforms of the Shah and his advisers encountered.

It was only natural that the Iranian government should try to reduce all external tension to a minimum during that period of internal upheaval; hence the great efforts to improve relations with the Soviet Union. Russia reciprocated by toning down anti-Persian propaganda, the Soviet assumption being, no doubt, that closer contacts with the Soviet Union would gradually induce the Persians to renounce their alliances with the West and withdraw from their military pacts. There may have been other reasons, such as the growing conflict with China, which caused the Russians to shore up their southern fences. Once the Tehran government had declared that it would not permit the establishment of rocket bases on its territory, the Soviet ideological experts began to modify their attitude towards the domestic reforms carried out by the Shah and his government. Previously they had maintained that the 'notorious reform' was carried out in the interest of the landlords and feudal circles, and that the main intention of those who had framed the law was to strengthen the rotten monarchical regime and to distract the popular masses from fighting for their rights.[48] Once the rocket-base assurance had been given, it was announced in Moscow that many misunderstandings had been ironed out and that the last barriers to good relations had been removed.[49] As for the Shah's reforms, it was now found that there was a real prospect of the emergence of a new coalition of social forces interested in pursuing a national policy,[50] that the implementation of the reform programme would objectively promote social and economic progress, eliminating the most archaic survivals of the Middle Ages, and that it would raise the material and cultural level of the Persian people.[51] A few years later comments on the reforms became even more enthusiastic: Persia was going through a period of serious economic change, a fundamental break-up of the social structure designed to take the country into the twentieth century. There were glowing reports about the striking results of the reforms, the prosperity, the hard-working young technocrats of the (ruling) dynamic New Iran party; the people of Iran were facing the future with confidence.[52] The Soviet leaders seemed willing to accept the monarchy and appeared indifferent to the entrenchment of a new *bourgeoisie*; so long as it pursued the right kind of foreign policy, a favourable and optimistic assessment could be expected of the domestic policies of the Iranian government.[53] For the Persian communists this line was, of course, unacceptable, and they continued to attack the 'anti-national, anti-democratic government': they contended that the White revolution was an utter failure, that there was deep disappointment with the Shah's dictatorship.[54] 'The Shah and other leaders know no limit to their treason to the country.'[55] The Persian communists, like their Turkish comrades, were given a free hand in their propaganda, but how effective could it be if it was in such striking contrast to the Soviet approach? This caused a great deal of heart-searching among the Tudeh militants and provoked further dissension and splits. Many left-wing 'deviationists' claimed that Soviet help for the Shah in his reforms was harmful because by raising the living standards of the masses, it would strengthen the hold of the government and weaken the Communist party.[56] The central leadership of the party was willing to admit that the reforms were not altogether demagogy, a sheer political swindle ('such a view could lead to sectarianism and isolate us from the masses'); their party's uncompromising opposition to the anti-national regime did not mean that it would reject out of hand every measure taken by the government. But, in the last resort, revolutionary change was still necessary, for by its violence and anti-democratic actions the government had ruled out a peaceful solution of the problems facing the country. [57] Reforms that had no support among the people were bound to be shortlived and could not produce the desired and much needed radical changes. [58]

The Soviet approach to Iran after 1962 showed little consideration for the immediate tactical interests of the Iranian communists. The overthrow of the Shah and his regime and the emergence of a communist Iran closely allied with the Soviet Union would have meant a great victory for world communism, and for the Soviet Union a breakthrough to the Persian Gulf and the Indian Ocean. It could have been plausibly argued that Iran was a weaker country than Turkey and that the overthrow of the Shah and of a relatively small number of his supporters would open the road to radical political change. 'Objectively', a sub-acute revolutionary situation undoubtedly existed; but such arguments ignore the 'subjective' factor, the weakness of Iranian communism, its internal splits and lack of discipline. The fact that the party was so unreliable must have caused concern in Moscow; in these circumstances a successful revolution in Tehran might have resulted in the emergence of a regime less than enthusiastic to cooperate with Moscow. Lastly, there were the risks involved in an isolated breakthrough in one country, however important: a victory in Iran might have been off-set by negative reactions in the neighbouring countries. Soviet political planning looked towards a more distant future. It was, of course, obvious that Soviet economic aid would help the present regime to consolidate itself, but it would also contribute to the growth of the State sector in the national economy and thus reduce the influence of capitalism. The young technocrats who had emerged as the new *élite* had already established cordial relations with their Soviet counterparts; gradually they would come to realize that they could manage without the archaic political system still prevailing. Meanwhile, the advantages of a non-communist Iran well disposed towards Moscow, and in which Soviet influence was constantly growing, were not to be belittled. Given the general framework of Soviet foreign policy, the violent overthrow of the regime with Soviet support was ruled out, and the Tudeh party alone was not able to accomplish it.

And so the official state visits continued, agreements were signed, and praise was heaped on the Shah. After 1963 these exchanges became so numerous that it is difficult to keep track of them. The Shah visited Moscow in July 1965; in the following year he went to five other East European capitals; to Rumania and Yugoslavia in May and June, to Bulgaria, Hungary and Poland in September. Everywhere he was welcomed as an honoured guest with greater pomp and circumstance than was usually accorded to the heads of the neighbouring communist states. The Sofia communiqué said that the Bulgarian people had the 'highest praise for the initiative of His Imperial Majesty the Shah in his campaign against illiteracy'. The Rumanians expressed feelings of 'high esteem' for the efforts made in Iran to make economic, cultural, and social progress. The Hungarians also lauded the Shah for his part in the campaign against illiteracy; they were 'following sympathetically the efforts of the Iranian people towards cultural, economic, and social development'. Ochab, the Polish president, praised his guest for his progressive foreign policy; 'we know and value these efforts', he said, and the Polish communiqué ended with expressions of deep appreciation for Iranian progress.

The Iranian communists were acutely embarrassed, and criticized their East European comrades for exceeding the limits of normal diplomatic courtesy; the Shah, after all, was no more than 'a reactionary monarch hated by his people'. Summarizing the significance of the Shah's visits, Soviet commentators stressed their practical value; West Europe and America exported to Iran ten times as much as they bought from her. Requests to increase their imports from Iran had been ignored and the country's foreign trade balance as a result had been constantly negative. The socialist countries, on the other hand, had developed their contacts on a mutually advantageous basis.[59] The statistics were a little over-simplified; they ignored Iranian exports of oil to the West as well as Western financial aid and capital investment. But it could not be denied that for Iranian products other than oil it was not easy to find markets in the West. Iran, to quote an extreme example, imported from West Germany goods valued at $206 million in 1966–7, but German investments in Iran during the period were a mere $2 million.[60]

As one result of the Shah's visits to East Europe, and of other trade negotiations, several commercial treaties were signed in 1966–7, providing for exchanges totalling about $380 million (Poland, 159 million; Czechoslovakia, 107 million; Rumania, 104 million; Bulgaria, 15 million). The East European countries showed great interest in oil imports from Iran, in view of the high prices demanded for Soviet oil and their own growing oil consumption. Of particular significance in this context was the 'oil-tractor' agreement with Rumania concluded in August 1966. In return for substantial deliveries of oil, Rumania was to supply Iran with 15,000 tractors, accessories, and spare parts over the next five years, a tractor-manufacturing and a tractor-assembly plant. Rumania was to gain a near monopoly in the supply of tractors to Iran. The agreement ran into difficulties in its early stages because Iranian experts were said to dislike the tractors which Bucharest wanted to deliver; they had originally been destined for China.

The Shah's trips to the Soviet Union and East Europe were followed by other official visits, including one by prime minister Hodeyda to the Soviet capital in 1967 and Kosygin's state visit to Tehran in April 1968. The Rumanian and Iranian premiers exchanged visits, the Shah's sisters went to Czechoslovakia and the Soviet Union, and a great many parliamentary and technical delegations also went to and fro. Not all of these exchanges were outstanding successes; if the Tehran government had hoped to gain Soviet support for its interests in the Persian Gulf, Mr Kosygin poured cold water on their expectations. A Soviet official statement about the Persian Gulf published one day before Kosygin's intended visit was officially confirmed, made it clear that Moscow was critical of the Iranian attitude.[61] Nor was there any good reason to take at face value the ritual statements published at the end of such meetings; the Soviet press noted after Hodeyda's visit that Iran was 'alarmed by Israel's continued aggression against the Arab states and the escalation of the criminal war of American imperialism in Vietnam'. Both sides were no doubt aware that neither Israel nor Vietnam was a major preoccupation for Iran, and that the Tehran government had no reason to feel particularly unhappy about the defeat suffered by

Nasser at the hands of the Israelis. But even the meetings that were only partly successful had a cumulative effect; they contributed towards a reorientation of Iranian policy after years of almost total dependence on the West. Its repercussions were felt in the foreign, political and military fields as well as in Iran's economy, to which we shall now turn.

The new confidence shown in Tehran in the middle sixties was one of the most striking by-products of the economic progress that had been achieved. After uncontrolled inflation in 1960–1, Iran's economy began to show an upward trend; between 1964 and 1967 there was an annual growth of almost 11 per cent while the cost of living rose by less than one per cent. The wheat and barley harvest rose from 3·1 million tons in 1962–3 to 5·2 million in 1967; for the first time Iran was able to export grain as well as to meet her own needs. Despite the sizable increase in agricultural output, its share of the gross national product steadily declined (from 34 per cent in 1959–60 to 24 per cent in 1966–7) as the result of the rapid pace of industrialization. *Per capita* income, one of the lowest in the world, rose from $197 in 1965 to $220 in 1968; according to the plan, it was planned to reach $307 in 1973 if the 57 per cent growth of the GNP contemplated in the fourth Iranian five-year plan (1968–73) was reached. The three main centres of industrialization were the Isfahan region, where big new steel works were erected, Ahwaz-Abadan, the centre of the oilfields and the petro-chemical industry, and the Tabriz district, where machine industry was increasingly concentrated.[62]

Economic help to Iran in the past had come mainly from the United States; US aid to Iran between 1954 and 1967, including government loans and grants and the US share of aid provided by the UN and the World Bank, totalled $1·9 billion. In 1967 it amounted to $190 million, of which $83 million were part of a programme of military aid. The US aid mission to Tehran was shut down at the end of 1967; American representatives had reached the conclusion that, given the rapid economic expansion, aid was no longer needed.[63]

Oil has been the key factor in Iran's economic development. Until nationalization in 1951, Iran was the leading producer in the

Middle East; as a result of the upheavals of the early fifties it had fallen back to third place after Kuwait and Saudi Arabia, even though the State income from the sale of oil rose more than three-fold between 1951 and 1965. Oil operations were still wholly managed by an international consortium of fourteen Western oil companies.[64] Successive Iranian governments had insisted on regaining for their country the lead in Middle East oil production and accused the consortium of slowing down production and thus hampering the economic development of the country. Prime minister Hodeyda publicly charged the oil companies with 'provocation',[65] and the Shah threatened that Iran would break the agreement with the consortium if new arrangements were not made. The dilemma facing the consortium was that a 20 per cent increase per year, as demanded by the Iranian government for a five-year period, was bound to cause a substantial fall in oil prices, since world demand was expected to rise by only 9 per cent per year in the near future (7 per cent in 1967). The oil companies argued that there was world overproduction of oil, that additional new markets did not exist, and that the idea that a producer could push up output regardless of whether the commodity could be sold was totally unrealistic.[66] In addition, it would have brought Iran into sharp conflict with the other producing countries, which were equally eager to increase their output. Against this, Iran argued that it needed the income from the oil industry far more urgently than sparsely populated countries such as Kuwait (not to mention Abu Dhabi), and that its entire economic future was in danger unless oil production (and consequently its own income) was increased to about 280 million tons in 1973.

The intricacies of Middle East oil policies are discussed elsewhere in this study, but they deserve at least a cursory mention here, for in Soviet-Iranian relations these issues have played an important part. According to the Soviet view, the international oil cartel not only organized the boycott of the nationalized Iranian oil on world markets between 1951 and 1953, but had also exerted pressure on Iran ever since.[67] The Soviet thesis that the West kept down oil production because it needed an economically underdeveloped Iran as a supplier of raw materials and as a market for industrial goods found some willing believers in

Tehran; so did the suggestion that the government ought to pursue an independent policy 'free from the shackles imposed by the consortium'.[68]

The Iranian communists, as usual, went much further in their attacks, claiming that the oil consortium was far stronger than the government, that the Shah and his advisers were in 'secret collusion' with the oil-plunderers, and that they were 'systematically betraying' their country.[69]

For all their complaints about the oil companies, there was no doubt in the minds of the Persian leaders that in the foreseeable future West Europe and Japan would remain by far their best customers. The Soviet Union, as a matter of principle, did not import substantial quantities of crude oil, and the purchases of the other communist states were small in comparison with the needs of the OECD countries. The one advantage of trade with East Europe was that it was conducted on the basis of a clearing agreement, and thus did not involve convertible currency. Iran paid with crude oil for the import of machines, and this was likely to ease the pressure on her chronic balance of payments deficit.

It would be tedious to enumerate in detail the various trade agreements between Iran, the Soviet Union, and the other East European countries. The 1963 deal concerned the joint building of a hydro-electric station and reservoir on the frontier river Aras, and Soviet assistance to Iran in breeding fish. Far more ambitious were the agreements of January 1966 and March 1967. The first provided for the delivery of natural gas from Iran, hitherto unused, to the Soviet Union for a period of twelve years, and a 42-inch pipeline was to be built from the oilfields of Khuzistan to the Soviet border west of the Caspian Sea; the flow of gas, amounting to 10,000 billion cubic metres per year (rising to 20,000 billion later on), was scheduled to start in 1970: its total value was thought to be about $66 million per year and likely to rise.[70] These gas deliveries were to pay for the various Soviet projects in Iran, such as the $230 million steel plant near Isfahan (with an annual capacity of 500,000–600,000 tons, and a possible expansion to more than 2 million), a machine-tool factory, compressors and services in building the pipeline, and about $20 million for the Aras dam. In addition the Soviet Union undertook to buy a sizable share of Iran's exports; almost all its wool exports, two thirds or more of lead ore, karakul skins, and henna – not to mention 40 per cent of Persia's caviar.

Trade expanded by leaps and bounds. In the early sixties the Soviet Union accounted for less than 3 per cent of Persian imports and had taken 13 per cent of its exports; in 1967 total trade turnover exceeded $70 million, more than double the figure for 1965.[71] As a neighbour, Russia had traditionally been one of Iran's chief trading partners, and was among its best customers for products other than oil up to the early thirties. Soviet economists were aware that Western firms held a secure place on the Iranian market and that there was still a certain amount of prejudice against Soviet machinery – 'largely inspired by competitors';[72] they had no illusions about the limit of Soviet-Iranian trade expansion. Soviet experts calculated that with the agreements reached the Soviet share in Iranian imports would not exceed 12 per cent by 1974.[73] It came only sixth in the list, behind West Germany, the United States, Britain, Italy, and Japan. Iran receives at present (1970) about $1,225 million annually from its sales of oil to the West and Japan; total Soviet credits are approximately one quarter that sum ($330 million) and extend over several years. A realistic appraisal of the magnitude of Soviet-Iranian trade and its prospects can be formed only by comparing these figures.

Among the Iranian debts to which the natural gas was mortgaged the politically most interesting item was an allocation of $110 million for Soviet military equipment, mainly trucks, half-trucks, and small arms. This arms deal did not cover sophisticated equipment and did not necessitate the presence of many Soviet instructors. The idea that Western officers in charge of Phantom jets and other CENTO weapons would have to rub shoulders with their Soviet counterparts in Iran had at first caused shudders in the Western capitals. The United States had provided virtually all of Iran's armament since the end of the Second World War, and the news in July 1966 that Tehran was considering the purchase of surface-to-air missiles in Moscow provoked a minor shock in Washington. The Tehran government explained its need for such sophisticated weapons with reference to the vulnerability of the Persian Gulf loading installations, especially at Kharg Island, to the Arab air forces – equipped by the Russians. 'We do not even have any anti-aircraft guns to protect us in the Gulf,' the Shah is reported to have said.[74] American surface-to-air missiles could be bought only for cash or on short-term credit at $2\frac{1}{2}$ per cent interest. The Soviet government, however, showed little enthusiasm for this particular deal,[75] and the Shah eventually accepted an American offer to modernize the Iranian air defence forces.

The Soviet-Iranian arms deal was welcomed, not surprisingly, by the Persian communists, who argued that this proved that there was no Soviet threat, for 'What country contemplates attacking another state while at the same time supplying it with defensive weapons?'[76] The Tehran government's arms policy was to play it safe. A high-level Iranian army delegation under General Bahram Anian, the chief of staff, went to Moscow in December 1967 to negotiate about further arms supplies for delivery in May 1968, while the Shah was seeking $600 million credits in America for the purchase over a period of six years of supersonic fighter-bombers, modern tanks, and other sophisticated weapons.[77]

The heavy preoccupation of the Persian government with military problems (a defence budget of $512 million in 1968) reflected the changed foreign political situation. As the danger from the north receded, as Britain gave up Aden and announced that it would withdraw from the Persian Gulf in 1971, there was growing concern in Tehran about the defence of its vital interests in that area. Bahrain had always been considered Iran's fourteenth province; any advance by pan-Arab forces in either the Persian Gulf area or South Arabia was considered an immediate threat to Iran. In the past the quarrel had centred on such relatively harmless topics as whether the Gulf should be named 'Persian' or 'Arab', or on Tehran's refusal to recognize Bahraini postage stamps. With Britain's withdrawal the whole question was likely to be reopened. Tehran would have favoured an agreement with Saudi Arabia and Kuwait, but any alliance with Saudi Arabia was looked upon with great disfavour by Moscow,[78] whereas the Emir of Kuwait was too afraid of radical Arab nationalism to pursue an independent policy. In 1968 diplomatic relations between Tehran and Cairo were restored and the Iraqi prime minister visited the Iranian capital. But it remained doubtful whether there could be a lasting reconciliation between Tehran and the pan-Arab leaders, the traditional animosity between Persians and Arabs quite apart. The Arabs still claimed Persian Khuzistan (a demand pressed in particular by the left-wing Ba'th), and Iran continued to regard Bahrain as part of its territory. The danger of armed conflict in the Persian Gulf after withdrawal of the British forces had been by no means entirely removed.

It is doubtful whether Iran, given a free choice, would really have chosen the Soviet Union as its neighbour, as the Shah once said in Moscow in an after-dinner speech, if only because Russia was so much larger and stronger. Since the question had been decided, not on the basis of free will, Iran had to make the best of it; once the cold war had receded, successive Iranian governments engaged, not unsuccessfully, in a balancing act: they collaborated with the Russians in building various enterprises in the north, while in southern Iran cooperation with the oil companies continued. The building of the big pipeline from the south to the Soviet border was in some ways symbolic: up to Saveh in the centre of the country Western firms were to build it; from Saveh on the Russians would continue the work. American setbacks in Vietnam and the British retreat from Aden and the coming withdrawal from the Persian Gulf strengthened the Tehran government in its belief that it had to accommodate itself (within limits) to the Russians, who seemed reasonable and helpful, had dropped all territorial claims, and no longer gave active support to the Iranian communists. Traditional suspicions had not disappeared, and the idea of a Soviet presence in Aden or the Persian Gulf did not fill Persian hearts with joy. The neutralist policy, moreover, had one serious flaw: it was based on the assumption that the global balance of power and the equilibrium in the Middle East would remain more or less stable. But if it changed in favour of the Soviet Union, there was the danger that the northern neighbours might not be satisfied with mere neutrality. The effects of such a development on Iran's position could not be taken lightly. To a large extent its future depended on the measure of domestic progress, the speed of modernization and industrialization, and the rise in the standard of living. In contrast to some other Middle East states, Iran is a nation with a long national tradition and thus, despite all transient difficulties, great reserves of strength. Progress and stability, to be sure, ultimately depends not only on the yearly rate of growth, but on the government's success in regaining the confidence of an *élite*, large sections of which were still disaffected, in bringing about a community of purpose between the leaders and the people. Accelerated economic growth *per se* would result in greater prosperity, but not necessarily in greater stability. Until these aims are realized, and radical changes within the regime had taken place, Iran is bound to remain doubly vulnerable.

4
Russia, Zionism, Israel .

Soviet attitudes towards Israel, unfriendly almost from the beginning, became more hostile as Moscow's relations with the Arab countries improved; but they were also affected by the existence of a 'Jewish question' inside the Soviet Union. The traditional Soviet and communist approach to Zionism before the establishment of the Jewish state was wholly negative. The Communist party in Palestine denied the very principle of Jewish immigration, let alone the idea of a national home, which did not make it exactly popular within the Jewish community. The Soviet decision in 1947 to vote at the United Nations for a Jewish state came as an agreeable surprise to Zionists; the Soviet Union was among the very first to grant the Jewish state full diplomatic recognition. This Soviet-Israeli honeymoon did not, however, last; it was only a brief and, in retrospect, somewhat incongruous interlude. There was at the end of the war a great deal of sympathy for the remnants of European Jewry. However hard-boiled the Kremlin's policy may be, it is not impossible that the Soviet leaders, too, were not immune to this general sentiment. Unwilling to revise their basic attitude towards Zionism, they nevertheless recognized the necessity to find a haven for the survivors of the holocaust. From the point of view of Soviet interests in the Middle East, moreover, a good case could be made for supporting Jewish statehood. The Jewish independence movement in Palestine fulfilled an 'objectively progressive' function, for it helped to weaken Britain's position in the Middle East, and, generally speaking, added to the unrest which in Soviet eyes was a symptom of the unfolding general crisis of capitalism. The Arab world was at the time still ruled by monarchs

(Farouk, the Hashemites) and reactionary *élites*; there was not much scope for an active Soviet foreign policy in these countries.

Soon after the establishment of the state, the first unfriendly commentaries began to appear in the Soviet press. This change in attitude was caused mainly by domestic factors. Stalin and his advisers had clearly over-rated the extent to which the Jews had been integrated into Soviet society. According to Soviet doctrine, the national problem had long ago been solved: this was one of the triumphs of Leninism-Stalinism. In fact, the situation was a great deal more complicated. While many individual Jews had been prominent Bolsheviks in the early years of the regime, the great majority of them were purged in the thirties. Most Soviet Jews were not party members and their attitude towards the regime was as ambivalent as that of other national minorities. During Stalin's last years they were singled out for persecution; individual Jews were arrested and some were executed, an un-official *numerus clausus* was introduced, and some professions were closed to them altogether. All this contributed to the alienation of Soviet Jews; there is some reason to believe that but for Stalin's death Soviet Jews would have been hit even more severely by a systematic campaign which was anti-semitic in everything but name. The establishment of the state of Israel struck a deep emotional chord among many of them, however irreligious and alienated from Jewish traditions. The arrival of the first Israeli ambassador to Moscow turned into a spontaneous popular demonstration without precedent in the Soviet capital. This was a cause of much concern to the Soviet leadership, and within a few months an anti-Zionist campaign was launched. It was to be made clear beyond any shadow of doubt that diplomatic relations with the state of Israel did not entail sympathy with Zionism; Soviet Jews were to have no ties with their co-religionists abroad; the Soviet Union was their homeland and they would not be permitted to emigrate to Israel. As the anti-Jewish purge became more intense in 1951–2, the accusations became louder and wilder. Jewish organizations and individual Jews, not necessarily Zionist, were denounced as inveterate enemies of the Soviet Union.

Soviet-Israeli relations, never particularly close, were naturally affected by this campaign; a few months before Stalin's death diplomatic ties were severed. The campaign ceased after the death of the dictator, those arrested were released, the preparations for show trials were discontinued, and after a brief interval diplomatic relations with Israel were resumed. But there was no dramatic improvement: the Jewish problem in the Soviet Union persisted; while Soviet Jews had no longer to fear for their lives, many anomalies in their status remained, and promotion in many fields remained difficult if not impossible; they were treated as a minority, but did not have the rights of political and cultural autonomy given to other national minorities. According to the official version, Soviet Jews had been completely assimilated; they did not need schools or newspapers of their own, and they certainly did not want to emigrate. But in fact, Soviet society being what it was, full assimilation was very difficult for them. There is little doubt that, given the opportunity, a sizable number would have left the country. Traditional, popular anti-Semitism had by no means been stamped out altogether in the Soviet Union; in addition, suspicion of the Jews persisted on the part of the party and state organs. Unlike other minorities, the Jews, or at least many of them, had relations abroad; their national and cultural centre lay elsewhere, they could not be relied upon in an emergency. Describing a vicious circle, this distrust in its turn caused further disaffection among the Jews. By the late nineteen-fifties only a few Jewish 'technicians' were left in the Soviet political leadership.

The attitude towards Israel was also increasingly affected by the growing Soviet involvement in the Arab world. Once the state of Israel was established, it ceased to be an agent of revolutionary ferment, and thus had no further value for the Kremlin. In the Arab countries, on the other hand, the anti-Western movement gained strength in the early nineteen-fifties. The anti-British demonstrations in Egypt and Iraq, the overthrow of Farouk, the mounting disturbances in Syria – all attracted Soviet attention. With the arms deal of 1955 the groundwork was laid for close political military and economic cooperation with Egypt and Syria. With all its hostility to Israel, however, the Soviet Union had apparently at first no desire to become involved in the Arab-

Israeli dispute, which it regarded as a national conflict of no direct concern to itself. But since the struggle against Israel figured very high on the list of Arab priorities Soviet diplomats soon realized that, short of giving substantial assistance to the Arabs against Israel, they would make little headway in the Arab world. While unwilling to accept the more extreme Arab demands (e.g. the destruction of the Jewish state), the Soviet Union began to give full support in the United Nations to all other Arab complaints. A massive propaganda campaign was launched against Israel, where there was growing concern about the large-scale Soviet arms shipments, including many weapons that the Jews could not get from the Western powers. There was little doubt in Israeli minds that these arms would ultimately be used, not against 'Western imperialism', but in that war against Israel which featured so prominently in countless speeches, articles, and solemn declarations issuing from the Arab world. Concern at the growing Soviet antagonism was shared by the left, traditionally pro-Soviet in its outlook, where it was felt that Soviet policy, while on the whole progressive and worthy of support, was blatantly one-sided in the Arab-Israeli conflict, giving full backing to the Arabs, irrespective of the merits of the case in the light of 'proletarian internationalism'. Eventually even the Israeli Communist party faltered; having stoically and faithfully supported Soviet anti-Israel policy for almost two decades, it split more or less on national lines. The extreme left was deeply pained by Russia's attitude, and depressed by its support for the Arabs in the Security Council, which, they thought, made any effective United Nations action for peace impossible. Above all, there was the problem of Soviet Jewry. If Israel was to grow and to develop, it needed hundreds of thousands of newcomers. Immigration from the Soviet Union, to be sure, had been stopped in the nineteen-twenties, but Jews had been permitted to emigrate to Israel from most of the 'people's democracies' (including Poland, Bulgaria, and Rumania). Was it altogether unrealistic to assume that one day the gates of the Soviet Union would also be opened? Soviet anti-Zionist and anti-Israel campaigns were followed in Israel more in sorrow than in anger, and many efforts were made to 'talk' to the Russians, to persuade them to reexamine their attitude. There was a great deal of sympathy for things Russian, not perhaps for the Soviet regime but certainly for Russian literature and music. The old Israeli establishment had modelled itself on the pattern of the radical Russian intelligentsia. The Soviet response, while negative on all basic political issues, was sufficiently vague to encourage the belief (among those eager to believe) that an improvement could be achieved if only Israel would reorientate its policy. An unsentimental analysis would have shown that a basic change in the Soviet attitude was well-nigh impossible. Unlike the 'people's democracies', the Soviet Union could not let any sizable number of Jews go, for this would have been an admission of the failure of Soviet nationalities policy. It would moreover have created a dangerous precedent and caused serious problems with other national minorities. Above all, it would have thwarted political efforts in the Arab world. As between the Arab states and Israel, the Soviet Union never wavered. The Arab world had a great revolutionary potential, in the sense that anti-Western attitudes were deeply ingrained, whereas Israel, having established a reasonably modern state, could not feel the same resentment towards the West, quite apart from its many ties with Jews in the Western world. Above all, and most decisively, the Arabs were the stronger battalions; the few Jews could not resist 60 million Arabs who, with Soviet help, would soon overcome their backwardness. All ideological reservations apart, there was the hard fact that Israel had only 2, not 20 million inhabitants, and even if it had radically changed its policy it would have remained in Soviet eyes far less important than the Arabs. For this reason, if for no other, Israeli attempts to bring about a change in Soviet policy were doomed to fail. The main themes of Soviet anti-Israel propaganda hardly changed between 1955 and 1968; there were merely ups and downs in the intensity of the campaign. After the rise of the Neo-Ba'th in Syria in February 1966, the line became harsher than before, but too much significance should not be read into these variations of the Soviet political barometer: on the whole there was remarkable consistency.

From summer 1957 onwards, the Soviet press and radio gave much publicity to the reports of individual Soviet citizens who, misled by Zionist propaganda, had been deeply disappointed by their bitter experiences in the 'Zionist paradise'. (A few Soviet citizens, mainly from the formerly Polish regions and the Baltic republics, were permitted each year to rejoin their relatives in Israel. The number of permits granted averaged between 50 and 150 a month.) The Soviet press was particularly critical of Israeli claims to have established a socialist society; the *kibbutzim* were described as labour camps in which idealistic workers were exploited by Wall Street bloodsuckers. Israel was attacked for having collaborated with Nazism in the past, and for whitewashing the Third Reich by accepting reparations from West Germany. Israel, according to the Soviet version, was a willing tool of American monopoly capitalism, engaging in ugly plots against the progressive regimes in the Arab world. On the subject of Israeli strength (or weakness) there was considerable ambiguity: Israel was described at one and the same time as a puppet and an imperialist power in its own right. Before the war of 1967 the general tendency was to stress its utter dependence on America, whereas after the war there was an inclination to describe it as in itself imperialist, inciting peaceful but gullible Americans against the Soviet Union, sowing enmity and distrust between the two super-powers. The activities of Israeli tourists in the Soviet Union and of Israeli diplomats in Moscow were frequently given attention in the press, and Soviet citizens were warned of the dangers of ideological contamination. Africans and Asians were exhorted not to accept Israeli technical help, for Zion's emissaries were agents of NATO and of world imperialism. They were acting on behalf of the big oil companies, which were eager to provoke a war in order to perpetuate their hold on the area. It was never made quite clear how a new war could help the oil companies, which wanted above all peace and stability. Since they were the first to suffer in any crisis, their feelings towards Israel, whose very existence complicated their relations with Arab governments, were anything but friendly. Israel was accused by the Soviet press and radio of producing poison gas, atomic bombs, and other means of mass destruction, usually in co-operation with West Germany. Soviet arms deliveries to the Arab countries, on the other hand, were not thought to be a matter of public interest.[1] Whenever clashes occurred along the Arab-Israel borders, only the Cairo or Damascus version was reproduced, and the impression gained by the unsuspecting Soviet reader must have been frightening: an aggressive state engaging incessantly in totally unprovoked attacks on its peaceful neighbours, a permanent danger to peace in the area and indeed to the whole world. Israel was furious about the systematic campaign of vilification; it probably under-rated the sales resistance of Soviet readers who, given their long experience, had learned to read *Pravda* and *Izvestia* with critical eyes and were not deeply affected by the stream of invective. Occasionally the propaganda over-reached itself and had to beat a temporary retreat. One example was the publication of a book, *Judaism without Embellishment*, which drew freely on traditional anti-semitic themes and contained particularly offensive cartoons.[2] It was withdrawn from circulation, but other books continued to appear, not much less aggressive and mendacious in tone. An article in *Komsomolskaia Pravda* put the number of Zionist followers in the United States at between 20 and 25 millions, and described them as having virtual control of America (59 per cent of all business enterprises, 70 per cent of the law firms, 80 per cent of the mass media).[3] Such crudities caused no little embarrassment to Western communists: 'Where do you get that kind of figure?' asked the chairman of the Communist party of the state of California. 'You get them from one kind of source, the Gerald L. K. Smiths and so forth, the anti-semites of the United States.'

The question of Soviet motives is an important one. There was a great deal of unabashed cynicism and Israelis were probably ill advised to get over-excited about what was the normal Soviet way to express disapproval of those whom it disliked or with whom it disagreed. There is no good reason to believe that the Soviet leaders were genuinely convinced that Israel had been the aggressor in every clash with the Arabs; Soviet comments after the Six Day War made it clear that the Russians had been unhappy about the extremism of certain Arab leaders and the excesses of Arab propaganda. But in addition to the anti-Israel polemics, normal by Soviet standards, there was an edge of extra hostility that cannot be explained within the framework of Marxism-Leninism, a shrillness and intensity which stemmed partly from traditional antagonism towards Jews and which often ascribed to them both superhuman cunning and inherently evil intentions. The 'Protocols of the Elders of Zion', the concept of Jewish world domination, had, after all, emanated from Russia. Old-fashioned anti-semitism was contemptuously rejected after the revolution, but the deeper instincts which had, *inter alia*, produced the 'Protocols' were by no means totally uprooted, and conspiracy theories became more fashionable than ever. A Soviet communist was conditioned to see plots everywhere and his task was to unmask them; this, to a considerable extent, determined his approach to Zionism, Israel, and the Jews in general. Those who made Soviet policy did not altogether disbelieve their own propaganda; it is usually not at all easy to establish with any degree of certitude where cynicism ended and conviction began.

Mention has been made of the Syrian *coup* of February 1966 which brought the Neo-Ba'th to power in Syria. From that date on there was a steady stream of Soviet announcements that Israel was about to attack this, the most progressive of all Arab states, alone or in combination with the US Sixth Fleet, or in collaboration with the reactionary forces in the Arab world. There has been such warnings in the past, but after February 1966 they became a permanent feature of Soviet propaganda. During the month of May 1966, to give but one example, there was a strong warning (7 May) by the diplomatic correspondent of *Izvestia*, Kondrachov, claiming that Israel had elevated provocations against neighbouring states to the level of official policy; one third of Israel's army had been moved to the Syrian border. *Pravda* returned to the same subject on 21 May; on the following day Radio Moscow announced that the danger of war in the Middle East was now extremely acute. To give additional emphasis to this warning, it was followed by an official statement by the Soviet government on 27 May; the Soviet Union would not remain indifferent to attempts to violate peace in the immediate proximity of its frontiers.[4] The next few days brought further articles and broadcasts and an official note on the same lines was handed to the Israeli ambassador in Moscow.

Between May 1966 and the outbreak of war the year after, not a single month passed without at least one such crisis. It is possible that the one in May 1966 was deliberately provoked; it followed the visit to Moscow by Yusef Zuayin, the new Syrian prime minister. One could think of a number of reasons which may have induced both Russians and Syrians to create a war scare: it was bound to strengthen the Neo-Ba'th regime internally, deter Israel from retaliating against the guerrilla forces operating from Syrian territory, compel Syria's enemies in the Arab world to give at least verbal support to the Arab sister country threatened by Zionist attacks, induce Nasser to cooperate more closely with the new Syrian regime. It must have seemed a clever stratagem involving no risks, for Israel, utterly dependent on the United States, would not dare to engage in large-scale military action against America's wish. But war scares in the Middle East have a self-generating effect, and in the long run they can be self-fulfilling. If the scare of May 1966 was deliberately provoked despite better knowledge, there is no reason to assume that all the subsequent scares were orchestrated in a similar manner.

The outbreak of war in 1967 and the war scare preceding it were part of a chain reaction which had been started by Soviet leaders in cooperation with their allies in the Arab world, over whom they perhaps lost control. Accident, misunderstanding, and misinformation played a great (and growing) role once the train of events had been set in motion. Conjuring up foreign political threats for domestic purposes had been one of Stalin's favourite tactics; in the late nineteen-twenties he invoked the threat of Anglo-French military intervention, when in fact there was no such danger. These war scares always followed a certain pattern; they were never totally implausible. There had, after all, been a war of intervention in Russia in 1918–19, and the Israelis had attacked Egypt in 1956. The belief in conspiracy as a main agent in politics has always had a strong appeal in the Soviet Union and the Arab world. Such inclinations are dangerous if coupled with the frequent use of disinformation as a political weapon; it seems to be well beyond human capacity to sow suspicion without ill effects on one's own judgement.

Within the Soviet establishment there was not complete unanimity with regard to Israel. Among the intelligentsia many felt unhappy about the thinly veiled anti-semitic policy directed against 'rootless cosmopolitans'; they realized that Soviet enmity towards Israel could be explained more easily by the requirements of power politics than by communist ideology. The Russian intelligentsia had traditionally regarded anti-semitism as morally and intellectually beyond the pale; other parts of Russian society had been more receptive. In theory, anti-semitism was a crime in the Soviet Union, but the constant anti-Israel campaign was bound to create the impression that Zionism was merely a synonym for the Jews.

For very different reasons, there were misgivings about the wisdom of Soviet Middle East policy among technocrats and even military leaders; they regarded economic assistance and arms shipments on such a lavish scale as a doubtful investment. The Soviet economy was still in need of capital and capital goods, and they failed to understand why priority should be given to foreign countries ruled by non-communists, and not too efficiently at that. Among the foreign political experts, too, counsels were divided: those dealing with the third world warmly endorsed the support given to Nasser and the Syrians; others, dealing with Europe and America, realized that the anti-Israel policy was not popular in the West, even among communists. It also provoked criticism among Russia's East European allies, partly for economic reasons (they had to foot some of the bills of Soviet Middle East policy), partly on political grounds. These then were the doves. The hawks were found mainly among the guardians of party orthodoxy, and those who disliked Jews and were glad to rationalize their feeling in ideological terms; there were not a few in the army, the leadership of the party, and the communist youth organization, the Komsomol, favouring a more dynamic and expansive foreign policy and demanding that Israel be 'taught a lesson'. Between the ideologists who backed the military regimes in Egypt and Syria and those who had strong reservations about them and did not rule out a betrayal on their part, there were the middle-grounders, firmly anti-Israel, who, however, refrained from giving free rein to anti-Jewish sentiments. This is not to suggest that there was a violent tug-of-war among the Soviet leaders; Israel was not of sufficient importance to preoccupy them for long; but the differences of opinion, although not extreme, were sufficiently wide to make it difficult at any given time to talk about a full political consensus; the days of total unanimity in the Kremlin had long since passed. If a war scare was launched at a certain point, this did not necessarily mean that the entire leadership had decided to intensify the conflict in the Middle East. The initiative might have been taken by a group of hawks without any prior consultation and decision at the highest level.

Such seems to have been the case with regard to the crisis in May 1967. The news about Israeli troop concentrations and the impending invasion of Syria which started the scare came from Soviet and Syrian sources. The Egyptians, as it subsequently transpired, regarded these fears as 'hallucinations',[5] but they decided for reasons of their own to act as if the warnings were justified. This still leaves open the question whether the Russians were acting on the basis of wrong information, a possibility that cannot be entirely excluded. Their whole appraisal of Israel, of its readiness to fight, and of the military capacity of Egypt and Syria were, as later appeared, quite mistaken. It is equally possible that for a variety of reasons the news about Israeli troop concentrations was deliberately fabricated against better knowledge.[6]

It can be taken for granted that most Soviet leaders did not at that time want a war between Israel and the Arab countries; there was genuine surprise and confusion as the conflict escalated after Nasser's closure of the Straits of Tiran. There is reason to doubt whether Moscow had been informed beforehand that Nasser was about to take this step, but once the decision had been taken the Soviet leaders faced a serious dilemma. They simply had to support the Arabs; the Soviet government statement on 24 May made it clear that they would stand by them if they were attacked; but they also made it known directly to Nasser, and by implication in their public pronouncements, that they would not support a 'holy war' against Israel such as the Arabs proclaimed. Soviet policy at this stage was to give political help to Nasser and to work for an 'acceptable, just, and peaceful solution' of the crisis – that is, to make it possible for Egypt to keep the gains it had just made. The Aqaba issue, according to Soviet comments, was not of great importance. Western propaganda, it was said on one occasion, was deliberately inflaming the problem, and on another: 'The impression is created that somebody is ready to take dangerous steps and kindle the danger of war in the Middle East in order to decide whether one or two or four ships will sail through the straits of Tiran.'[7] In the early stages of the crisis the main blame was put on America, which wanted to divert attention from an escalation of the war in Vietnam, [8] and a leading Soviet commentator wrote that the events in the Middle East should not be regarded in isolation.[9] It happened to be a mistaken appraisal of the situation, for the Middle East crisis had nothing at all to do with the bombing of the demilitarized zone in Vietnam. Later the anti-American motif was toned down; clearly negotiations with Washington had got under way and the ground-rules of the dispute had been established for the two super-powers. America and Russia would not intervene and they would work (within narrow limits) for a de-escalation of the conflict. Both Moscow and Washington sent notes to that effect to Cairo and Tel Aviv, but while Nasser privately promised that he would not fire the first shot, his spokesmen announced that war was now inevitable and that the combined might of the Arab armies would crush Israel within a few days.

At this stage Moscow no longer had control over Egypt and Syria. It could not press in the United Nations for a solution that was unacceptable to Nasser (such as a return to the *status quo ante*). Soviet spokesmen complained about the lack of American willingness to restrain Israeli extremists, and contrasted Cairo's 'constructive proposals' with Israeli 'irresponsibility'.[10] But their hands had been forced by the precipitate actions of their Arab allies; the war scare was about to turn into a real war, the political barometer was fast reaching danger-point, 'black crows were circling over the Middle East'.[11] By that time the political picture had become almost hopelessly blurred: according to the original Soviet version, Syria had been threatened by a combined Israeli-Jordanian invasion sponsored by the CIA and the oil magnates. But on 30 May Hussein signed a pact with Nasser and thus joined the anti-Israeli front. What had been described as a confrontation between 'reactionaries' and 'progressives' now became a national conflict, and while Soviet spokesmen were not at a loss for ideological explanations, these were by no means shared by all other communist parties, let alone the non-communist left in Europe and America.

While the Soviet leaders, like the American, preferred not to take any further action for the moment, both Arabs and Israelis tried to anticipate what action the Soviet Union would take in the event of armed conflict. Nasser and the Syrians thought they would not need Soviet military help provided Moscow prevented the Americans from intervening. Of this they were assured by the end of May, and it gave them great confidence, for they were convinced that the war against Israel would be a walk-over if no other powers interfered. In its statement of 23 May, the Soviet government had declared that the aggressors would face not only the united strength of the Arab countries, but also a firm riposte from the Soviet Union and other peace-loving states.[12] No one apparently bothered to find out what a 'firm riposte' meant in military and political terms: in the general euphoria it was probably not thought worthwhile to clarify such details. There is no reason to assume that the Arab countries had asked for and received a firm undertaking from the Soviet Union that there would, if necessary, be Soviet military intervention; the complaints by Boumedienne and many Arab newspapers that the Soviet Union had left its allies in the lurch after 9 June were quite unjustified.

The Israelis were naturally deeply concerned about possible Soviet action. Most of them, expecially the army leaders, thought Soviet military intervention unlikely, but in view of American uncertainties the unspecified Soviet threats could not be taken lightly; there had been warnings from Washington about the possibility of Soviet intervention. Eshkol and the foreign ministry made a desperate last-minute effort to convince the Soviet Union that Israel had no intention of invading Syria, that there had been no troop concentrations, and that the Soviet attacks on Israel had been altogether unjustified. But the Soviet diplomats were not at that stage interested in historical truth and abstract justice; their task was to threaten Israel with dire consequences if it decided to break the Egyptian blockade. This the Israelis were unwilling to accept, and after 1 June, with the danger to the existence of the state increasing daily, it was decided to act as if the Soviet threats had no substance.[13]

As far as can be ascertained in retrospect, it had been the Soviet assumption that full-scale war would not break out in the Middle East, and a quick Israeli victory was thought even less likely. Up to the very outbreak of war the line pursued by Federenko, the Soviet delegate at the UN, was that there was no particular urgency, that Israel and its backers were creating an atmosphere of artificial hysteria, and that no emergency meeting or specific action was needed. His attitude did not change during the first two days of the war; according to Soviet press and radio reports, the Egyptian and Syrian armies continued to advance into Israel and the Arab air forces continued to attack even after they had ceased to exist. As they had done in the past, the Soviet mass media published only the Arab communiqués; it was not until the night of 6 June that Moscow realized the magnitude of the defeat, and on 7 June instructions were given to Federenko to ask for an immediate cease-fire and unconditional Israeli withdrawal. The Soviet representative, who had until then prevented any action by the Security Council, now argued that the Middle East crisis was of the greatest urgency, and accused the United States of sabotaging the work of the Security Council because it was not willing to act quickly enough.

At first the Arab states rejected the Soviet proposal of a cease-fire, whereupon Federenko put the blame on Israel. Meanwhile anti-Israel protest meetings were taking place in Soviet factories and the leaders of the Soviet bloc were asked to come to an urgent meeting in Moscow on 9 June; Rumania did not sign the communiqué issued after the meeting, but Yugoslavia, exceptionally, did. It is unlikely that the posssibility of armed intervention was discussed at this meeting, if only because Arab resistance had by that time ceased. All the communist leaders could do in the circumstances was to decide on concerted political and economic action to prevent a total collapse of the 'progressive' regimes in the Arab world. It was suggested at the time that the Soviet Union might have decided to intervene had Israeli forces advanced beyond Kuneitra towards Damascus. In retrospect even that appears doubtful, because no Soviet forces were ready for such an expedition at short notice; everything had happened much too fast. On 10 June the Soviet Union broke off diplomatic relations with Israel; the other communist countries (again with the exception of Rumania) followed suit within the next few days. It is not certain whether there was unanimity in Moscow about the wisdom of this step, for it must have been clear that a break in diplomatic relations would from then on limit Russia's freedom of action in the Middle East, and make it even more difficult to bring pressure to bear on Israel in the days to come. Moscow had warned Israel so often that its very existence was at stake that Israel had almost become inured to it; short of military action, the break in diplomatic relations exhausted the Soviet arsenal, but in view of mounting dissatisfaction with the Soviet Union in the Arab world, the leaders in Moscow felt they had to take some action to reassure their allies and a diplomatic break was the least they could do. Israel, it was said, was flouting world opinion; if it did not immediately withdraw to the former borders the Soviet Union and its allies would impose sanctions 'with all their possible consequences';[14] what kind of sanctions was not specified.

The full extent of the Arab defeat did not emerge from the Soviet press even during the first weeks after the war; President Nasser's 'grave setback', itself a euphemism, became a 'difficult moment'.

The Soviet political and military leadership did not, of course, fail to realize the seriousness of the defeat; immediate measures were taken to rush arms, military instructors, and economic aid to Egypt and Syria. Substantial arms shipments and a hundred MiGs were flown to Cairo within a few days of the armistice.[15] But for the moment the main emphasis was to be in the the political field. The Soviet Union asked for an emergency session of the General Assembly of the United Nations, and when it convened on 19 June Prime Minister Kosygin appeared as the first speaker. Israel had committed a perfidy without precedent, he said, by provoking a total war of aggression against Egypt and Syria. He demanded the condemnation of Israel, the immediate retreat of

Israeli troops, and the payment of reparations to the Arab states for the damage they had suffered. It soon appeared, however, that the Soviet proposal would not gain a majority, and even a more modest Yugoslav proposal reducing the demands to one (withdrawal of Israeli troops) ran into opposition. The feeling of the majority, as subsequently expressed in the Security Council resolution of 22 November 1967, was that the withdrawal of Israeli forces from the occupied areas should be combined with the termination of all states of belligerency, freedom of shipping, and the mutual acknowledgment by all parties of the sovereignty, territorial integrity, and political independence of every state in the area.

The Soviet campaign in the United Nations was not very successful; the watered-down Soviet proposal, rejected by the Arab states as not far-reaching enough, was defeated in the General Assembly. The Security Council decision, which later on became the basis of Soviet and Arab policy, at first aroused little enthusiasm among the Arabs; Syria did not accept it and boycotted Gunnar Jarring, the Swedish mediator appointed by the United Nations. It was the aim of Soviet policy after the Six Day War to isolate Israel, to compel it eventually to give up the conquered territories. Less than a week after the end of the war Israel began to feel the full blast of Soviet displeasure, expressed in a sustained propaganda campaign almost unprecedented in its ferocity; seldom had a small country been given so much publicity in the Soviet mass media, which asserted that there had been few examples in history of such treacherous aggression as had been committed by Israel against the Arab states.[16] Israel was accused of barbaric war crimes: 'The aggressors are killing prisoners of war and defenceless peasants. They publicly execute men, women and children. . . . Even Western correspondents compare these crimes to those perpetrated by the Nazis.'[17] *Pravda* first used the term 'genocide', which was to be freely used from then on.[18] There were reports that Israeli soldiers had fired indiscriminately on passers-by in Arab villages well after the fighting had ended, that they had used wounded Arabs for target practice, and burnt whole families alive. Many Arabs had been subjected to horrible tortures. The personification of this new Israel was

Moshe Dayan, 'a pupil of Hitler and the darling of the Nazis all over the world, a man of immense brutality, cowardice, and hypocrisy'.[19] A former lackey of the British, this would-be Napoleon had developed an insatiable appetite, dreaming of an Israeli empire from the Nile to the Euphrates.[20] *Krokodil*, the Soviet satirical weekly, renamed him 'Moshe Adolfovich' and compared his campaign to Hitler's attack on Poland in 1939.[21] At his orders, Israeli soldiers had bayoneted children and raped women; the reports that they had also blown up some houses and that drunken Israeli officers and soldiers had desecrated Arab holy places came almost as an anticlimax.[22]

The campaign was not restricted to Israel; world Zionism figured equally prominently – a pack of gangsters and the tool of Wall Street bankers. Active in more than sixty countries, Zionism was not a political movement, but a criminal conspiracy directed against all peace-loving peoples. Drawing its inspiration from the teachings of Judaism, it had always been racialist in character; it was based on tyranny and slave labour; ultimately it aimed at world domination. But fortunately, owing mainly to Soviet help, these sinister plots had been uncovered in time and would be frustrated. The Israeli triumph had been a Pyrrhic victory, for in their main aim they had failed; the 'progressive' Arab regimes had not been overthrown. There was no doubt that the Israelis would fare as the Nazis did before them.

The effects of this massive propaganda campaign could not be ignored. It was hardly likely to appeal to intellectuals and the politically well-informed, but the sheer repetition of atrocity stories was bound to have a certain impact on the public at large. Outside the Soviet Union the campaign proceeded less crudely, but its aims were essentially the same and the political and psychological climate was certainly more favourable than before the Six Day War. Before 5 June 1967, the great majority of left-wing public opinion, including many communist parties, had either supported Israel or at any rate shown misgivings about Soviet policy. Israel had been openly threatened with extinction by the Arab leaders, and the Soviet version that this had been the work of only a few reactionaries and adventurists among them, and that Nasser and the Syrians had never been part of it, was given little credence. Israel's decision to go to war on 5 June was more often than not justified on the left as an act of self-defence. But once the war had ended, the general attitude began rapidly to change. Israel was no longer in immediate danger; it had shown that it could take care of itself. The Arab refugees, on the other hand, became an object of pity, and Israel's failure to provide a constructive solution provoked much criticism. Israel refused to withdraw its troops from the territory it had conquered; it now acted as an occupier. Houses were blown up, Arab civilians exiled or arrested. It seemed only natural that left-wing opinion should become more receptive to anti-Israel arguments.

Propaganda played an important role after 10 June 1967, as it had before the outbreak of the war. But, propagandist accounts apart, the Arab defeat had to be explained, both for Soviet domestic consumption and to answer the critics of the Soviet Union in the Arab world. On 9 June President Boumedienne of Algeria had openly criticized the Soviet Union for being unwilling to take greater risks in its support of the Arab cause. Later on newspapers in various Arab countries, including even Egypt, began to spread 'anti-Soviet' views (to quote a *Pravda* correspondent): the reactionaries, aided and abetted by the Chinese, were making 'dirty accusations'.[23] When President Boumedienne went to Moscow in June 1967 there was some blunt speaking. In answer to his inquiries about Soviet military assistance to the 'progressive' countries in the Arab world, the Soviet leaders asked for his view about the consequences of nuclear war. But Boumedienne, who had temporarily assumed a leading role in the Arab camp, was not put off so easily: an atomic war, after all, was likely to affect New York and Moscow much more than Algiers or Cairo.

Gradually a coherent Soviet version of the origins of the Six Day War and the Arab defeat emerged. The Israelis, of course, remained the chief villains. They had defeated the Arab armies mainly owing to the element of surprise; to believe Beliaev and Primakov, who provided the first detailed authoritative comment,[24] the attack had come more or less like a bolt from the blue. The Israelis were better equipped; just before they struck they had received major arms shipments from the imperialist powers. There were also hints of more direct military cooperation between Israel and America, but Soviet commentators preferred not to be too specific about this. They did not give wide publicity to Nasser's allegations (subsequently withdrawn) that the Sixth Fleet and the British had provided the Israelis with air support. This would have immediately exposed the Soviet Union to the charge of not having extended equal help to the Arabs. The Israelis, it was maintained, had been successful because they were fanatical and cruel. Like the Germans under Hitler, the majority of Israelis had accepted the chauvinist, imperialist policy of their leaders.[25]

There was also some criticism of the Arabs: Nasser had been betrayed by the 'military *bourgeoisie*',[26] especially in the air force command. Soviet commentators even mentioned the names of some of these 'reactionaries' who had deliberately sabotaged the Arab war effort because they thought the progressive changes taking place in the UAR a greater danger than Israel. Certain Arab propagandists were also taken to task; Ahmad Shukairy's extremist slogans ('throw the Israelis into the sea') had done great harm to the Arab cause. Nasser and the Syrian leaders (who had been as extreme in their declarations), were, publicly at least, exempt from criticism; their behaviour had been statesmanlike throughout the crisis; they had been the victims of calumny spread by the Western press. Not the new, progressive Egypt and Syria had been defeated by the Israelis, but the remnants of the old order, which unfortunately were still quite strong.[27] But given Nasser's (and the Egyptian people's) fervent wish to purge these reactionary and anti-Soviet elements who had thwarted the Arab war effort, they would overcome their present weakness, become much stronger, and eventually regain the lost territories. Such encouragement was, however, frequently mixed with criticism of the Arabs, not only for their ultra-radical slogans in the past, but also for their intransigence in the present, which 'objectively played into Israel's hands'. Some Soviet commentators thought Arab unwillingness to recognize Israel unwise, and were concerened about the 'ultra-leftists' who suggested a new round immediately, even if it meant certain Arab defeat.[28] Arab opposition to the Security Council resolution was also wrong: 'justified though it was, it actually played into the hands of Israel, enabling her to drag out the solution of the main issue – the withdrawal of troops'.[29] On occasion Soviet observers admitted that in a strange way Israel was objectively playing a progressive role: it had been a factor making for Arab unity and for progressive development (that is, radicalization) in the Arab world.[30] This was, in other words, Hegel's cunning of reason, the price that had to be paid both for Arab unity and for the road to socialism. But it was a high price, for it compelled the Arab states to spend large sums on defence rather than economic development, and it provided 'fertile soil for leftist adventurism', which, disregarding the practical position, called for an immediate new round of fighting.[31]

The Arab-Israeli war had political repercussions in East Europe out of proportion to its intrinsic importance, and apparently it also provoked some dissension within the Soviet Union. While Soviet propaganda remained on the whole bitterly hostile to Israel, there were occasional dissenting voices claiming that, after all, there was a difference between Hitler's war and the events of June 1967,[32] and that it should be made clearer that the Soviet people was not anti-semitic. Soviet statements oscillated between open threats of Soviet intervention and possible annihilation of the state of Israel,[33] and communiqués that were remarkably moderate in tone, omitting even any reference to Israeli aggression.[34] Neutral observers in Moscow reported that there was a good deal of sneaking admiration for Israel's achievement, among both the military and the political leaders, and deep disappointment with the Arabs, even if for obvious reasons it could not be publicly voiced.

In East Europe the Arab-Israeli war was one of the reasons for the further polarization in the communist camp. It helped to trigger off both the Czech thaw and the Polish cultural pogrom in the spring of 1968. Pro-Israel sentiments had been fairly pronounced in some East European countries, despite (or because of) the Soviet line; there was identification with a small country which had successfully resisted the pressure exerted by much stronger forces. In Poland, on the other hand, where the leadership faced an acute internal crisis, the Jews became pawns in the struggle between rival factions: they were made scapegoats for the riots that broke out in March 1968. 'Cleanse the party of Zionists' became the new watchword (as if there had been any Zionists in the Communist party of Poland). It was a deeply cynical performance, and no one could say what its long-term results would be. It was the first time that a communist regime had openly sacrificed internationalism, hitherto one of the basic tenets of communist ideology, in theory as well as in practice. There were few victims, but the political implications were more far-reaching than those of the Slansky trial in Czechoslovakia. What happened in Poland heralded a movement in the communist world away from traditional beliefs towards a new order in which nationalism (and national enmities), rather than Marxism-Leninism, became the main ideological cement. Polish 'anti-Zionism' found some admirers in the Soviet Union,[35] provoked open resistance in Czechoslovakia and Yugoslavia,[36] and was the cause of acute embarrassment to communist parties in the West.

Some of the smaller European communist parties (the Dutch, Austrian, and Swiss, for instance) had been critical of all-out Soviet support for the Arabs, and there was no blind acceptance among the bigger parties either. Soviet spokesmen found it increasingly difficult to justify the break in diplomatic relations with Israel. Moscow had maintained diplomatic relations with Nazi Germany and fascist Italy; it had not severed its ties with Greece, despite the *coup* in 1967; the decision not to maintain relations with Israel was unprecedented and raised awkward questions.[37]

After the end of the Arab-Israeli war a great many diplomatic journeys were undertaken between Moscow and the Arab capitals. The Soviet generals were the first to visit Cairo. Podgorny, President of the Supreme Soviet, visited Cairo, Damascus, and Baghdad in June-July 1967 to reassure the Arab leaders that Soviet help would be continued. In January 1968 a Soviet delegation headed by Kyrill Mazurov, a member of the Politburo, visited Cairo; he had been preceded by Marshal Tito. Boumedienne was the first Arab leader to call on the Kremlin; he was followed by Atassi of Syria, Arif, the Iraqi President, King Hussein of

Jordan, and in July 1968 by Nasser himself. Two top-level gatherings of communist leaders, in Budapest in July and in Warsaw in December 1967, were devoted to deliberations on the Middle East situation. The Arabs wanted more arms and economic aid; the Soviet leaders, as far as can be ascertained, expressed complete sympathy with the Arab aim of eliminating the consequences of Israeli aggression. At the same time they made it clear to their guests that a military solution of the conflict was out of the question in the near future. They also tried to put their exchanges with the Arab world on a basis of reciprocity; they could not indefinitely underwrite military and economic aid on an ever-growing scale.

The Arab-Israeli conflict had facilitated Soviet activities in the Middle East in the fifties and early sixties. The Soviet investment in Egypt and Syria had been eminently worthwhile, but after about 1965 returns began to diminish. The defeat of the Arab states had been a blow to Soviet prestige and had necessitated further heavy investment in these countries. But despite this outlay, relations between the Soviet Union and the Arab countries were not markedly closer in 1970 than before the war. It was not at all clear whether the Soviet position in the Arab world had become more secure, with the exception of Egypt, which had certainly become more dependent.

The Israeli victory in 1967 had come as a surprise to Moscow. The Soviet leaders had under-rated Israel because they were convinced that 'Jews do not fight'; the traditional Russian image of the Jew had changed little since the revolution. The realization that Jews did fight if their national existence was at stake did not make the Kremlin any more friendly towards Israel; on the contrary, there was a great deal of annoyance, righteous anger, and the desire to teach the Israelis a lesson. But the war also reopened discussions in Moscow as to how far Soviet hostility to Israel should be allowed to escalate, taking into account both Soviet self-interest and the 'international duty' of the Soviet Union. Hostility towards Israel, both emotional and political, was deeply ingrained in some powerful circles in Moscow, but there were also voices asserting that Soviet support for Arab national aspirations did not necessarily entail full identification with them.

5
The Soviet Union and the
Arab World

Egypt

In the nineteen-fifties conditions in the Arab world favoured a radical break with past policies. The new leaders of Egypt were eager to establish closer contacts with the Soviet Union. A new class and a new generation had come to power, and they felt the need for a new and more daring approach in domestic and foreign policy alike. Unlike Turkey and Iran, the Arab world had not preserved its sovereignty in its recent history; there was a great deal of resentment against the West, which had dominated the Middle East for so long and still kept much of its influence through defence pacts and economic links. And, again unlike Turkey and Iran, the Arab world had no common border with the Soviet Union and was not directly exposed to Soviet pressure. The Soviet Union was thought of as a powerful but distant country whose support against the encroachments of the West should have been enlisted by the Arabs long before. Of domination from that quarter the radical Arab leaders were not afraid, for the Soviet Union did not behave like the old colonialist powers. To communist influence they felt quite immune: asked about the danger of communist penetration, Nasser once said; 'All our people are politicians and very smart. . . . I am certain that no communist will, whatever happens, influence Arab nationalism. On the contrary, the ideas of Arab nationalism will finally and forever prevail.'[1]

The Soviet leaders were aware of the mental reservations of their new allies in the Middle East, but this did not worry them unduly, for they were convinced that the logic of events would gradually drive the Arab leaders (or their successors) towards closer political collaboration with the Soviet Union, and that an ideological *rapprochement* would eventually follow.[2]

By 1958 Soviet political, military, and economic ties with Egypt had become very close: it was the honeymoon of the new alliance. The USSR had supported Egypt during the Suez crisis, it had underwritten the first stage of work on the Aswan dam, and was soon to undertake the second, main stage as well. Substantial arms shipments had been delivered to Egypt and a loan agreement totalling $175 million had been signed. Nasser went twice to Moscow in 1958; the second time in connection with the Iraqi revolution and the American landing in Lebanon. Khrushchev promised every possible help; he would issue warnings, but made it clear that there would be no Soviet armed intervention.[3]

Amid these protestations of lasting friendship, careful observers could detect warning signs well before the year had ended. Syria had merged with Egypt in February 1958; the Soviet government did not comment, but for a number of good reasons it was not over-enthusiastic. During 1958 Nasser had become more conciliatory towards the United States; he wanted American wheat and financial support for his economic projects. Above all, events in Iraq precipitated a crisis. The Iraqi revolution, which Nasser had followed with high expectations and not a few designs of his own, had gone sour: the radical nationalists in Baghdad turned against the local Nasserists and entered into a close alliance with the communists. Moscow praised Kassem as a truly democratic ruler; Iraq had suddenly become a more democratic country than Egypt; the Iraqi revolution rather than the Egyptian represented a higher stage of political development.[4]

Nasser accepted the challenge: in a speech in Port Said on 23 December 1958, and in a series of addresses between January and April 1959, he conducted a major propaganda campaign against communism, the enemy of Arab nationalism and unity. Communism was equated with Western imperialism, the communists wanted 'to dominate us and establish a terrorist, bloody dictatorship'; they were foreign agents, and Khrushchev's representations on their behalf was 'intervention in our affairs'.[5] Moscow mildly rebuked Nasser, but preferred at first to ignore his outbursts. The communist press, less restrained, criticized the internal situation in Egypt and Syria, as it had done all along; the suppression of democracy, the persecution of Arab communists, and the murder of one of their leaders were the main targets of attack. The *World Marxist Review* complained about the climate of fear in Egypt, the ruthless dictatorship, Gestapo methods, unbridled terror, unemployment, poverty, and concentration camps.[6] The propaganda war abated a little in February, but reached its highest pitch in late March and early April, after the bloody suppression by Kassem and the communists of the Mosul uprising. Some of the most bitter insults were exchanged in April 1959; these had been preceded by an exchange of letters between Khrushchev and Nasser, of which some details were later revealed: Khrushchev had called the president of the UAR a 'passionate and hot-headed young man' who had 'taken upon himself more than his stature permitted', and had accused him of trying to annex Iraq.[7] Nasser replied that 'but for my hot-headedness our country today would be a Western base for rockets and atomic bombs against the Soviet Union. . . . With the same hot-headedness we shall face the new danger as we have faced enemies in the past. . . . We will also win against the new agents of communism.'[8] Soviet spokesmen had always stressed the decisive part of the Soviet Union in saving Egypt in 1956, but Nasser now disparaged its role during the Suez crisis: 'we did not see the smallest hint of help from a single foreign state, including the Soviet Union.'[9] And a few days later:

We were trying to convince ourselves that the communist parties in our countries were independent of international communism. We found out that they were not, and that was why I called them communist stooges. They carried out orders and instructions to liquidate patriotic and national elements in order to place our country inside the zone of communist influence. We were suddenly faced by flagrant interference in our internal affairs by Russia.[10]

and this despite the fact that Khrushchev in his personal notes to the Egyptian president had acknowledged that Cairo's attitude towards communism was a matter of domestic policy which concerned the United Arab Republic alone.[11] Accusing the Russians of trying to establish a 'Red Fertile Crescent', Nasser claimed that the large reservoir of goodwill built up by Moscow in three years of friendship had been lost in less than three weeks after the Mosul revolt. *Pravda* countered by criticizing an unnamed public figure in the Arab world for his policy of immediate and mechanical unification of all Arab states, whether they wanted it or not. All who did not agree with his ideas were declared to be communists, Zionists, and enemies of the Arab people.[12] In April and May further letters were exchanged between Khrushchev and Nasser, and it appears that the former succeeded in mollifying the Egyptian leader. In a speech in India in May, Khrushchev emphasized that 'properly speaking we have no conflict with Egypt', and on another occasion it was said in Moscow that even an anti-communist campaign by a recipient of Soviet aid would not affect the fulfilment of past commitments and the prospects of further assistance.[13]

At this stage the dispute suddenly subsided. Less than a year later Nasser declared that it was his duty to pay tribute to the tact and disinterestedness which the Soviet Union had demonstrated towards Egypt: 'In spite of the divergence of opinions, Moscow never put pressure on us, never threatened to stop her aid.'[14]

Both sides were clearly eager not to burn all bridges. The Soviet Union regarded Egypt as the key country in the Arab world, and it did not under-rate Egypt's potential role in Africa. Subsequent events in Iraq seemed to confirm this appraisal. For Iraq began to backslide: the 'progressive elements' were persecuted under Kassem and all but annihilated under his successors. Too much had been invested in Egypt to withdraw support lightly; the impression created in the third world would have been most unfortunate from the Soviet point of view. The communist movement in Egypt was small, split into several factions, and ineffectual; there was no real alternative to Nasser's leadership in Egypt, or indeed in the Arab world. Consequently, Moscow decided to ignore the attacks and to supply the aid that had been promised.

In August 1960 the agreement for the second stage of the Aswan dam was signed. The High Dam was to be the outstanding symbol of the achievements of Nasser's regime: it was to expand

Egypt's cultivable area from 6 to 7·3 million acres, provide all-year-round irrigation to another 700,000 acres, facilitate navigation on the Nile, provide cheap electricity for industrialization. It was believed at the time that as a result the national income of Egypt would rise by some 29 per cent. Soviet support for this project ('a symbol', a 'shining beacon of progress' – Mikoyan) was of paramount importance. Nasser was at ease working with the Russians who, he said, had proved loyal partners in all their undertakings; their terms were fair, interest charges low (2½ per cent), and no strings were attached.[15] Soviet comment was that 'in contrast to the West we have not tried to use the High Dam as a means to put pressure on Egypt', and an American observer noted that Russia had now succeeded in assuring herself of close ties with the UAR for at least the next decade.[16]

Further exchanges between Cairo and Moscow took place on all levels: Patriarch Alexius visited Egypt, while Field-Marshal Abd al Hakim Amer led an Egyptian delegation to Moscow to discuss Soviet military aid. When Nasser met Khrushchev at the United Nations General Assembly in New York in October 1960 the hatchet was finally buried; all that remained to do, Nasser said, was to 'review the crisis in a spirit of mutual understanding in order to strengthen the basis of our friendship'.[17]

From his point of view, a break with the Soviet Union would have been a major calamity; it would have made him dependent on the Western powers, from whom he was unlikely to get the necessary support for both his economic projects and his military ambitions. Relations with America, to be sure, improved in 1960; American shipments provided food for many Egyptians, more help was promised, and John Badeau, well known for his sympathies for the Arab cause, was appointed American Ambassador to Cairo. John F. Kennedy engaged in a prolonged private correspondence with Nasser; the general impression in the Middle East was that America was about to become 'more neutral' in the Arab-Israeli dispute. Yet there were also constant irritations, such as the 'Cleopatra' incident and the Douglas amendment to the Mutual Security Act,[18] both of which Nasser attributed to Zionist intrigues. Above all, his policy continued to clash with American interests all over the Middle East and Africa.

Egypt had increasingly come to support Soviet policies in the United Nations and elsewhere; its proclaimed positive neutrality was gradually wearing thin. The denunciation by the Egyptian press of 'Kennedy's massacre in Cuba' caused no more than raised eyebrows in Washington, but the Congo was a different matter; Cairo, with or on behalf of the Soviet Union, intervened directly in this conflict and there ensued a bitter quarrel with Washington.

Developments inside Egypt made a lasting reconciliation with the West less and less likely and a further *rapprochement* with the Soviet Union almost a foregone conclusion. In July 1961 Nasser undertook a sharp turn to the left 'to protect the revolutionary regime from feudalism, monopolies, and exploiting capitalism'; after the breakdown of the union with Syria further drastic measures were adopted. The aim of the decrees was to stamp out 'capitalist reaction', which Nasser thought had been responsible for the Syrian secession and now threatened his own rule in Egypt. Some 400 banks, factories, and public utilities were nationalized, some private properties were seized, maximum land-ownership was reduced to 100 *feddan*, workers were promised a share in profits, 5,000 political opponents were arrested, and many foreign nationals expelled.

Control over large sectors of the Egyptian economy passed into the hands of the State bureaucracy. It is immaterial in this context whether these measures were indeed 'socialist' in character (as Nasser claimed), or whether it was simply another case of State domination of the economy of which there are many examples in history, from Pharaonic Egypt to Mussolini's Republic of Salò. From the Soviet point of view, the decrees were definitely a step in the right direction, because they were 'objectively undermining the foundations of private ownership and preparing the conditions for the liquidation of capitalist relations'.[19] Egypt was on the road of non-capitalist development, not a third road, a cross between capitalism and socialism, but a road leading to socialism.[20] Nasser in his early days had flirted with fascism; the Free Officers' movement in 1952 had been patriotic and radical in character, without any clear ideological content. It had been in favour of 'socialism', but so was everyone else at the time. The radicalization of the regime took Moscow by surprise. The official Soviet appraisal did not change at once; a leading Soviet correspondent visiting Egypt at the time wrote that the policy was as yet far removed from building socialism, and the decrees only partly changed the situation in the villages where the *bourgeoisie* had consolidated its positions.[21] It is instructive to compare the accounts of the same correspondent published a few years later, when he was to write about the great progress that had been made on the road to socialism, and about the friendship he encountered everywhere.[22]

There were occasional setbacks. Even after the hatchet had been buried in 1960 the Egyptian press continued to attack international communism, and Soviet spokesmen retaliated in kind from time to time. *Pravda* in May 1961 complained that the Egyptian press had opened its columns to the 'vilest anti-Soviet slander' and, recalling the political and economic support that had been given to the UAR, it reminded freedom-loving Arabs of their proverb, 'Cut not the tree that provides the shade.'[23] Was Soviet economic aid after all not altogether unconditional? The Egyptians were not deterred: the Soviet Union, they claimed, was again interfering, challenging the UAR's sovereignty and dignity instead of basing relations on equality.[24] Hostile slogans made their appearance, such as 'Destiny has shown you to be imperialists and also agents of world Zionism, suckled by the Jew Marx.' When Anwar as-Sadat visited Moscow at the head of an Egyptian parliamentary delegation, he was told by Khrushchev that while the Egyptian leaders still understood little of socialism, they would end up as communists 'because life imposes communism on man'. How, he asked, could the Russians have confidence in Nasser, seeing that he was losing his grip, unable to solve his country's problems?[25]

It looked as if a major storm was again brewing, but the conflict subsided very quickly. It was to be the last serious open clash between the two countries for many years; occasionally criticism made itself heard, but there were no more orchestrated campaigns. The new provisions of the National Charter of 1962, which allocated 50 per cent of the seats in parliament to workers and peasants, were noted with satisfaction in Moscow; so was the fact that 'for the first time the workers openly observed their proletarian festival' (1 May).[26] Trade relations, which had tailed off after 1958, again picked up and 1962 was a record year for Soviet economic aid. Long-range TU-16 jet bombers and Mig fighters were supplied to the Egyptian air force and a great many official visits were exchanged.

These were the years of intense ideological discussions in the Soviet Union about the concept of the 'independent state of national democracy' (enunciated in 1960), about socialism of the national type, and the character of the national liberation movement. More and more Soviet Middle East experts came to accept the view, voiced at first only by a few, such as G. Mirsky,[27] that the regime in the UAR (and in some other developing countries) was basically progressive; the world outlook of these revolutionary democrats had undergone an evolution; though they were not representatives of the working class, they were able to change direction and move towards socialism.[28]

It is more than doubtful whether the Soviet leaders decided to modify their policy *vis-à-vis* the UAR as the result of academic disputations of this kind. It is far more likely that the discussions among the experts reflected divided opinions within the leadership. Khrushchev, 'erratic, but tending towards an abandonment of accepted doctrinal compromises', went further than any other Soviet leader in reappraising his attitude towards Nasser;[29] in 1964, without apparently consulting his colleagues in the Politburo, he granted Egypt a new substantial loan and made both Nasser and Abd al Hakim Amer (as well as Ben Bella) 'Heroes of the Soviet Union'.

In 1964 Nasser had been ten years in power; other third world leaders had come and gone, but his influence and prestige had steadily grown. Khrushchev had no more doubts about his pro-Egyptian policy; the warnings of Arab communists that, some economic reforms apart, no essential changes had taken place in the policy and character of the regime were impatiently brushed aside.[30] When Nasser, in anticipation of Khrushchev's visit in 1964, abolished the emergency laws under which political prisoners (including many communists) had been held without trial, *Pravda* hailed it as a 'historical step'.[31] Soviet persistence and patience had been vindicated.

Khrushchev's visit to Egypt was the culmination of this policy. He was welcomed in Cairo with great enthusiasm, in contrast to the reception given to Chou En-lai, who had been to Egypt shortly before. The Soviet leader stressed on every occasion the disinterested character of the economic help extended by his country, and the fact that there was full agreement between Moscow and Cairo on all important international issues. All went well but for the hosts' constant harping on Arab unity; irritated by the unceasing stress on nationalism, Khrushchev condemned on several occasions the purely nationalist approach to unity, contrasting it with the communist approach, with its revolutionary class basis.[32] Soviet commentators obliquely referred to these incidents, but tried to avoid giving offence, claiming that the concept of Arab unity had of late undergone a substantial change; the question of the 'unity of the Arab working people', they said, was being raised with increasing acuteness.[33] Soviet arms supplies were also discussed on this state visit; Marshal Grechko and other high-ranking Soviet officers were members of the Soviet party. Khrushchev revealed that Field-Marshal Amer had jokingly turned to him after Grechko's speech and said: 'Give us more arms.' Remarking wryly that 'apparently all military men are alike' in constantly asking for more arms, he said that there would be no difficulties regarding additional arms if that became necessary.[34]

Ali Sabry's visit to Moscow followed in September 1964. Sabry, then prime minister, wanted to discuss the use of the new loan of $250 million that Khrushchev had promised the Egyptians. The largest project covered by the new agreement was an iron and steel complex with an initial annual capacity of more than a million tons; other projects included a power station, a lubricating oil plant, and twenty training centres for workers.[35] Both sides stressed that Soviet-Egyptian friendship had reached a new peak, largely owing to Krushchev's personal initiative. In a memorandum written in Yalta a few weeks before his death, Togliatti, the Italian communist leader, described Khrushchev's visit to Egypt as one of the most important victories obtained by the Russians over the Chinese.[36]

A few weeks later Khrushchev was overthrown, and it was at

first by no means certain that the new collective leadership would display the same warmth and willingness to support Egypt. The Arab communist leaders who had been greatly annoyed by Khrushchev's excessive enthusiasm for Nasser used the opportunity to stress the need to differentiate between the 'non-capitalist path' and the building of socialism. Soviet ideological experts suddenly decided to give a higher grading to Algeria than to the UAR.[37] Cairo was apprehensive; though Cairo Radio announced that relations between states were not based on the preferences of individuals, one of Nasser's aides was quoted to the effect that the *Rais* had been visibly affected by the report of Khrushchev's dismissal. Haykal, who only a short time before had heaped extravagant praise on the fallen leader,[38] had second thoughts: was it not a fact that Khrushchev was the only Soviet leader with whom the Egyptian revolution had clashed in a 'fearful and intense battle'; he had not been far removed from Stalinism and had committed many mistakes; he had not been the first to call for a *rapprochement* with Egypt; his opponents had preceded him in their admiration for the Egyptian revolution.[39] Haykal no doubt somewhat exaggerated the intensity of the admiration the Soviet leadership felt for the Egyptian revolution; Moscow continued to have serious reservations about the character of the Egyptian regime, even though comment was guarded. What made them opt for Egypt and what precluded a Soviet reorientation at this stage was the growing rivalry with China and the defeat of 'national democracy' in other parts of the world. China was showing at the time a certain activity in the Middle East; Chou En-lai had been to Cairo in late 1963 and paid a longer visit in 1965. A Soviet rebuff to Cairo would have led with near certainty to an Egyptian *rapprochement* with China and this was the last thing the Soviet leaders wanted.

'Grading' the countries of 'national democracy' was in those years a favourite pastime in Moscow. Algeria usually scored higher than the UAR, mainly because the Russians had serious misgivings about the Arab Socialist Union, Egypt's state party which, despite many efforts, had failed to become a real political force comparable to the Algerian FLN.[40] But such Soviet reasoning and the optimistic assessments about the course of events in Indonesia and Ghana had a fatal flaw: Ben Bella, on whom the Soviets had put so many hopes, was overthrown in August 1965; Sukarno and Nkrumah fell early in 1966. Of all the hopefuls in the third world only some minor African countries remained, and of course Castro, but his loyalty to the Soviet Union had always been a little suspect. As a result, Nasser's prestige again soared in Moscow, even though there was a tendency among political observers there to be less sanguine about the prospects of the national liberation movement in general.[41]

There had been differences of opinion between Khrushchev and his colleagues in the politburo, but few of a basic character, as became apparent soon after his fall; the others had objected more to his character and style than to his policy. Within a few weeks after his dismissal, Nasser was given assurances that Soviet policy towards Egypt would not change; Jakob Malik, a deputy foreign minister, went briefly to Cairo to see him, and was followed in December 1964 by a more highly placed leader, Alexander Shelepin, a member of the Politburo.[42] Shelepin went out of his way to praise Egyptian foreign policy, especially in the Congo, and promised that Soviet economic help would continue.[43] Field-Marshal Abd al Hakim Amer attended the November festivities in Moscow that year; his visit was hailed as a 'new milestone in the strengthening of friendship and solidarity between the two countries', and he signed a new military agreement with Malinovsky, the Soviet defence minister, details of which were not published at the time.[44] The stage was thus set for a resumption of contacts on the highest level, and Nasser went to Moscow in August 1965. The topics that were discussed ranged widely, including Vietnam, the Soviet-Chinese conflict, Soviet help for the new Egyptian five-year plan. Nasser promised to support Moscow at the forthcoming Afro-Asian conference; it was thought at the time that this conference would witness a Soviet-Chinese showdown, which the Soviet leaders regarded with some trepidation.[45] But the basic aim of the meeting in Moscow was, according to Haykal, the Soviet wish (expressed by Brezhnev) 'to know you better as a human being', to strengthen personal relations and 'establish personal friendships'.[46] The

Soviet leaders certainly missed no opportunity to flatter Nasser. Haykal reported that Nasser was asked on one occasion by Marshal Malinovsky why he did not wear the order of Hero of the Soviet Union which Khrushchev had bestowed on him; Mikoyan added that the Soviet Union continued to regard Nasser as a 'real hero of heroes'.[47]

Compelling reasons induced the Soviet leaders to continue the Egyptian alliance and Nasser was at least equally interested in ensuring that Soviet support should not cease. He had by now come to depend on Soviet arms supplies; Egypt's economy, in an uncertain state at the best of times, had been further weakened by the war in the Yemen. His position in the Arab world had deteriorated: he had quarrelled with Syria, and there was open conflict with Jordan, Saudia, and Tunisia. The war in the Yemen was going badly and of his great friends in the third world only Tito was left. He could have worked for a *rapprochement* with the American leaders, some of whom were only too eager to reestablish a working relationship. But they had offended him on so many occasions and he had retaliated by such a deliberate policy of irritating and provoking the Americans that even the patience of the most long-suffering American diplomats began to wear thin. Aware that his isolation, part inevitable, part self-induced, was growing, the Soviet alliance became more important for Nasser than ever.

Two other major visits by Soviet leaders to Egypt took place before the Israeli war in 1967. Kosygin made a state visit in May 1966, and foreign minister Gromyko came for a shorter stay in late March 1967. Kosygin dutifully made the rounds: he saw the land-reclamation projects at Al Tahrir, the industrial complex at Helwan, the Aswan dam. He told the National Assembly that he admired Egypt's social and economic progress and its steadfast anti-imperialist struggle, and promised further economic and military support.[48] There was no need to discuss further credits; the loan of the year before was still only half taken up. The final communiqué dealt with the aggressive activities of the imperialist forces and the growing danger of war.[49] There seemed to be no specific problems of any urgency; Moscow wanted to demonstrate (as two *Pravda* correspondents put it) 'the falseness of the theory that the Soviet Union had cooled towards the third world and no longer attached great importance to the Afro-Asian states'.[50]

Kosygin also had a meeting with Ahmad Shukairy, the head of the Palestine Liberation Organization, later on denounced by the Russians as a nationalist hot-head whom no one had ever taken seriously. Kosygin gave an impression of militant solidarity with Nasser, but remained in fact a little vague on some essential points, such as the Soviet commitment in the event of an armed conflict with Saudi Arabia or an Egyptian preventive war against Israel (a possibility mentioned by Nasser in a speech shortly before Kosygin's arrival).

The talks between Gromyko and Nasser in March 1967 were shrouded in unusual secrecy. The visit came unannounced; it was suggested that it had to do with the situation in Arabia, or perhaps with Egypt's inability to make the repayments due. But would the presence of the foreign minister have been needed for discussions of this character? The Yugoslavs announced that the question of the UN peace-keeping force in Gaza would also be discussed,[51] a most intriguing piece of information in view of what happened less than two months later.

There were many indications that all was not well in Egypt even before the disastrous war against Israel. Soviet economic aid extended to the UAR since 1954 totalled $740 million;[52] in addition, the communist countries of Eastern Europe had extended aid and grants estimated at $540 million. Military aid was more difficult to assess; estimates varied between $900 million and $1·6 billion, far more than had been given by the Soviet Union to any other country. United States economic aid to Egypt during the same period totalled $1·1 billion – mostly in 'Food for Peace' shipments of grain. The US had provided the bulk of Egyptian grain imports, but in view of growing Egyptian hostility towards Washington (Nasser's famous 'Jump in the lake' speech; the burning of the American library in Cairo; the shooting down of an American civilian aircraft), it was doubtful whether aid would be continued, and the Soviet Union faced an additional commitment of exporting to the UAR up to 2·5 million tons of grain a year, worth perhaps $300 million, with only a remote possibility of repayment.

Soviet commentators emphasized the 'remarkable successes' in Egyptian industry and agriculture;[53] work on the Aswan dam proceeded on schedule. Under competent management, the Suez Canal functioned reasonably well and had become a major source of income. But despite the enormous investments the strains and stresses in Egypt's economy were more palpably felt every year; consumption was outstripping production, the cost of living was rising steeply. Egypt was no longer in a position to pay its foreign debts. It owed the International Monetary Fund about $300 million and the total UAR foreign currency reserves were equivalent to only about 8 per cent of her foreign debts. Soviet observers regarded the inadequacy of agrarian reform as the main stumbling-block; a new rural *bourgeoisie* had emerged; the more prosperous sections of the peasantry were going over to a capitalist mode of production.[54] They also blamed the mixed economy; capitalists were still appropriating public funds for private profit.[55] Egypt's three main sources of foreign exchange were the Suez Canal (about $220 million in 1966), the cotton crop (about $336 million in 1966), and, to a lesser extent, tourism. But over half of the yearly cotton crop was already mortgaged for years to come to the USSR and Eastern Europe. The continuing population explosion prevented any real and lasting improvement in the standard of living; the Aswan dam and the other industrial projects were just sufficient to prevent a further decline. Egypt was an unlikely place to serve as a communist show window in the third world, but despite grave misgivings the Soviets had not given up hope, and they advised Nasser to press ahead with his industrialization drive regardless of obstacles. But it must have dawned on some Soviet economic experts by 1966 at the latest that Egypt was even less likely than Cuba (where the Soviet Union had entered into similar commitments) to attain self-sufficiency and economic independence. There was always the chance that one day Egypt would be able to put its hands on the oilfields of Arabia or Libya; seen in this light, the build-up of the army could perhaps be regarded as a productive investment.

Egypt's very weakness was its strength *vis-à-vis* the Soviet Union: it needed immediate and massive help. Had the Soviet

Union refused to help, Cairo would have been compelled to turn to another big power; given the world situation in 1966–7, and above all the declining fortunes of its other protégés in the third world, Moscow simply could not afford to lose Egypt. In economic terms the alliance was a major liability, but the Soviet Union had become reconciled to the idea that in the modern world big powers had to pay a high price for political influence.

The original Soviet military agreement with Egypt, periodically reviewed, provided for the delivery of about 150 MiG 15s and 17s, some 40 Ilyushin tactical bombers, several hundred tanks, two destroyers, and three submarines. More and more sophisticated weapons were subsequently supplied, including the most modern Soviet tanks, TU-16 jet bombers, MiG 21 aircraft, Komar and Ossa rocket-vessels. Soviet commanders became frequent guests in Cairo: Marshal Grechko, Admiral Gorshkov, as well as the chiefs of staffs of the Soviet navy and air force. There was close military cooperation, and hundreds of Soviet military experts were permanently stationed in Egypt to maintain liaison and to act as advisers and instructors. There were also reports about secret treaties providing Russia with naval bases in the Mediterranean and the Red Sea, airstrips and other military installations in the Western Desert and Upper Egypt.[56] These were not military bases in the traditional sense, for this would have created political complications; there was no question of surrendering Egyptian sovereignty in peacetime. But the arrangements made it possible for the Soviet navy to refuel, to have repair work done, and to rotate crews far away from Soviet territory.

Over a decade the Egyptian armed forces had been built up by the USSR. We do not know how satisfied the Soviet military leaders were with the results of their work. They certainly regarded Egypt as the strongest military power in the area. True, there had been some warning signs, such as the failure of the Egyptian expeditionary force in the Yemen, but for a number of reasons Moscow seemed to favour Egyptian involvement in South Arabia and, having cooperated with the Egyptian army for so long, they could not fail to identify themselves with it.

Political relations between Moscow and Cairo were bedevilled by an excess of ideological analysis, and this has also, to a certain extent, affected Western writings on the subject. These investigations into ideological similarities and differences created a great deal of confusion, partly because of semantic difficulties, for 'scientific socialism' is far from having the same meaning in Cairo and Moscow. But there was also an inclination to exaggerate the importance of the ideological factor in the relations between the two countries. Soviet commentators are aware of the strong religious and national elements in the new Egyptian ideology, and have, on the whole, taken a more lenient view of these 'remnants of the past' than of the Nasserist pretensions to establish its own Arab socialist ideology. Above all, they have been unhappy about Egyptian reluctance to accept Soviet notions of class (and class struggle) and the rejection of the central concept of the dictatorship of the proletariat.[57] Soviet experts noted more in sorrow than in anger that though their Egyptian friends had somehow instinctively chosen the right path in recent years, they were still ideologically very backward, and had therefore to be closely watched.

The analysis of Soviet-Egyptian relations in terms of the class struggle and the dictatorship of the proletariat does not take one very far, for in the last resort both Soviet communism and Nasserism are two different forms of national socialism, with the former on a somewhat higher level of ideological sophistication. The dictatorship of the proletariat is a central concept in Soviet ideology, but it is hardly a reality in Soviet life. The whole discussion about the leading role of the working class (allegedly existing in Russia) as distinct from leadership by the intelligentsia and the bureaucracy (as practised in Egypt) is sterile. For the Soviet Union, like Egypt, is run by a bureaucracy consisting mainly of party officials, the 'technical intelligentsia', the army, and the secret police. What really bothered the Soviet experts was the absence of an effective state party; they had argued for a long time that the Arab Socialist Union, with its six million members, could not be the cadre party which Egypt, like every progressive country, needed. They had suggested that within the ASU leadership should pass to an *élitist* group; Soviet advisers had been instrumental in convening study seminars in Cairo, setting up an ideological training centre, and promoting a variety of publications, including the periodical *Al Tali'a* (Vanguard).[58] All to little avail, for the ASU continued to lead a shadowy existence; important political initiatives emanated from Nasser and his inner circle, several high-ranking army officers, some technocrats, a few intellectuals, and the police and secret service chiefs. The absence of a central political party reflected, as the Russians saw it, the 'ideological weakness' of Egypt; Arab radicalism was a mood rather than a doctrine; no one could say with any certainty how it would react at a time of stress. Fifteen years earlier such an unsatisfactory state of affairs would have prevented any real alliance between the Soviet Union and a foreign country, but in the changed world of the nineteen-sixties it seemed to matter less. Egypt under Nasser had chosen the 'non-capitalist way'; the regime was opposed to the West and supported the Soviet Union, and this was the main criterion. The Soviet leaders had learned from bitter experience that ideological unity was of little benefit if the parties concerned did not also give full and active support to Soviet policies. Moscow had not been spoiled by its erstwhile allies from Tirana and Bucharest to Peking. During the Czechoslovak crisis of 1968 they were let down by most communist parties, whereas Nasser and his friends gave them much-needed support. The leaders in the Kremlin, both Khrushchev and his successors, were eminently practical men, and they drew the obvious lesson: what mattered in the last resort was unquestioning loyalty, not ideological conformity. Nasser was one of the main beneficiaries of the new polycentrism in the communist world.

The extent of Soviet responsibility for the war of 1967 and Egypt's defeat will not be altogether clear for a long time to come. It is unlikely that the Soviet Union wanted a war at that stage; on the other hand, it decisively contributed towards its outbreak through some major errors (at best) of judgement: the assumption that Nasser and the Arab leaders were satisfied with the *status quo* with regard to Israel and that therefore their bellicose speeches could be safely ignored; the belief that the great quantities of Soviet arms would be regarded as mere status symbols; the conviction that Egypt under Soviet guidance had gained much strength and that the Soviet Union would be able to control events in case of a major crisis. All these assumptions were proved wrong within a very few days in the summer of 1967; Soviet policy and Soviet prestige were affected by the Egyptian collapse and a basic reappraisal of the whole relationship with Cairo became necessary. An explanation had to be provided for the Soviet public: Egypt had been described for many years in the Soviet press as a progressive country with tremendous achievements to its credit, in contrast to Israel, ruled by a reactionary, anti-popular government and in a state of permanent crisis. Israel, needless to say, was also much the smaller country. The same correspondents and political analysts who had described Nasser's regime in glowing terms, the Beliaevs, Primakovs, and Ivanovs, cannot have found it easy to admit that something must have been radically wrong in their accounts. The official explana-tion was that Israel had intended by means of a surprise attack to overthrow the progressive regimes in the Arab world, but that this scheme had failed owing to the resolute stand taken by the Soviet Union.[59] Soviet commentators also mentioned the 'com-plicated internal political situation' in the UAR created as a result of the defeat.[60] The setback was explained by the Russians with reference to 'apostasy and treason' on the part of some high-ranking officers and of the reactionaries in general, the former landowners, sections of the petty *bourgeoisie* and the intelligentsia and, of course, the religious fanatics of the Muslim Brother-hood.[61] But this was not quite convincing. Why had the regime suffered economic and military setbacks in the first place? There were some frank articles, and one can well imagine that comment not scheduled for publication was even more outspoken. The Arab armies, it was said, had been composed largely of peasants, most of them poorly educated;[62] the officers had been self-seeking, using their privileges to improve their personal posi-tion.[63] Soviet arms and equipment had not been properly used; 'the surprise attack did not explain everything'.[64] Above all, there had not been sufficient contact between the leadership and the 'popular masses', and the demand was now voiced to purge the State apparatus of all 'reactionaries', to reorganize Egyptian political life, to give greater participation to the 'popular masses' in running the country. Soviet observers welcomed the purge of more than 600 officers and the conspiracy trials, including that of the former minister of war, Shams el Din el Badran, and Radwan, the former minister of the interior. According to the Soviet post-mortem, the Egyptian revolution had failed to change the old state machine radically, for the army officers as a 'class' had been 'susceptible to corrosion'.[65] The participation of the 'popular masses' was not, of course, meant quite literally, nor was the opposition to military men in principle. The Soviet leaders wanted above all more power for the 'Russian party' in Cairo, and the dismissal of all those who, as *Pravda* put it in February 1968, 'spread doubts about the nature of Soviet-Egyptian relations and called for a resumption of friendly relations with the United States'. The call for agreement with America was not confined (according to *Rose el-Yusef*) to the 'secret thoughts of those now behind bars, but was also heard on very different lips which voiced the spirit of defeatism and the secret desire to rob the people of their victories and to strike at socialism'.[66] The friends of Russia, men 'known for their progressive views', were Ali Sabry, vice-president and subsequently leader of the ASU, Shaarawi Gomaa, minister of the interior, Amin Howeidi, then head of Nasser's private secret service and minister of state, Muhammad Fayek, minister of national guidance, and the Cairo ASU secretary, Abdel Magid Ferid. There were also the communist intellectuals ('progressive elements known for their Marxist views') who had been given prominent positions in press and radio and for whom Moscow now demanded greater scope in the party apparatus.[67] Nasser's own position between these warring factions was by no means clear. The army, his traditional source of power, had lost face in the war, and he could no longer be quite certain of the loyalty of the new officers who had replaced his old comrades. The demonstrations of workers and students in February 1968 were manifestations of a serious malaise. Nasser was grateful for the 'resolute help and the tremendous efforts made by the Soviet leadership', as he put it in a cable to the Soviet Presidium.[68] But he was also aware of the growing resentment against the Soviet presence in Egypt, the almost total dependence which had resulted from his policy. Once

Lord Cromer, the British Resident, had been Egypt's real ruler; Nasser's agents no doubt told him that the parallel between Lord Cromer and Vinogradov, the new Soviet ambassador, was being freely drawn in Cairo after the war. From time to time Nasser made half-hearted attempts to assert himself and to follow an independent line. The faithful Haykal launched a trial balloon in his weekly column, asking in a cautious and roundabout way for more freedom of manoeuvre in Egypt's foreign policy, only to beat a hasty retreat when the Russian party counter-attacked. In an interview with an American periodical, Nasser belittled the number of Soviet military advisers ('less than a thousand' – certainly an understatement) and described his own foreign policy as non-aligned.[69] But it was perhaps symptomatic that only a heavily censored version of this interview was published in Egypt.

As Nasser reviewed the situation of his country one year after the war, he must have decided that he had no choice but to put all his hopes in the Soviet alliance. The decision cannot have been easy; it had been his great ambition to restore real independence to Egypt and for a while, during the late fifties and early sixties, he appeared to have succeeded. But he had always wanted to accomplish too much in too little time: industrialization and a social revolution in Egypt, supremacy among the Arabs, a leading role in the third world, a campaign in the Yemen, and the liberation of Palestine. After the Six Day War Egypt urgently needed economic aid, and above all it needed arms for which it could not pay. Nasser admitted as much: 'We have so far paid not one penny for the arms we obtained from the Soviet Union to equip our armed forces. Actually, were it a question of payment, we have no money to buy arms . . .'[70] There was no chance of receiving the aircraft and missiles free of charge from anyone but Russia. He was, of course, aware that by burning the bridges to America he weakened his bargaining position *vis-à-vis* Moscow. But he was no longer concerned about the price that would eventually have to be paid. He still maintained that there were no strings attached: 'Why does the Soviet Union give us all these things? I wish to tell you frankly and clearly that the Soviet Union has never tried, not even in the time of our greatest trials, to dictate conditions to us or to ask anything of us. . . . We went on [in Moscow] asking for hours, but they did not make one request of us. Even when I told them I felt ashamed that we were making so many demands while they had asked nothing from us . . . they told us: We take this stand on the basis of our ideology. . . . We have nothing to ask . . .'[71] After his state visit to the USSR in 1968 he welcomed the presence of Soviet naval forces in the Mediterranean, the new shield of the 'progressive Arab states'.[72] His old friend Tito, whom he had seen on his way back, disapproved of Moscow's Mediterranean ambitions and warned him of the dangers of total dependence,[73] but Nasser, plagued by illness, was now a man near despair, talking in apocalyptic terms about a new war. He had made concession after concession to the Russians, purging the army and the State apparatus of all people considered undesirable in Moscow. One observer noted that the Arabs must have found it difficult to square these concessions with what used to be their fierce attachment to Egyptian sovereignty and independence.[74] But Nasser was now in a great hurry. His pride had been deeply wounded; everything was now to be subordinated to the coming war against Israel. There was the old problem, as Haykal wrote in August 1967 and again in July 1968, that the Soviet Union wanted to avoid a head-on collision with the United States. But this did not mean that Moscow would refrain from giving help in a coming war; if only the Arabs showed enough self-assertion, they could induce the Russians to attach more importance to the Middle East than to Vietnam. These were almost literally the same arguments the Syrians had used before the Six Day War.[75]

Russian hopes had been dimmed by the outcome of that war. Soviet visitors to Cairo discovered aspects of Egyptian life they had overlooked before: 'Here a string of young girls carrying thirty kilogram baskets of rubble on their heads runs along while an overseer chases them with a stick. Quicker! quicker! quicker! It is unbearable for a Soviet citizen to watch, but you must not interfere.'[76] Nevertheless, the Soviet Union continued to give economic help. Mazurov, a Soviet deputy prime minister, repeated at the opening of the Aswan power station in January 1968 that Soviet aid would continue until all traces of the aggression had disappeared. Moscow undertook to supply within three months 300,000 tons of wheat to help Egypt to overcome a critical shortage. Soviet work on the Helwan complex continued; it was announced that production would meet all the domestic iron and steel requirements and leave about 500,000 tons of steel for export. But the new mills were not to be completed until 1976.[77]

Of the greatest immediate importance was the military help. Even before the end of the war, on 8 June 1967, a Moscow-Cairo airbridge had been established to fly war material into Egypt. A year after the war Western specialists estimated that the Soviet Union had replaced 300 of the 365 jet fighters that had been lost, 50 of the 69 bombers, 450 of the 550 tanks; the stocks of Styx-type anti-shipping missiles were replenished and ground-to-ground missiles of the modified Kennel type with a range of 45 miles were provided for the first time, thus introducing a new element into the Middle East arms race.[78] In October 1968 the value of arms deliveries since the Six Day War was estimated at $2·5 billion.

With all that there cannot have been many illusions in Moscow about Egypt's short-term military prospects. What if, owing to Nasser's impetuosity, yet another situation developed over which the Russians would have no control? There were frequent Soviet warnings against 'rank demagogy and adventurist exhortations', usually attributed to Chinese influence in the Middle East.[79] The Soviet generals asked for, and received, a far greater say in Cairo than before the war; perhaps they thought that the mere presence of 3,000 Soviet military experts and instructors would act if necessary as an effective brake.

The question whether Nasser was expendable must have occurred more than once after the war to those responsible for Soviet Middle East policy. Moody, unpredictable, unable to fulfil his promises, he surely appeared at times a major liability to his Soviet allies. But no other Egyptian leader, certainly no member of the 'Russian party' in Cairo, enjoyed the same prestige in his country, let alone in the Arab world. Nasser was the only charismatic leader, and miraculously his prestige was not irremediably shaken by his defeat – or so it seemed. Wider issues were also involved: given the assumption that Soviet power was to be asserted in its own backyard, support for Egypt seems in retrospect almost inevitable. But the Soviet endeavour to make Egypt a showcase for socialism was clearly based on a miscalculation; the country was too poor, nor was it well suited for a Soviet-style regime. Egypt's weakness was in some ways an asset, for it made the country permanently dependent on the Soviet Union. A defeated country was more likely to remain a faithful and loyal client than a victorious and prosperous one. With loyalty at a premium in the communist world, this was not a consideration to be ignored.

From Egypt's point of view, the interim balance was almost wholly negative. The alliance with the Soviet Union, from the original arms deal of 1955 on to 1970, was largely the work of one man. Ideologically Nasser was truly uncommitted; he belonged to the generation which, in the case of an Axis victory, would have turned with equal ease to fascism. He was a radical nationalist, not a socialist, let alone a Marxist. He could argue in his defence that Egypt's desperate poverty had left him little freedom of choice, that America made all kinds of conditions that were offensive to an Arab patriot, that Egypt's interests clashed everywhere with those of the West – in Israel, in Africa, in the Arab peninsula. The Russians regarded him as a chosen instrument; for the Americans he was at best an unfriendly neutral. They wanted him to concentrate on economic construction at home, not to make war against Israel, not to intervene in Africa, not to manufacture rockets or nuclear weapons; they tried to restrain him with regard to all the things that were dear to his heart, whereas the Russians had been in every respect far more sympathetic.

In the last resort it was a tragic story of overweening ambition. To achieve his aims, Nasser needed massive foreign help. He was forced to gamble, persuading himself and trying to convince others that they could receive such help without any loss to Egypt's independence. Persistent, clever, but lacking real wisdom and foresight, he grossly overestimated the strength of his country, its immunity to 'foreign ideas', and, in general, the significance of radical Arab nationalism in the modern world. Whenever Nasser suffered a setback during the seventeen years of his rule, he had sought shelter in closer proximity to Moscow. After 1965 many of his plans were frustrated, and the *rapprochement* seemed to have become permanent. Looking back in 1968 on his achievements and failures, and above all on the tremendous discrepancy between promise and fulfilment, Nasser must have had his moments of despair. But there was still the hope that the front of his enemies would crumble, that with one swift, masterful *coup* he would destroy them all and enter history as a great leader and liberator.

Only the future will show whether the trend of Nasser's policy, the ever-growing dependence on the Soviet Union, is reversible. Given Egypt's geographical position and the balance of power in the area which Nasser had tried so hard to upset, it is probably premature to speak about a 'point of no return'. It still depends in the last resort on the scale of priorities of Egypt's leaders. Those to whom the heavy burden of succession has fallen are not to be envied.

Syria

Summing up on Syria in 1958, I wrote that this was the most militantly anti-Western of all Arab countries and that it had moved closest to the Soviet Union. Not as the result of 'Soviet propaganda', but as the culmination of an internal radicalization.[80] After more than a decade full of dramatic events – the union with Egypt and its dissolution, *coups* and counter-*coups*, one war and innumerable war scares – there is no reason to revise and little to add to that appraisal. While refraining from open criticism, the Soviet Union had been far from enthusiastic about Syria's union with Egypt. The *World Marxist Review*, more outspoken than the Soviet press on such occasions, had called it a 'deplorable example': Syria had been subordinated to Egypt; the unity that had been imposed from above was artificial in character; Syria was ruled by undemocratic means; the Egyptian *bourgeoisie* had simply extended the sphere of its activities.[81] When Syria again became independent in September 1961, the

Soviet Union was the first of the big powers to recognize the new regime.[82] The new Syrian government, headed by Mamun al-Kuzbari, favoured a neutralist foreign policy, but was opposed to agrarian reform, let alone communism, which it regarded as hostile to Islam and Arab nationalism. In the elections that took place at the end of 1961 the new leaders received a comfortable majority. It seemed, as a Soviet historian noted, that everything had been put back to where it was before: the 'golden age of *bourgeois* democracy' had returned.[83] But a parliamentary majority meant little in a country lacking a democratic tradition; the new regime had powerful enemies among the intelligentsia and the army officers, especially those of the younger generation. In March 1963 the government was overthrown by a military *coup* headed by Colonel Amin el Hafiz and the leaders of the Ba'th Party. Since then and up to the time of writing the Ba'th has remained in power. But the *coup* of 1963 was by no means the last one, for the party was taken over by a new group of army officers and politicians. All the early Ba'th leaders were ousted; in 1968 that party had nothing in common but the name with the movement that had come to power five years earlier.[84] The year 1963 marked the zenith of its influence and popularity. The Ba'th is a nationalist and socialist party, with members in many Arab countries, whose origins go back to the late nineteen-thirties. In 1963 Ba'th governments came to power in both Syria and Iraq, but their leaders showed little political ability; torn by internal divisions and weakened by the refusal of the military to accept civilian leadership, they suffered almost instant eclipse. A Soviet commentator has provided a vivid, and on the whole accurate picture of conditions in Syria in 1963:

While this political merry-go-round continued, Syria presented an extraordinary spectacle: ministers and senior officials appointed to their posts exclusively on the principle of 'reliability', but often having no idea of the real situation and its economic problems, and interested only in political cabals; officers, each of them thinking that his hour would come at any moment, and that a battalion of soldiers or a dozen armoured cars would be enough to seize power; journalists trying to guess who in fact would carry out the next *coup*. Plots, rumours of plots, denial of rumours of plots, suspicious troop movements. No one trusts his neighbour, everyone tries to outsmart his partner; superiors look searchingly at their subordinates: Who will be the next to strike? . . . There was a popular anecdote at the time in Damascus about an officer who came up to the headquarters building. The sentry asked what he wanted. 'To carry out a *coup d'état*.' 'Don't you know the standing orders? Wait in the queue round the corner.'[85]*

The Soviet attitude towards the old Ba'th had never been very friendly: the Ba'thists were accused of terrorism, adventurism, anti-communist propaganda: their socialism was a sham, they behaved like fascists and Spanish falangists. The frequent professions of friendship for the Soviet Union made by their leaders left Moscow unimpressed.[86] This negative communist appraisal of the Ba'th was no doubt influenced by the fact that Syria, unlike Egypt, had a fairly substantial communist party, and that the Ba'th, in contrast to the Egyptian ASU, was a cadre party with a well-defined political programme. It was weaker than Nasserism and at the same time more difficult to infiltrate. The collapse of Ba'th rule in Iraq was welcomed in the Soviet Union and a similar fate was predicted for the Syrian government: 'chaos prevails in any country which the Ba'thists rule'.[87] But the Syrian Ba'th managed to cling on to power; the main struggle was fought out inside the party, between the regional (Syrian) command and its general leadership (the All-Arab National Command). The contest was mainly between the old, civilian leaders of the party (such as Salah Bitar and Michel Aflaq) and a group of young, ambitious, and radical army officers who were steadily gaining influence. The former gradually lost control, and the prime minister Amin el Hafiz, himself a military man, took a middle-of-the-road position between the two factions. Soviet observers were quick to note these developments, welcoming the victory of the 'healthy, honest, energetic, patriotic elements' over the 'treacherous, discredited clique of old-style politicians'.[88] When the Syrian government decided (in January 1965) to nationalize

---

* The freshness of the comments of the writer of this account, G. Mirsky, is unfortunately not at all typical of the general level of Soviet political reportage on or analysis of the Middle East. Mirsky's articles and books, however much mistaken on occasion, often display an intelligence and originality sadly absent in most Soviet political writing.

over a hundred companies, and when the communists were released from prison, there was a marked improvement in the Soviet attitude: 'Enthusiasm reigns in the workers' quarters of Syrian towns.'[89] The Ba'th remained 'petty *bourgeois*' as far as its class character was concerned, but it was now noted in Moscow that its slogans ('some directly borrowed from the communists') had many supporters among workers and peasants.[90] In some respects, the Ba'th programme did not go far enough for Moscow; the trade unions, the communists claimed, had not been given enough authority. On the other hand, even in 1965, the Syrian communists detected a tendency towards ultra-radicalism among the left-wing Ba'th likely to antagonize the middle classes; lack of understanding of their just demands was bound to play into the hands of the reactionaries.[91]

The internal Syrian crisis reached its climax towards the end of 1965, when the regional party leadership under Salah Jadid, the army chief of staff, demanded the resignation of Amin el Hafiz. Hafiz refused to comply. According to one Soviet source, there had been a quarrel about foreign policies; according to another, Hafiz believed that the ultra-leftists would by their hasty action discredit the idea of building socialism in Syria.[92] Bitar, the main exponent of the civilian leadership, agreed to form a government on condition that the military stayed out of politics. The All-Arab Command dissolved the regional (Syrian) leadership and assumed the functions of supreme political authority in Syria. This was the eighth government since the Ba'th had come to power in 1963. It was to be as short-lived as most of its predecessors, for the military, who still wielded real power, immediately plotted its overthrow. On 23 February 1966, in the bloodiest of all *coups* so far (the eighteenth since Syria had become independent) the left-wing Ba'th returned to power; Amin el Hafiz, Bitar, and the other old party leaders were arrested. Nuredin Atassi became the new head of state and Dr Zu'ayin was made prime minister, while effective power rested in the hands of a small group of colonels. Most of the new rulers belonged to ethnic and religious minority groups, mainly the Alawites and, to a lesser extent, the Druzes and Ismailites. Soviet observers were aware of this fact and expressed some concern; they wrote that people in Syria talked too much and too easily about socialism in various parts of the world,[93] but they were agreed that, by and large, the February *coup* was not a *coup* like its predecessors, but a great progressive event, and that under the new rulers, who had declared their intention of carrying out a policy of socialist transformation, relations between Moscow and Damascus would become much closer than ever before. It was hoped in particular that the Syrian communists would soon be given an opportunity to take a leading part in the new regime.

The communists, who had been in opposition both during the Nasserist period and after 1961, were inclined to take a more critical view of the Ba'th than Moscow, but after the January 1965 decrees they modified their line. The Ba'th policy of nationalization, their Central Committee stated, was an important step forward.[94] Hints were dropped that they were ready to cooperate with the Ba'th which would need their political know-how and particularly their ability to mobilize the masses. Above all, they could serve as a bridge to Moscow. There were, of course, conditions attached: Khalid Bakdash, one of their leaders, would have to be allowed to return from exile, and some of their representatives would have to join the new government.[95] Negotiations between the Ba'th leaders and the communists began in February 1965; the former, despite their slogans about 'left-wing unity', could not reach agreement among themselves about the measure of freedom to be given to the communists. Eventually the Beirut communist press (*Al Nida, Al Akhbar*) was permitted to circulate freely in Syria, but Bakdash was allowed to return only after the February 1966 *coup*. The neo-Ba'th, after purging many of its old members, appointed communists to cabinet posts, but it was never quite clear how many there were, because the communist ministers were co-opted as individuals rather than as representatives of their party. The Ba'th was reluctant to admit that communists were now sitting in their inner councils, denouncing the news of this fact as yet another 'imperialist provocation'. Soviet and communist spokesmen were less inhibited about the subject and flatly announced that 'communists and members of other progressive groups' had at last joined the Damascus government.[96]

Not all Ba'thists were happy about these developments, but they were told by their leaders that it was a political necessity. The Ba'th lacked a mass basis; some sources put its membership as low as 2,000 not counting several hundred army officers. It needed all the outside support it could get. A rebuff to the communists would have jeopardized the close contacts with Moscow. The Soviet leaders had reservations about the neo-Ba'th, but these were outweighed by the opportunities offered by this enthusiastic new ally. Moscow showed immediate readiness to help: a protective screen was erected around Syria to shield it from its enemies and detractors. Throughout 1966 and early 1967 the Soviet mass media published frequent announcements about alleged conspiracies to overthrow the new regime, hatched from within, in the other Arab capitals, and, needless to say, by Israel. Nasser was advised to establish close links with the neo-Ba'th, thus ensuring the survival of the regime. The new rulers of Syria did not make it easy for their protectors. The violent manifestos issued by the Syrian government, its incessant attacks on the 'reactionary forces' in the Arab world, caused a great deal of concern in Arab capitals and fears about a 'Soviet Cuba in the Middle East'.[97] During the first weeks and months of the new regime the Soviet leaders were uncertain about its chances of survival, and there were great sighs of relief in May and June 1966, when it was reported from Damascus that the opposition was too weak and disunited to take any effective action against the neo-Ba'th: 'The tide was running in favour of the new government.'[98]

There was a great deal of coming and going between Damascus and Moscow after February 1966. Military contacts had existed for a long time; Mamduh Jaber, the then Syrian defence minister, had gone on an official mission to the Soviet capital in October 1964. Marshal Grechko had told him on that occasion that the Soviet Union was ready to assist Syria materially and morally to defeat imperialism and its supporters.[99] Naturally, the Syrian generals were above all interested in the material implications of this promise and discussed their shopping list in considerable detail. After the 1966 *coup* the flow of Soviet arms increased; there were unconfirmed reports that the Soviet Union had asked for two bases in exchange for the war material that was about to be supplied.[100]

Several weeks after coming to power, Prime Minister Zu'ayin went to Moscow with a request for Soviet political support. He also wanted help for the ambitious Euphrates dam project, the Syrian equivalent of the Aswan dam. It involved the building of a reservoir lake of about 350 square miles, the irrigation of some $1\frac{1}{2}$ million acres of land, and the building of a huge hydro-electric complex. Politically, the project was far more problematical than the Aswan dam, for Syria had not bothered to consult Turkey and Iraq, the other riparian states. Turkey, with which Syria's relations were traditionally bad, could largely thwart the scheme by building a dam of its own, as indeed it had announced it would do. Iraq, on the other hand, was likely to suffer; a million Iraqi farmers were bound to be affected by the Syrian dam. Disregarding these objections, the Syrians went ahead with the project on the basis of a West German promise to finance and supervise the building of the dam. When Damascus broke off relations with Bonn in 1965, in protest against West Germany's recognition of Israel, it became necessary to find a new sponsor. Zu'ayin's efforts in Moscow were successful; the Soviet Union agreed to step in and to underwrite a substantial part of the project – 'a crushing blow for West Germany and Western Imperialism' as the Damascus newspapers put it.[101] The first Soviet dam experts arrived in Damascus in May 1966 to great official acclaim; the government declared that this project would be the basis of the new Syrian five-year plan: 'We are determined to build the dam, over our own bones if need be.'[102] Russia also agreed to help Syria in extending its railway network, to renovate the Homs-Aleppo line, to build a new line from Qamishli in eastern Syria to Latakia on the Mediterranean coast, and also to provide new equipment.[103] An oil agreement with the USSR had been signed in 1965, and in April 1966 a further Soviet offer was submitted to develop Syria's oilfields.

For a little while the Euphrates project was given so much publicity that the impression was created (to quote a Lebanese newspaper) that the country's entire future depended on whether or not the dam was built. There is reason to doubt whether this enthusiasm was ever widely shared: not only was the Euphrates project much smaller than the Aswan dam, it was also much less vital for the country's economy. It was regarded primarily as a symbol of political achievement of the neo-Ba'th, a group of politicians without genuine interest in economic problems.

The future of the regime remained uncertain and the construction of the dam was at best several years ahead; more effective slogans were needed to mobilize the public, to dramatize the achievements of the new regime against the 'enemies of Syria and socialism'. Soviet-Syrian cooperation in the field of propaganda and political warfare manifested itself in the creation and orchestration of artificial crises; political tension was kept high for weeks on end. Sometimes the initiative emanated from Moscow, more often from Damascus. Every few weeks it was announced that the Israeli army, in cooperation with Jordan and Saudi Arabia, was about to attack Syria, that the CIA and the British oil companies were hatching plots, that Syrian reactionaries were engaged in sinister intrigues. A state-of-siege mentality was systematically inculcated and the tone of the official Damascus press, never a paragon of moderation and sobriety, became quite hysterical during the summer of 1966: Syria was under imperialist attack, the reactionaries were trying to isolate it. The country could rely only on the Soviet Union, and (perhaps) on Egypt.

It is not easy to establish in retrospect with any degree of accuracy how much of this was deliberately fabricated and how much was genuinely believed by the instigators. The apprehensions of the neo-Ba'th were not entirely unjustified; the hold of the regime was precarious, the measures taken against the middle classes and the Islamic clergy diminished what popularity it had. Even the communists admitted that, in hastily nationalizing some small enterprises, the cart had been put before the horse. Khalid Bakdash found it necessary to reassure the small shopkeepers: they would be defended against all those who stood to the left of the communist party.[104] No doubt there were plots against the neo-Ba'th, but the more serious ones came from inside the regime, such as the conspiracy of Colonel Selim Hatoum. He had played the leading role in the February *coup*, but subsequently quarrelled with his colleagues, escaped to Jordan, returned to Damascus during the Six Day War, and was executed by his captors. Hatoum was accused by Damascus and Moscow of having been an agent of both China and the CIA. The truth was less complicated: Hatoum had suffered defeat in a struggle for power in which ideology played only a secondary role.

Among the men who had come to power after February 1966 there were several radical socialists, such as the trade union leader Khaled el Jundi, who was arrested after the Six Day War. But for most of the new leaders, especially the army officers, the fashionable socialist phraseology was little more than a smoke-screen behind which an unceasing struggle for power and personal aggrandizement went on. Despite the revolutionary slogans, the attachment of these men to the cause of socialism (let alone 'revolutionary democracy') was more than a little suspect: they were riding high on what they thought was the wave of the future. Arab socialists outside Syria were at first perplexed; by backing the neo-Ba'th, the Soviet Union was pursuing a policy that was not based on either moral or revolutionary principles, for these individuals were 'known opportunists'; in respect to the Ba'th, most of them were transients, who had neither shared in the party struggle nor adhered to its ideology.[105] That the new leaders had been disloyal to the traditional Ba'th ideology was not Moscow's concern; the decisive question was whether they would be loyal to their new partners. There could be no certainty on this count in Moscow, where at times misgivings were expressed about the boastfulness of the neo-Ba'th, its lack of moderation and its instability. But the Russians could not hope to educate their new allies within a short period; at most they could act as a realistic and moderating influence and keep some control by means of frequent consultations and meetings. There were many such con-tacts between the Syrian and Soviet leaders during the months preceding the Six Day War. Hafiz el Asad, the Syrian war minister, went to Moscow, as did the other strong man of the junta, Salah Jadid, heading a Ba'th party delegation in January 1967. This was a real innovation, for up to that date all contacts between Moscow and the Arab governments had been on the government level. The Soviet representatives noted (to quote the official communiqué) the importance of the progressive measures carried out by the Ba'th party in Syria which opened up socialist prospects for the country's development.[106] But in fact the Ba'th leadership was, not to mince words, less interested in the 'socialist transformation of Syrian society' than in the perpetuation of its own rule and in an activist foreign policy. For a long time Syria had been the most militant Arab country in its attitude towards Israel, outdoing the other Arab governments in its insistence on immediate war. It had been the chief base from which the Arab guerrillas staged their raids into Israel. This, and the dispute about the Jordan waters, had been the sources of permanent tension between Israel and Syria. Successive Ba'th governments had failed to gain the support of the other Arab countries for a combined attack on Israel, and the neo-Ba'th government was even less likely to receive support for the proposal, in view of its violent campaigns against the 'reactionary' Arab countries. But it did not desist from its policy and the Soviet leaders had to decide how far to go in their support. Moscow gave Damascus full diplomatic assistance, making solemn declarations that the Soviet Union would not remain indifferent to any attempts to violate peace in a region in direct proximity to its borders.[107] But such promises, far from restraining the Damascus junta, contributed to further tension in the area. The neo-Ba'th leaders thought that with Soviet backing they could pursue even more militant policies. Nor did the defence agreement with Egypt signed in December 1966 have a salutary effect (Kosygin was said to have helped to bring about this reconciliation between Damascus and Cairo); the new guarantee made them only more inclined to undertake aggressive policies.

The leaders of the neo-Ba'th played a fateful role in the events preceding the Arab-Israeli war: the battle at Lake Tiberias in early April 1967, the new wave of Fatah attacks, the internal crisis in Syria culminating in yet another campaign against the 'reactionaries', and ultimately the war scare, were designed to help the neo-Ba'th junta to overcome their internal difficulties[108]. In this they succeeded, but at what a price! The war scare made war a reality; the baseless rumour that fifteen Israeli brigades were about to attack Syria precipitated Egypt's mobilization. In the war that followed Syria did not acquit itself very well; after the bombastic speeches of Zu'ayin and the other leaders, the hasty retreat from their impregnable positions on the Golan heights came as a shock. One reason for the defeat was the withdrawal of many units from the front line to strengthen internal security – the Syrian leaders were more worried about the enemy within than about the Israelis. Their caution in a way paid off, for during the first year after the war there was no serious challenge to their power, despite the army's dismal performance. The opposition was still ineffective; the government ruled with an iron hand, giving internal security absolute priority in all its political activities. The Syrian army assumed most of the functions of the political police. As plots from within remained the main danger to the regime, frequent purges were carried out in both the army and civilian circles. Immediately after the war ended the Soviet leaders assured Damascus of their continuing support: Podgorny's visit to Damascus and Zu'ayin's trip to Moscow were part of these emergency consultations. Later, in March 1968, Marshal Grechko went to Syria to coordinate military ties between the two countries, and a neo-Ba'th delegation went again to Moscow for 'ideological discussions'.[109] But while the Soviet press expressed admiration for the brave stand of the Syrians against the Israeli aggressors, the Russians were more than a little irritated with their impulsive allies, who had involved them in an adventure over which the senior partner in the alliance had lost control. Soviet commentators reporting from Damascus complained about the Syrian ultra-leftists with their suicidal plan of a new people's war, even if that involved Israeli occupation of still more Arab territory.[110] On various occasions Syria's unwillingness to collaborate with the other Arab countries was criticized; so was its opposition to the Security Council resolution of 22 November 1967, and the refusal to enlarge the government and establish a popular front. The new appointments made in Damascus inspired little confidence in Moscow. The new Syrian chief of staff was Mustafa Tlas, a theoretician of guerrilla warfare and translator of Che Guevara, not one of Moscow's favourite revolutionary heroes. When the Ba'th leaders met Brezhnev and his colleagues early in 1967, and again in summer 1968, it was stated in the joint communiqué that the exchange of opinions demonstrated that both parties held 'similar or identical views' on world affairs.[111] Yet both sides were no doubt aware that this statement was only half true. Despite all protestations to the contrary, ideology played a lesser role in Syrian politics than, say, in China or Cuba, and Syria found it therefore much easier to accommodate itself to the Soviet Union, provided that Soviet help was forthcoming. It needed a protector and it had something to offer in return. Syria was a country with many natural resources, even though under the rule of Nasser and the Ba'th the Syrian economy had declined. As a field for large-scale Soviet investment and a potential showcase for both the achievements of communism and the advantages of Soviet help, Syria was a somewhat more promising choice than Egypt. But the neo-Ba'th had no real sound basis; the regime was thoroughly unpopular; here was not one leader even remotely comparable in stature and mass appeal to Nasser. Its radicalism, coupled with the traditional Syrian xenophobia, made a reconciliation with the West unlikely, but it did not necessarily make them trustworthy allies. The events leading up to the Arab-Israeli war in 1967 had shown that the Syrian rulers were uncontrollable, their record on the home front had demonstrated that their radicalism was largely verbal, and that under their leadership Syria was unlikely to make much progress. In Syria the Soviet Union had found a promising but highly problematical ally; the problems were different in character but no less grave than those facing Egypt. The regime was ruling through fear; its overthrow was likely to lead to violence and counter-terror, similar to the events in Baghdad in 1963. Deeply committed to the neo-Ba'th, the Soviet Union followed events in Syria with much concern.*

* Within the neo-Ba'th there were differences of opinion about the extent of the collaboration with the Soviet Union. Some leaders favoured total submission; others were for an independent pro-Soviet line. The former, headed by prime minister Zu'ayin, were defeated in October 1968 by the faction led by Hafiz el Asad, minister of defence.

Iraq

The overthrow of the monarchy in 1958 marks the great divide in recent Iraqi history. General Abdel Karim Kassem, the military dictator who succeeded the Hashemites, cooperated closely with the communists; within a few months they became one of the country's strongest political forces. Many key positions passed into their hands, including, to all intents and purposes, the revolutionary tribunal under Colonel Mahdawi, set up to carry through a large-scale purge in the country.[112]

Major and minor public figures suspected of lack of enthusiasm for the new regime were imprisoned, and many were executed, with or without the benefit of a trial. 1959 was later remembered in Iraq as the 'Year of the Red Terror'; the country seemed to be on the verge of a communist take-over. But communist strength was not so formidable as it appeared; the party leadership, as one of its main figures later admitted, was too young, without experience or theoretical training, and the party as a whole had grown too fast.[113] Kassem, while using the communists, had no intention of allowing them to dictate his policy. Gradually the communists' power was curtailed, and once it emerged that they were not after all going to rule the country, the party had to pay the price for the terrorist excesses that had been committed at its instigation. The communists had made a basic political mistake: they had tried to settle accounts with their enemies without being able to carry the job through to the end. After 1959 their fortunes began to decline. Through the new 'Association Law', Kassem prevented the legalization of the Communist party, recognizing instead a totally unrepresentative rival group led by Daoud al-Sa'igh; the real party (*Itihad al Sha'b*) became illegal. The communist press was banned and the many front organizations came under attack in October 1960.[114] One by one the key positions in the various political and social organizations that had mushroomed after July 1958 under communist guidance were lost to the party – the associations of teachers, journalists, peasants, and women, as well as the General Federation of Trade Unions (May 1961); they kept their hold on the students union only for a little longer. Since the communists had acquired their positions not by democratic means, but by packing meetings with non-professional elements, it proved surprisingly easy to replace them with supporters of the regime.[115] Many individual communists were arrested in connection with the terrorist excesses that had been committed. Speaking at the congress of the CPSU in October 1961, Salim Adil (*alias* Husain Radawi), the Iraqi party's first secretary, said that 112 communists or pro-communists had been sentenced to death and 770 to imprisonment by military courts, mainly for their part in the Kirkuk disturbances and other riots in 1959.[116] Two years later Salim Adil was himself executed. By November 1960 the last communist supporters had been removed from the government on charges either of deviationism or of incompetence. Mahdawi's People's Court ceased to function, and by early 1961 there was talk that the communists might again have to go underground.[117]

The gradual decline of communist power was a great disappointment to the Soviet Union. During 1958 and 1959 Iraq had been the most promising Arab country, much more so than Nasser's Egypt. Diplomatic ties between Moscow and Baghdad were resorted almost immediately after the revolution of July 1958 and the Soviet Union offered to assist the Kassem regime in every possible way. In March 1959 Iraq was granted a development loan of $500 million for a period of six years, to finance fourteen big industrial projects, including a steel mill and several factories. Soviet engineers were to work on a new Baghdad-Basra standard-gauge railway (involving another $180 million loan). The Soviet Union also undertook to improve lands in southern Iraq and navigation on the two main rivers, and to install an atomic reactor in Baghdad.[118] Soviet military aid given to Iraq was estimated at $120 million by April 1960.[119] The Soviet media refrained from attacking Kassem even after he had turned against the communists, but continued to praise the Iraqi revolution. Baghdad had become an 'important source' from which Arab fighters for freedom were seeking material and moral help: a complete phase in the Arab national movement had ended and a new one had opened.[120] Relations with Baghdad remained cordial even after the communists had been removed from key positions. Anastas Mikoyan, accompanied by the minister for foreign trade. visited Baghdad in April 1960 and announced that the Soviet Union had now both economic and military superiority over the West, and that it was ready to share its achievements with Iraq.[121] In September 1960 the Iraqi chief of staff, General Abdi, went on a prolonged visit to Moscow; so did Mahdawi and the Iraqi minister of education. Kassem declared on many occasions that, though no communist himself, he wanted to be on friendly terms with the communist world and needed its support.[122] Having removed the immediate threat of a communist take-over, he had no desire to destroy the party altogether, for he was aware that he might still need it against his many foes, such as the Nasserists and the Ba'thists. Many of the death sentences imposed on communists by military courts were not carried out.

Up to 1960 Kassem's foreign policy had been orientated towards the Soviet Union; the bitterness of the attacks in the official press against 'Western imperialism' easily surpassed even Egypt's anti-American and anti-British campaign. During 1960 there was a marked change; relations with the Western powers improved, and Kassem and the Baghdad press began to stress Iraq's neutrality; there was occasional criticism of the Soviet Union, even at the time of Mikoyan's visit. The following year the pendulum again swung in the opposite direction: Kassem blamed Britain, not the Soviet Union, for the Kurdish rising (of which more below) and he also invited British resistance when staking his claim to Kuwait. For the difficulties encountered in the negotiations with the Iraq Petroleum Company also Britain was blamed, all of which impelled him to look for a new *rapprochement* with Moscow. Trade between Iraq and the Soviet Union continued to expand: the share of the Soviet bloc countries in Iraq's foreign trade rose from 17 per cent in 1960 to 21 per cent the year after; a new cultural agreement was signed and military collaboration continued.

After two years of Kassem's rule the first flush of pro-Iraqi enthusiasm in Moscow had passed, as the limitations of the regime became painfully obvious. There was growing criticism of the persecution of 'patriots and democratic elements' in Iraq; one Soviet periodical wrote that the streets of Baghdad were 'red with their blood', that a wave of reactionary poison was spreading, that the dregs of society had again crawled out from dark corners and gateways.[123] There was Soviet criticism of the Iraqi agricultural reform, which, it was argued, was proceeding far too slowly, of the hostile attitude towards the Soviet Union on the part of some Iraqi newspapers, of the tendency to appease the Western powers.[124] But on the whole such criticism was still muted and infrequent; it cannot be even remotely compared with the intensity of the attacks directed against Kassem's successors in 1963. The Soviet leaders clearly had not written off Kassem entirely, the tacit assumption being that he was, like Nasser, unpredictable, and that while keeping him at a certain distance, nothing should be done to cause a final break. Kassem's growing isolation, the ridiculous cult around his personality, the nonsensical political schemes emanating from his government, made it virtually certain that the days of the regime were numbered. But the communists, even while persecuted by the government, could not afford to dissociate themselves from Kassem altogether; later on they were to claim that it was a wicked slander to suggest that they had ever supported Kassem: they had been ('as everyone knew') the most consistent fighters against his dictatorship. But in fact they had collaborated closely with Kassem during the early phase of his rule, and they had every reason to be afraid of his overthrow, since they were too weak to succeed him themselves. The massacres of 1959 had left deep scars; many people were only waiting for the hour of retaliation and Kassem's pan-Arab rivals happened to be the communists' worst enemies. Much as they had come to dislike and to despise Kassem, the communists had a vested interest in the continuation of his reign.

The Kurdish Problem

The Kurdish issue made it increasingly difficult for the Soviet Union to persist in its attitude of low-key, distant benevolence *vis-à-vis* the regime. For the Kurds were not just an internal Iraqi problem that could be ignored by outsiders; once open warfare had broken out between them and the Baghdad government, the Soviet Union was bound to become involved.[125] There are substantial Kurdish minorities in Iran and Turkey; more than a million of them live in Iraq, mainly in the Sulaimaniya and Arbil districts, but also in the region of Mosul and Kirkuk. Individual Kurds suffered no discrimination in Iraq; indeed, some of them rose to leading positions in the State. But there was marked reluctance on the part of the Iraqi authorities to make concessions to the Kurds as a minority, let alone to recognize them as a separate nation, and the more pan-Arab the Iraqi government of the day, the less likely it was to accede to Kurdish demands. A major Kurdish rising had taken place in 1943 under the leadership of Mullah Mustafa Barazani, the head of the Barazani tribes; in October 1945 he crossed with his men into Persian Kurdistan, where, under Soviet auspices, a Kurdish republic was established at Mahabad. The political basis of this republic was the Democratic Party of Kurdistan (DPK), a popular front consisting of various left-wing nationalist bodies and the Kurdish communists.[126]

After the withdrawal of the Soviet troops from Iran this republic collapsed and Mullah Mustafa, who had established an alliance with the DPK, crossed with his men into the Soviet Union, where they remained for more than a decade. After the revolution of 1958 they returned to Iraq and were warmly welcomed by Kassem, but within a year it appeared that the hopes of the Kurds for national self-determination were not likely to be fulfilled; tension rose and in 1961 sporadic clashes occurred between the Barazani tribes and Iraqi forces. Kassem at this stage decided to support those Kurdish tribes which resented the ascendancy of the Barazanis, and there ensued a period of intertribal warfare in which the DPK and the Barazanis defeated their opponents. By September 1961 this had turned into a full-scale rising; the insurgents seized many police posts in north Iraq and several cities were firmly in their hands. Government troops staged a counter-offensive and bombed Kurdish villages. But access to the mountainous strongholds of the Kurds, difficult enough in summer, proved impossible in winter, and the main body of the insurgents was undefeated. The government has not succeeded in reimposing full control ever since, and a state of intermittent warfare has continued, involving at times up to two-thirds of the Iraqi army.

The Kurdish rising posed a difficult choice for the Soviet Union, and even more so for the Iraqi communists. Whereas the Kurdish communists gave qualified support to Barazani, Iraqi communists urged Kurds and Arabs to join forces in the struggle against imperialist plots aimed at the disruption of the nationalist ranks. The secession of Kurdistan from Iraq and the scheme to establish a Kurdish government was in communist eyes an imperialist plot. The Iraqi Communist Party announced at the time that while supporting the right of the Kurds to self-determination, it opposed both pan-Arab chauvinism and extreme nationalist tendencies among the Kurds.[127] But this line was by no means clear and consistent; while they were still hoping for a reconciliation with Kassem they tended to cold shoulder the Kurds. When the persecution of the party became more intense they expressed support for the just demands of the DPK and denounced the Baghdad government for 'savagely attacking' the Kurds.[128] In a resolution adopted in March 1962 the Iraqi communists reiterated their support for Kurdish autonomy within the Iraqi state. But, as one commentator added, the realization of this immediate aim did not affect the legal right of the Kurds to press for the establishment of an independent Kurdish state, to include the Kurds of Turkey and Iran as well. Meanwhile, there could be no doubt that autonomy for the Iraqi Kurds would have wide repercussions among the Kurds in the neighbouring countries and thus give additional impetus to the struggle against CENTO and other imperialist plots.[129] For years the Iraqi communists tried to steer a difficult middle course between Kassem, Arab nationalism, and the Kurdish independence movement.

Soviet policy followed similar lines; at first the Kurdish rising was not even reported in the press. Kassem exonerated the Soviet Union *expressis verbis* from any complicity in the rising, putting all the blame on Western imperialism. After Kassem's fall in June 1963 a new major campaign was launched against the Kurds, and now, with the total suppression of communism in Iraq and the deterioration in Soviet-Iraqi relations, Soviet reticence gave way to warm support for the Kurdish cause. The Soviet delegation raised the issue in the United Nations; according to the accounts by Soviet observers, the 'fascist clique in Baghdad was perpetrating genocide'; crimes against humanity were being committed in Kurdistan; more than 200 villages had been destroyed, and thousands killed in the napalm bombings.[130] In an official declaration dated 9 July 1963, the Soviet government announced that it regarded the campaign against the Kurds as a threat to peace, especially in view of the fact that the fighting was taking place near the Soviet border, in an area which 'the imperialists would like to use for an attack against our country'.[131]

The Ba'th government which had been responsible for the Kurdish campaign of 1963 was overthrown in November of that year and General Arif stopped the war in February 1964. But not for long; in the spring of the following year fighting broke out again; the Baghdad press, which had first denied these reports as foreign fabrications, then argued that the government was only exercising its natural right to destroy the rebel bands.[132] Soviet commentators noted on various occasions that neither the DPK nor Barazani wanted to secede from Iraq; that they stood for a reasonable and peaceful solution of the Kurdish problem within the framework of a progressive policy for Iraq.[133] 'Even if the Iraqi government asked us to separate, we would not agree,' Barazani is said to have told a Soviet correspondent. On other occasions the Soviet press criticized 'extremist circles' among the Kurds which were stubbornly resisting a peaceful solution, thus 'objectively helping to prolong the war' with their unrealistic demands.[134] The Kurdish issue was a thorny problem for all concerned, and the efforts of Prime Minister Bazzaz in 1966 to find a settlement evoked some sympathy in Moscow. A new truce (the third) was eventually signed in June 1966; Bazzaz solemnly declared that the problem could be solved only by full recognition of all Kurdish national rights. The Soviet Union welcomed this step, stressing that the just demands of nearly a quarter of the country's population had to be fulfilled.[135] But the Bazzaz government was overthrown before it could carry out its promises and by September 1966 the Iraqi communists were noting that government policy had scarcely changed: the army was still in Kurdistan, economic sanctions had not been fully lifted, many Kurdish nationalists were still in prison.[136] They announced that they were supporting the Kurdish national leadership, despite the fact that they were no longer part of it. When it was clear in March 1967 that the government did not intend to carry out the policy outlined by Bazzaz, the communists called on the democratic forces in Kurdistan and its armed units (known as the Peshmerga Army) not to surrender their arms. Not that the Kurds had intended to do so anyway.[137] Communist influence had decreased among the Kurds over the years, partly because of what Kurdish nationalists considered merely 'lukewarm communist support' for their cause, partly as the result of unending internal splits and dissensions within the communist ranks. Over the years many issues had divided them – whether the party organization in Kurdistan should be dissolved and become part of the Popular Front, how closely they were to cooperate with Barazani, whether they were to keep their ties with the DPK, and what their attitude was to be *vis-à-vis* Bazzaz. The prestige of the party and its political effectiveness was seriously affected by these splits and the quarrels between the communists and the Kurdish leadership.[138]

Iraqi attempts to pacify the Kurds continued both before and after the *coup* of July 1968, but a lasting solution was unlikely to be found under a regime that put pan-Arabism first. From the Soviet point of view, and for the Iraqi communists, this conflict constituted both a challenge and a source of weakness. As in most other Middle East national clashes (excepting only the Arab-Israeli conflict), the Soviet Union was reluctant to give total support to one side, but anything less than full support was unlikely to reap political gains.

After Kassem

The overthrow of Kassem in February 1963 had been a major setback for the USSR. His domestic policy was criticized in Moscow more outspokenly after his fall than before: the 'cult of personality', the arbitrary rule, and above all the 'rejection of support by the progressive forces'. But Soviet commentators insisted even after his fall that in foreign affairs Kassem had on the whole followed an 'anti-imperialist course'.[139] The policy of the Ba'th which had come to power in February was viewed with grave concern; all those who had been persecuted in the early years of the Kassem regime welcomed the opportunity to get even with their tormentors, and a new wave of terror erupted. Leading communists were brought to trial and sentenced to death, many more were lynched by the National Guard. The Soviet press denounced the terrorist methods of the new ('fascist') government, while the Iraqi press retaliated by attacking 'Muscovite imperialism' and the 'hangmen of the Soviet people'.[140] The Ba'th regarded this settling of accounts with the communists as an internal affair; if the Soviet Union chose to interfere in Iraq's domestic politics, relations between the two countries were bound to deteriorate, but this would not be Iraq's fault.[141]

There is no saying how far this crisis would have gone but for the new *coup* on 18 November 1963, which brought General Abdel Salam Arif to power. His regime was far less ideological in character than the Ba'th; the execution of communists ceased and an attempt was made to normalize relations with the Soviet Union. In December 1963 the Soviet ambassador was told by the new Iraqi foreign minister that he hoped the strained relations between the two countries were a thing of the past.[142] The Arif dictatorship promulgated several nationalization decrees affecting Iraqi and foreign banks and also certain major industrial enterprises. The Soviet Union and the Iraqi communists welcomed these steps, while noting that they were less far-reaching than the Egyptian nationalization policy.[143] There was faint Soviet praise for the liberal views of Abdel Rahman Bazzaz, the first civilian prime minister for many years, who promised elections and tried to reduce the influence of army officers in the government.[144] The communists were less forthcoming and criticized Bazzaz's 'contradictory and suspect' policies; while the Soviet Union praised Bazzaz's Kurdish policy, the Iraqi communists continued to oppose it.[145] But with all their criticism and the complaints about the undemocratic nature of the regime and the fate of arrested party members, they thought Arif's rule greatly preferable to that of the Ba'th. They expressed their willingness to cooperate with the Arab Socialist Alliance (the new state party) despite the fact that they thought it would 'hold in check the contradictions among the nationalist forces'.[146] Soviet economic and military support continued: by 1966 economic help was extended to thirty-seven different projects, including work on the Baghdad-Basra Railway. Under the 1967 cultural agreement fifty Iraqi university graduates were to be trained in the Soviet Union, and Soviet professors and researchers worked at Baghdad University.

Among the many visits of Iraqi politicians to Moscow, that of Prime Minister Bazzaz (July 1966), the Iraqi defence minister, and Adnan Pachachi, the foreign minister (April 1967) deserve mention. The acting chief of staff, Major-General Abdel Rahman Arif, was on a mission to Moscow in April 1966 when the news of the death of his brother, the President, reached him. He returned at once to become Iraq's new chief of state. The second Arif was a weak and irresolute man, always inclined to postpone a decision on important problems and to steer a middle course between radicals and conservatives in the Arab world. Naji Talib and Taher Yahia, his prime ministers, proved equally ineffectual, and there were repeated charges of corruption against the government. The communists soon began to predict a new *coup* and an attempt to get rid of Arif, 'whom even his cronies do not consider fit to be president'.[147] The *coup* came two years later; it was carried out not by the Nasserists (as the communists had predicted), but by Baqr, Amash, and Takriti, the Ba'th generals, who had been the stalwarts of the anti-Kassem movement in 1963. There was a growing discrepancy between the Soviet attitude towards the Iraqi government and the stand of the Iraqi communists. Despite occasional criticism, Soviet commentators put the stress on the achievements of the regime, on the fact that almost three-quarters of Iraqi industry had been nationalized, on the curtailment of the monopoly of the Iraq Petroleum Company, and, of course, on the Soviet-Iraq oil agreement.[148] Moscow's attitude was not nearly so warm and friendly as towards Syria and Egypt, but the normalization of relations was noted with satisfaction.

The Iraqi communists, on the other hand, continued to attack the regime with great bitterness, not only because of the continued arrest of some of their comrades,[149] but in protest against the 'reactionary, anti-democratic, treacherous' character of the regime in general. The third Iraqi Communist party conference, meeting in January 1968, denounced the 'evil regime' that had caused the imprisonment, death, or dismissal from army ranks of thousands of efficient officers and soldiers, and had sent only token units into the war against Israel.

It expressed equally strong opposition to the deal with French and Italian oil firms and the arms agreement with France. On several occasions in 1966–7 the communist leaders declared that their party would in future follow a revolutionary policy aiming at the overthrow of the Arif regime.[150] This kind of propaganda shed doubt on Soviet professions of friendship; when challenged on this, the official explanation was that the Soviet Union did not bear responsibility for individual communist parties. But in this particular case the explanation did not stand up to examination, for the communist radio broadcasts (*Voice of the Iraqi People*) from which the revolutionary appeals emanated was stationed in Bulgaria. Early in 1968 it was announced that this station would close down, officially on the ground that the traitors who had carried out the 1963 *coup* had destroyed each other and that the Iraqi Communist party had regained its strength.[151] The real reasons were no doubt somewhat more complicated. It was Soviet policy to remain on reasonably good terms with Arif while he was in power, and even his successors were given the benefit of the doubt; the Iraqi Ba'th party had, according to the Soviet press, improved since 1963; it now included new people among its leaders, and the war against the Kurds had been called off.[152]

Soviet long-term policy *vis-à-vis* Iraq had gradually come to resemble that pursued *vis-à-vis* Turkey and Iran: the main aim was to neutralize what had once been the West's northern tier. This could be best achieved by expanding trade relations with these countries, by cooperation in the military field, and, as far as possible, by refraining from polemics. The Iraqi communists were left to fend for themselves in a political constellation that was not unpromising for them. The weakness of the regime, the frequent changes, and the continuing instability in Baghdad helped to create a political climate conducive to a new and perhaps more effective communist bid for power.

Yemen and South Arabia

At the end of the nineteen-fifties the Yemen was still one of the most backward countries in the world. Its ruler, Imam Ahmad, and a small group of the Sayyids (members of the Zaydi sect) literally owned the country, and the main aim of their despotic rule was to perpetuate the existing state of affairs. The economic situation was slowly deteriorating; religious obscurantism effectively barred any progress. It seemed an unlikely ally for the 'progressives' in the Arab world, but its geographical position at the junction of the Red Sea and the Indian Ocean, and the fact that the old Imam was anti-British, qualified the country for membership in the national liberation movement. The Russians, too, were trying to gain influence there; a treaty of friendship between the Yemen and the USSR was signed in 1955, and a trade agreement the year after. Al Badr, the Crown Prince, visited the Soviet Union in 1956, and the Soviet press waxed enthusiastic about the traditional bonds of friendship between the two countries. The late Imam Yahya was praised as a patriotic leader, and the modesty of the Crown Prince's residence was contrasted favourably with the luxurious palaces of other Arab rulers.[153]

Russian engineers began work on the construction of Hodeida harbour, which was completed in 1961; considerable quantities of Soviet arms were sold to the Yemen by the Soviet Union. These included T34 tanks as well as other armour, old-fashioned (Yak 11) aircraft, field and anti-aircraft guns. Military instructors and advisers were provided to teach the 'Victorious Royal Regular Army' (to give it its official name) parachuting and other arts of modern warfare. Soviet leaders assured the regime of their moral support in the conflict with the British over Aden. Egypt's relations with the Yemen were even closer, and for a brief period the Yemen formally became part of the United Arab Republic.

Intense opposition to the regime was widespread, and it was only the masterful personality of Imam Ahmad – skilled in maintaining a balance between the disruptive forces and inspiring a mythical fear in his subjects – which held together the disintegrating fabric of the archaic body politic.[154] He died in September 1962; his son and successor, Al Badr, was overthrown a fortnight later. He was succeeded by a republican regime headed by Abdullah as Sallal, which carried out some overdue reforms, but remained unpopular and found itself unable to impose its authority on the country. Egypt dispatched both experts and regular troops to help Sallal, and to gain a foothold on the peninsula, but the Egyptian expeditionary corps made a poor showing; it was bogged down in the difficult mountainous regions of the country, where its technical superiority could not be developed, while the loyalist tribes led by the Crown Prince conducted successful guerrilla operations against the invaders. What had begun as intertribal war soon turned into a general offensive against the Egyptian occupation. The republican regime was recognized by Washington, whereas Britain preferred to await the outcome of the struggle. Saudi Arabia provided help for the Royalists, though not on so lavish a scale as Nasser's support for the Republicans. The Soviet Union was among the first to recognize the Republican regime, and a Soviet spokesman later declared that the supply of Soviet weapons as well as the help extended by the Egyptian army had 'played an important part in strengthening the republicans against the forces of reaction'.[155] Soviet engineers were building an airport at Al-Rahaba, and Soviet technicians were maintaining Soviet tanks and jet fighters stationed in the Yemen. There were no official reports from Moscow about the Soviet engagement in South Arabia; while it frequently attacked foreign imperialist intervention in the Yemen, the Soviet press was reluctant to reveal details about Moscow's role in the conflict. Needless to say, claims by Yemeni Royalist forces to have shot down Soviet planes were not confirmed in Moscow. But there could be no doubt about the growing Soviet interest in the Yemen: Prime Minister Sallal returned from a visit to Moscow in March 1964 with an agreement on economic and technical cooperation and an aid programme. The reclamation of deserts for farmland was envisaged as well as the construction of roads and the building of various factories. As the Republicans failed to assert themselves, Soviet writers, betraying their disappointment, noted that with the exception of a few 'patriotic officers' there was no one who could be relied upon; the masses had no political education, political parties did not exist, and the rich merchants ('more interested in building villas, night-clubs, and swimming pools than schools and hospitals') were still the mainstay of the Republican regime.[156]

The civil war in the Yemen, which petered out towards the end of 1968, claimed hundreds of thousands of victims and caused a great deal of destruction. Despite the use of napalm and poison gas, the Egyptians and the republican forces failed to win a decisive victory against the Royalists. The Egyptian expeditionary corps had to be constantly reinforced to prevent a military catastrophe, and the war gradually became a major burden on Egypt's economy. Its political and psychological effects were equally disastrous. The Egyptians and the Sana government put the blame for their lack of success on 'Saudian gold' and imperialist machinations; the more realistic Soviet writers, on the other hand, held that the continued resistance of the Imam's supporters had to be attributed to the loyalty of the backward Yemeni tribes to their religious leader. For both political and military reasons, the Soviet leaders pressed for the establishment of a strong Yemeni army, but Nasser opposed any such scheme, as well as direct Soviet arms deliveries to Sana, in which he saw a potential threat to Egypt's influence in South Arabia.[157] It was realized earlier in Moscow than in Cairo and Sana that the Republicans could not hope to achieve a decisive victory and the Russians therefore recommended a negotiated peace. A cease-fire agreement was signed in November 1963, followed by peace talks in Alexandria in September 1964 and again in August 1965, when Nasser and King Faisal concluded an agreement covering the settlement of the conflict. But neither this nor the subsequent negotiations at Khartoum and Beirut in 1967–8 brought an end to the civil war. While pledging full support for the Republican regime, Moscow did not refrain from criticizing the 'extremists' in Sana, who by their unrealistic demands and adventurist actions were damaging their cause and playing into the hands of the imperialists.[158] This referred *inter alia* to the refusal of the Republicans to negotiate with members of the Yemeni royal family. Nor did the Russians accept the rosy picture of the military situation painted by Sana as the war went into its sixth year. A juxtaposition of Yemeni and Soviet announcements in December 1967 and January 1968 makes interesting reading. While President Irani announced that calm had returned, Moscow reported a new Royalist counter-offensive. When the Yemeni minister of the interior declared that the situation in the Sana sector was extremely reassuring, Tass countered with a declaration that the situation continued to deteriorate.[159]

After the Six Day War Egypt was no longer in a position to keep its expeditionary force in the Yemen, and the troops were withdrawn. This resulted, not surprisingly, in the fall of Sallal in November 1967. He was replaced by a three man Presidential Council of moderate Republicans. As the last Egyptians left Sana in December 1967 there was an excellent chance for the Royalists to make good their promise to take the capital within a few days of the Egyptians' withdrawal, but they encountered stiffer resistance than expected, and their assault failed. The Royalist leadership was inept, and in this critical situation the Republican regime received further military help from the Soviet Union, and to a lesser extent from China, Algeria, and Syria. In an emergency airlift in November and December 1967, the Soviet Union ferried about 10,000 tons of equipment to Hodeida airfield within three weeks.[160] It supplied one squadron of MiG 19s, as well as Ilyushins, complete with ground crews and instructors, while Syria provided most of the pilots. There were also volunteers from the National Liberation Front, the party now governing the new South Yemen People's Republic. But once the immediate danger to the capital had been averted, the Republicans began again to fight among themselves. There were artillery duels in the centre of Sana in August 1968, and so far as control over the countryside was concerned, the issue largely boiled down to who paid most, and to whom.[161] After six years of a cruel and destructive civil war which had seen foreign intervention on a massive scale, an uneasy peace returned to the Yemen.

The situation in South Arabia had been confused enough throughout the fifties and sixties; with the retreat of the British from Aden and the South Arabian Federation it became altogether chaotic. Britain began to withdraw its troops in August 1967, and in November of that year Aden and the whole Aden Protectorate became independent as the People's Republic of South Yemen. This had been preceded by a bitter civil war between two nationalist organizations, the Cairo supported FLOSY and the independent left-wing National Liberation Front (NLF). After the defeat of FLOSY, Qahtan al Sha'bi, the leader of the NLF, became the first prime minister of the new Republic. His party stood for union with Yemen (Sana), but found itself almost immediately faced with more urgent preoccupations. Within six months of achieving independence the country had slipped towards anarchy and civil war. At a party conference in March 1968, the left wing of the NLF raised the banner of rebellion and decided to distribute arms to the 'Popular Guards', intending to create a counterweight to the army and the security forces, which it charged with 'a feudal mentality'. Some army officers were removed by the rebels, while others were arrested. The army, the only stable and certainly the strongest element in the new state, reacted by confronting al Sha'bi with an ultimatum: the officers had to be released and some of the leaders of the extreme left in their turn were to be arrested. Meanwhile, the NLF left wing continued openly to defy the government, seizing the eastern districts of the country and setting up 'popular councils' to administer them. They dismissed civil servants, senior army officers, and members of the security service, confiscated property, and attacked the government for pursuing a *bourgeois* liberal policy' instead of 'popular democracy'. Led by the former minister of defence, Salem al-Baidh, they called for armed resistance to the army until a regime composed of labourers, poor farmers, and soldiers was established throughout the country.[162] The army and the NLF majority immediately struck back; the 'opportunist leftists' were accused of undermining the economy, torturing political enemies, and a great many other misdeeds. The situation was further complicated by the renewal of FLOSY activities from their base in the Republic of Yemen (Sana), unsuccessful left-wing attempts to seize power in Aden and Hadra-maut, and friction between the army command and al Sha'bi, the prime minister. Several further revolts were reported, and the number of unemployed grew as the former main source of revenue, the entrepôt trade through Aden, dried up. Before independence the South Yemenis had received from Britain a yearly subsidy of about $60 million to balance their budget, this sum representing nearly 70 per cent of the total.[163] This subsidy was discontinued after the removal by the South Yeminis of the last British military advisers. The salaries of government employees were cut and the new government faced a desperate economic situation as well as a political crisis.

The Soviet Union had watched events in Aden and South Arabia for years with great interest. Aden, as *Pravda* noted on the day it achieved independence, held a key position in strategic communications and a key port on the route taken by oil-tankers between the Persian Gulf and Europe.[164] The Soviet Union had displayed considerable activity in the Horn of Africa opposite Aden; Chinese competition in these parts had only added to the Soviet concern. In the struggle between FLOSY and the NLF Moscow had remained neutral; the main thing, Soviet spokesmen said, was that the patriotic organization that came to power should serve the interests of the working class and the people.[165] To them the NLF programme, which advocated the confiscation of the land belonging to the sultans and opposed a military agreement with Britain, seemed promising. The first Soviet ambassador arrived in South Yemen in February 1968, and was followed by a Soviet military mission. Soon after the establishment of the new state, Soviet ships and aircraft were given facilities in Aden's harbour and airport.[166] The South Yemen defence minister went to Moscow to ask for increased military help; later on there were requests for Soviet financial aid.

As the civil war spread the Soviet Union had to decide whether to support the rebels or the government. The slogans of the NLF left wing were certainly radical, but there was an enormous discrepancy between their programme, and what really could be done in view of the backwardness of the country. Its leaders were by no means orthodox communists; some of them had found their inspiration in Cuba, where they had spent a long time, while others received their guidance from Mao's China. Such ultra-revolutionaries were hardly likely to appeal to the Soviet Union, and Moscow made known its displeasure with the ultra-radical resolutions of the Zingibar party congress. Soviet spokesmen claimed that the extremists had been incited by the Mao clique to oppose the legal government; their 'adventurist policy' was very dangerous and had to be decisively rejected.[167]

The Soviet investment in Yemen and South Arabia was not big in absolute terms. But Soviet arms, the biggest export to South Arabia, have played a decisive role at a critical moment in the Yemen's recent history. Despite the distance, the Soviet Union did not hesitate to send in ground-crews, albeit in small numbers. After the British withdrawal, the risks involved were relatively small. The bitter Egyptian experience must have taught the Russians that only massive military intervention would save the 'progressive forces' from defeat and that, in all probability, internal strife in one form or another would continue for a long time to come in Arabia. Western experts who had argued that South Arabia was too distant and unimportant for the Soviet Union to become deeply involved were proved wrong. The Soviet Union was definitely interested in South Arabia as a land-bridge to East Africa, even though the importance of Aden was greatly reduced while the Suez Canal remained closed. It wanted to get a foothold in Aden and Arabia for geopolitical reasons that were not dissimilar to those that had first induced Britain to establish bases there. It is unlikely that the ultra-radical initiative to establish communist rule in the caves of Hadramaut will have a great effect on events elsewhere in the Arab world. Soviet opportunities were further enhanced as the result of the overthrow of al Sha'bi in June 1969 by a junta advocating even closer relations with the USSR.

Jordan

Jordan has been referred to in the Soviet Union as the kingdom created by Winston Churchill between cigar and brandy,[168] but its right to exist has not been questioned. The Nabulsi national front government, which established diplomatic relations with the Soviet Union in 1957 and which opposed the Baghdad Pact, was warmly acclaimed at the time, and political support has been given to Jordan ever since in its struggle against Israel. That communism in Jordan was suppressed did not surprise the Soviet leaders and probably did not weigh heavily in the scales; the situation in the other Arab countries was not different. The pro-Western orientation of King Hussein, on the other hand, the fact that the Jordanian army refused Soviet arms and continued to receive its equipment from the West, was a black mark against him. For these reasons Soviet attitudes to Jordan were never truly cordial. When King Hussein declared in an interview in 1966 that Zionism and communism probably had the same objectives, *Izvestia* wondered whether the King was not 'looking at the situation from the moon or Mars'.[169] Before the Six Day War the Soviet press attacked Jordan as a basis of American imperialism which, in cooperation with Israel, would attack the 'progressive forces' in the Arab world. The situation suddenly changed when Jordan joined Egypt and Syria in the battle against Israel, and gave a better account of itself than either of them. Upon this the Soviet Union made it known that it would be willing to supply arms and equipment to rebuild the Jordanian army. American aid had been discontinued after King Hussein had accused Washington of having intervened in the war on Israel's side. The King seems to have been tempted at one time; he declared in July 1967 that he would turn to the Soviet Union if the West did not renew its supply of arms. President Ayub of Pakistan apparently played the role of mediator; Hussein met him in Karachi on the eve of his visit to Moscow in September 1967. Following Ayūb's intervention, Hussein received an invitation, and one month later he went on a state visit to the Soviet capital. According to official communiqués, his aim was merely to explain Jordan's position to the Soviet leaders, but Marshal Grechko participated in the talks, and Hussein, accompanied by Marshal Zakharov, inspected Soviet military equipment. He said that he would welcome Soviet artists and scientists to Jordan, but as for the arms, the Soviet negotiators did not apparently entirely dissipate his fears about the possible strings attached. The Soviet leaders themselves felt a little uneasy about the presence of the monarch, and Podgorny in his welcoming speech made a reference to the effect that the anti-imperialist struggle brought together strange bedfellows, as the great Lenin had already realized many years earlier.[170]

Hussein's visit to Moscow resulted in a cultural agreement and a declaration by the King that the Arab nation was grateful to the USSR for its assistance. But a military pact was not signed; Hussein was aware that this would result, as in Syria's and Egypt's case, in a total break with the West, and this he was not willing to risk. He must have been aware, too, that a refusal was bound to result in greater pressure by the communists and the Nasserists for a government of national unity to 'reorganize the army and to rearm it with supplies from friendly socialist governments'.[171]

The political survival of King Hussein and his regime over so many years is a near miracle, and the stresses created by the Six Day War have further reduced its long-term prospects. The King's overthrow would have reopened the question of Jordan's future; its transformation into a Syrian or Egyptian style dictatorship was one possibility, but there were several others, such as annexation, war, civil war, and perhaps even big-power intervention. Hardly anyone was interested in precipitating yet another Middle East crisis that might have incalculable consequences. But the ferment inside Jordan could not be contained and the King's position and that of his regime remain therefore extremely precarious.

The Persian Gulf

The Persian Gulf area has been for a long time the scene of many conflicts, ranging from feuds among the Gulf sheikhdoms to the hostility between Arabs and Persians. Iraq has claimed Kuwait, Iran regards Bahrain as one of its provinces, and Saudi Arabia wishes to annex Muscat and Dhabi. There is tribal and religious strife, and a struggle between 'revolutionary nationalists' and 'reactionaries' superimposed on it all. These various crises have from time to time over the last few decades reached boiling-point, without, however, causing great alarm outside the area. The situation changed in the late nineteen-fifties with the growing importance of the Persian Gulf as a leading world oil-producer and the danger that oil supplies would be affected. The British decision to withdraw from the Persian Gulf by the end of 1971, announced in January 1968, opened a new period of turmoil.

The importance of Gulf oil in Soviet Middle East policy is discussed elsewhere in this study, but Soviet interest in the area predates the Persian Gulf oil boom by many years. It existed well before Molotov in 1940 informed the German ambassador in Moscow that 'the area south of Batum and Baku in the general direction of the Persian Gulf is recognized as the centre of aspirations of the Soviet Union'.[172] The Russian advance towards Kuwait, Bandar Abbas, and the Persian Gulf figured prominently in British calculations from the eighteen-nineties; there were 'endless rumours' of Russian plans to secure from the Persian government a lease of Bandar Abbas, and Russian writers talked freely about various projects in the same area.[173] The railway from Syria to Kuwait planned by the Russian Count Kapnist in 1898 confirmed Lord Curzon's worst fears, and he made it known that the concession to Russia of a port of the Persian Gulf would be not only a deliberate insult to Britain, but a wanton disruption of the *status quo* and a deliberate provocation to war.[174]

The opportunities that opened to Russia in the Persian Gulf after an interval of more than five decades were wider than those before 1914; it was no longer merely a question of access to warm waters and bringing pressure to bear on the British. With the extension of the Soviet sphere of interest into East Africa and South-East Asia, the Persian Gulf acquired new importance as a bridgehead. At the same time renewed Russian interest in the Indian Ocean was probably not unconnected with the fear of China, and the idea that the Indian Ocean could mark the beginning of a line to contain China.[175] 'For over a century Russia had leaned on one side of the Middle East door to the Indian Ocean and Britain on the other', one observer commented, 'and now British power is finally to disappear from the area.' But as the Russians burst through the door they had to cope with a situation that in one essential respect was very different from the days of Curzon and Sazonov: all the countries in the area had become independent; the era of colonialism and semi-colonialism had passed. During the fifties and early sixties the Soviet Union was feeling its way in the politics of the Persian Gulf; its attitudes and comments were frequently contradictory. Soviet writers could not make up their minds whether the United States and Britain were bitter rivals there, or whether they were working hand in glove. Kuwait remained 'virtually a colony' in their eyes, even though it had attained independence, and the same was true, *a fortiori*, of Bahrain.[176] In 1953 a Soviet writer gave full support to Iran's claim to Bahrain, stating that union with Iran was the aspiration of the people of Bahrain.[177] In later years such backing was no longer given, not, perhaps, because the Soviet line on the subject has radically changed, but simply because in 1953 the Soviet Union was not yet deeply involved; before about 1956 there was in fact no official line. When Khrushchev visited Egypt in 1964 he was exceedingly insulting about the Emir of Kuwait, the 'little ruler' who accepted bribes and was 'trading in the riches of his people. He never had any conscience, and he won't ever have any.'[178] The Al Khalifa family, the rulers of Bahrain, fared no better: they were squandering vast sums on their caprices and 'embezzlement was flourishing'.[179] But this did not prevent the establishment of diplomatic relations between the Soviet Union and the Gulf states. The Kuwaiti minister of finance and industry visited Moscow in November 1964, and a little later a Soviet delegation went to Kuwait to sign an economic and technical cooperation agreement. Kuwait was rapidly upgraded in Soviet esteem. By 1966 the Soviet press noted that its 'international authority had grown'; its policy of non-alignment was praised, and the Prime Minister (and heir-apparent) was commended for his willingness to cooperate with the Soviet Union.[180]

Soviet relations with Saudi Arabia, another Arab country with vital interests in the Persian Gulf area, have been uniformly bad in recent years. The USSR had been the first country to recognize King Ibn Sa'ud after he became ruler of the Hedjaz in 1926 – this, a Soviet source said, was 'essential to the independence and free development of the area'.[181] The backwardness of his country did not at that time preclude the establishment of fairly close relations. When Amir Faisal became King in 1964, Moscow noted the reforms carried out by the new monarch, such as the introduction of a balanced budget and the limitation of the expenses of the Court.[182] But the reforms weighed less heavily in the scales than Faisal's opposition to Nasser's designs. The fact that Faisal not merely suppressed communism in his own country, but actively worked for an anti-Nasserist, anti-communist alliance in the Middle East, soon made him in Soviet eyes the 'avowed henchman of imperialism and Arab reaction'.[183] His visits to Iran and various Arab and North African countries in 1965 were condemned as an attempt to by-pass the Arab League and to establish an Islamic alliance. Such an alliance would have added to the strength of the conservative camp in the Middle East, and it was therefore at once denounced in Cairo and Moscow as an imperialist plot. The assistance given by Faisal to the Yemeni royalists, and to Jordan and the Syrian opposition, added fuel to the campaign against him.

There was a lull in the cold war between Cairo and Riyadh in 1964, and again after the Six Day War, but relations between Saudi Arabia and Moscow remained bad even while there was a temporary reconciliation between Faisal and Nasser. Faisal feared that the Soviet Union would take over from Nasser in the Yemen, using South Arabia as a springboard for expansion into the Persian Gulf. Moscow, on the other hand, accused the Saudi King of far-reaching ambitions: 'It is not just a matter of threatening . . . South Yemen and Aden; he also wants to drive through to the Indian Ocean. Those who reduce Faisal's role to that of a lackey of the Americans are mistaken, for he has his own policy for the South Arabian peninsula.'[184]

But the Persian Gulf imbroglio transcends the West-East conflict. Faisal's championship of Arabism against Iran in the Persian Gulf had, within limits, Nasser's blessing, whereas the Soviet leaders, if faced with a choice between Faisal and the Shah, were by no means willing to support the former. Other elements in this free-for-all in the Gulf were the Iraqi involvement, the new Federation of the small Gulf principalities, and, of course, the various 'progressive forces' on the Arab peninsula. In January 1968 Mr Eugene Rostow expressed the hope that Iran, Turkey, Pakistan, Saudi Arabia, and Kuwait would form a nucleus around which security arrangements could in future be built. This speech was immediately attacked as an attempt to hatch plans for 'knocking together a [Western] military bloc, to strengthen the position of the oil companies, and to combat the national liberation movements';[185] no such defence pact was necessary, since the Soviet Union would protect the Persian Gulf states against any foreign aggressor. There were indications that it was Soviet policy within the area not to become too closely identified with any one side, but to appear as the friend and protector of all (excepting only Saudi Arabia), so as to be able, in the event of a conflict, to play the role of mediator according to the pattern established at Tashkent. But what was the reward of the honest broker likely to be? Much depended on the development inside the various states. With the enormous oil revenues from Qatar and Dhobi (more than $300 million for 350,000 inhabitants), there was no doubt that a federation of Arab emirates would be economically viable. It would be a mistake to think, a Soviet observer wrote, 'that the Sheikhs do not recognize the twentieth century'.[186] But to what extent would their subjects benefit from the profits? The conflict between rulers and ruled in the Middle East had not by-passed the Gulf area. With some exceptions, the rulers have spent their money wisely, but this alone is hardly sufficient to stem the revolutionary tide.

During the late fifties and early sixties a number of 'liberation fronts' came into existence, mostly with Egyptian help. Several such organizations existed in Bahrain, another in Dhufar and Oman. Most of these groups were, however, rent by internal ideological and political strife which inhibited their development. After the Six Day War Egyptian influence decreased. The Arab National Movement (ANM), with its headquarters in the Lebanon, which served as a meeting-place for most of the local liberation fronts, had all along insisted on its independence of Cairo. Among the militants and leaders of this movement there were many ex-Palestinians, especially schoolteachers and trade union officials. After the Arab-Israeli War of 1967 the Saudi and and the Bahrain and Dhufar National Liberation Fronts gravitated to Damascus rather than Cairo; their presence in Cairo must have been an embarrassment for President Nasser, in view of the financial support provided for Egypt by Saudi Arabia and the oil Sheikhs. Communists have been active within most of these groups, some of them pro-Soviet, others inspired by Peking. A Western observer noted in 1968 that the methods of the NLF which had worked so well in Aden were likely to be successful in the Gulf too. FLOSY, which had been based on the urban community of Aden, had been defeated by the NLF, which had concentrated on operations in the hinterland. It had been NLF strategy in South Arabia to exploit tribal allegiances in such a way as to gain control of the countryside and to isolate the towns. But the opposition offered by the traditional regimes in the Gulf was likely to be tougher and better organized.[187]

Russian policies in the Persian Gulf have followed a consistent line over a fairly long period. There have been aspirations, but not a blueprint, let alone a time-table for conquest. Russia has been probing the area, and wherever the situation was promising it has taken steps to increase its influence; recent developments have made it a foregone conclusion that the Soviet Union will be drawn even more into the Persian Gulf, and the return of Soviet influence as one of the central factors in Gulf politics does not really come as a surprise. The survival of the Gulf states now depends on their own staying power, the measure of collaboration between them, and their ability to resist pressure. It is unlikely that the traditional structures will survive for very long, but their successors still have a chance to retain their independence with a little luck and if they succeed in finding outside support. Gulf oil will have a great deal of attraction for years to come, and those who own it hope that they will be able to play the Soviet bloc against the West, and vice versa, as Iran has done for many years with considerable success.

6

Oil for the Lamps of Eastern Europe?

Oil concessions represent in the Soviet view the foundation of the entire edifice of Western political influence in the Middle East, of all military bases and aggressive blocs. If this foundation cracks, Soviet writers have argued, the entire structure would begin to totter and then come tumbling down.[1] They refer, in more prosaic language, to the undisputed fact that Western influence in the Middle East in based *inter alia* on the activities of a number of major oil companies, which supply between 50 and 60 per cent (up to 80 per cent, including Libya and Algeria) of the requirements of Western Europe in oil, and that, on the other hand, an enormous part of the national income of the oil-producing countries (88 per cent of the export earnings in Iran, 92 per cent in Iraq, 93 per cent in Saudi Arabia) is derived from this same source. These are impressive figures, but there is an asymmetry between the position of the Middle East oil-producers and the European consumers: while OECD Europe was in the nineteen-sixties the only customer for Arab oil, Arab oil was not the only source of energy for OECD Europe.

One specific aspect of oil politics is of considerable relevance in the context of the present study – the growing Soviet interest in Middle East oil. On Middle East oil in general there is an enormous literature, both on a highly technical level and of the blood-sand-oil-and-intrigue variety, and the present writer cannot hope to compete with either. According to one school of thought, oil and the activities of the Western oil companies are the key to the understanding of Middle East politics; more recently Western experts have pointed to the increasing Soviet (and East European) need for Middle East oil as a major motive for Soviet bloc policies in the area. The present writer does not subscribe to a simplified oil-theory-of-history; in spite of their great economic significance, the oil companies have not during the last decade acted from a position of political strength. While Cuba has been able to resist the United States and Albania has succeeded in defying the Soviet Union, even the smallest Middle East oil producers have not found it difficult to play one oil company against another; the oil companies have been able neither to provoke wars nor to prevent wars. There has been a striking discrepancy between their economic strength and their political power. For individual countries, to be sure, the presence of oil has been a factor of paramount importance. It has had a great impact on their internal politics, as well as on their relations with the outside world. But it has always been a complicated and confusing process, bewildering for the tidy political scientist, and sadly disappointing for the believer in conspiracy theories of history.[2]

Soviet Oil

In the early years of the oil industry Russia was one of the world's major producers; around the turn of the century it held first place: European consumption was to a large extent covered by Baku and Grozny oil. In 1929 Soviet oil exports were surpassed only by those of Venezuela; in 1932, a peak year, more than 6 million tons were exported. With the turn towards autarchy, exports decreased, and during the second world war, with its heavy destruction and dislocation, the Soviet Union had to import substantial quantities of oil products. Once economic recovery had got under way after the war and new oilfields were discovered, oil production more than trebled within a decade (38 million tons in 1950, 129·5 million tons in 1959). The Soviet share in world production rose during this period from 5·5 per cent to 13 per cent, and in 1960, with production at 148 million tons, it moved to second place among the world's producers.[3]

Following the expansion in domestic oil production, the Soviet Union appeared on the world market as a major exporter: exports to countries outside the Soviet bloc rose from 1 million tons in 1950 to more than 20 million in 1960. In 1961 Soviet oil provided 35 per cent of the local demand in Greece, 22 per cent in Italy, 21 per cent in Austria, 19 per cent in Sweden. The British market was closed to Soviet oil, but West Germany received 10 per cent of its supplies from the Soviet Union, and Japan 7 per cent. At this stage leading Western oil companies became alarmed not so much by the actual quantity of Soviet oil that was exported to the West (less than 10 per cent of the demand of the non-communist countries) as by the political and economic implications and the disruption of the highly elaborate pricing system; above all, the 'Soviet oil offensive' seemed only the beginning of a far more massive onslaught on Western markets.[4] They asserted that the Soviet take-over had cost the Middle East and Venezuelan governments $486 million, that sales to the West were subsidized (the countries of East Europe had to pay approximately twice as much for Soviet oil), and that at the same time East European markets remained closed to Western firms; it was not only the oil firms and Middle East governments that were affected: the West as a whole had suffered, and there was a real threat of Soviet political domination over buyers.[5] It was argued that the main aim of the Soviet oil offensive was political, and that it therefore constituted a real danger to Western security. By disrupting Western oil operations, the Soviet Union was acquiring a means of exerting influence in the uncommitted countries, and eventually also in parts of Europe. Although the Soviet Union could not hope to reap financial profit by selling oil at cut-rate prices, Western observers assumed (rightly, as it later appeared) that the hope of obtaining a hold on the business of oil supply sufficiently large to ensure substantial profits at a later stage was not absent.[6] Other experts suggested what while political motives did play a certain part in the Soviet oil offensive, the exports were profitable business from Moscow's point of view, even at the low price level. The Russians did not want simply to disrupt the old price schemes, but to become charter members of a new club of oil producers, based on a more stable commodity agreement.[7]

The Soviet answer to these attacks was that, far from dumping oil on Western markets, Russian oil exports to that area between 1956 and 1959 had totalled only 24 million tons, about 4 per cent of its imports. The USSR was determined to recapture its pre-war place among oil-exporting nations and would not help to maintain artificially high prices.[8] This policy brought the Russians into competition with the other producing countries, including the Arabs. However, on many subsequent occasions Soviet spokesmen argued that Soviet oil exports were rising not at the expense of other nations, but because of the steady increase in the consumption of oil throughout the world. Between 1925 and 1935 the Soviet share of the West European market had been about 14 per cent, between 1955 and 1965 it was only 6 per cent; could one in the circumstances really talk about 'flooding the markets with Red Oil'? 'We sell oil in order to buy goods in return,' the chief Soviet spokesman explained.[9] The period between 1957 and 1961 was one of price-cutting in the oil industry, which eventually led to the establishment of OPEC (the Organization of Petroleum Exporting Countries). Founded in late August 1960 by the Middle East producing countries and Venezuela, its aim was to adopt a uniform attitude to oil companies which reduced oil prices unilaterally and without consultation.[10] Several weeks earlier, Esso had announced a cut in oil prices with special reference to Soviet oil penetration; the Russians had made a four-year contract with Italy to sell crude oil at approximately $1 per ton f.o.b. Black Sea terminals.[11] This was to cover about 20 per cent of the yearly Italian requirements, and the Soviet Union was to receive in exchange much-needed 40-inch-diameter pipe, synthetic fibres, pumps, and other goods. 'At this price,' one American oilman commented, 'it's hardly worth taking oil out of the ground in Texas.'[12] But the Russians maintained that some independent Western companies were offering even bigger discounts, that the Soviet Union was prepared to cut prices only as much as necessary to get a specific sale, and that it was occasionally underbid. Soviet spokesmen complained, in effect, that major American oil companies were waging a cut-throat price offensive against them.[13] They did not deny that the oil-export drive could also be a political weapon. The stoppage of oil to Israel and Soviet operations in Ceylon had shown this; Gurov, head of *Soiuznefteksport*, declared on one occasion that the deliveries of Soviet oil had played a 'major role in the independence struggle of the heroic Cuban people'.[14] Soviet exports of oil continued to rise from about 32 million tons in 1960 to 54 million in 1967, but then began to level off, somewhat to the surprise of most experts (the reasons for this will be discussed later on). As American companies boycotted tanker operators who worked with the Russians, the Soviet Union built up its own tanker fleet; pipelines to East Europe, including the famous *Druzhba* (Friendship) line, were also built during this period. Of the Soviet exports, a growing proportion went to West Europe and Japan; Russia's best customers in 1967 were Italy, Finland, West Germany, Japan and Sweden, in that order, with Japan much in appearance as a major new customer. Exports to the underdeveloped countries had never constituted more than a small portion of the total Soviet oil trade.[15] The Soviet Union had been East Europe's chief supplier of oil since the second world war, but the communist countries had been compelled to pay $16–20 per ton (Bulgaria 16, Poland 17, Czechoslovakia 18, Hungary 20), whereas Italy and Japan paid less than $8.[16] This price differential caused a great many complaints on the part of the East Europeans.[17] The Soviet standard answer was that their deliveries to East Europe were carried out on the basis of barter deals and that the East European countries also overcharged the Soviet Union for their machinery, which was not of top quality.[18] The price of Soviet oil in East Europe was somewhat reduced in 1966–7, and this market became less attractive for Moscow. The bloc countries began to show growing interest in direct deals with the oil-producers: Rumania and Bulgaria imported Iranian oil; other East European countries signed agreements with Iraq. After 1965 domestic consumption increased, the whole pattern of Soviet oil policy began to change, and its interest in Middle East oil became more pronounced. To understand the implications of these changes it is necessary at this point to review briefly Middle East oil production and its political and economic significance both for the producer countries and for West Europe, their leading customer.

Oil in the Middle East

The basic facts about Middle East oil are well known – namely, that it constitutes by far the most important economic asset of the area, that it is unequally distributed, that it is exceedingly cheap in comparison with oil produced in other parts of the world, and that there are seemingly unlimited reserves of it. It is sometimes forgotten, however, that the Middle East has only very recently assumed its present importance as one of the world's chief suppliers. The first important discovery in Iran was made in 1908; oil was found near Kirkuk in 1927, at Bahrain in 1932, and in Saudi Arabia in 1936, but up to the Second World War the Middle East provided less than 5 per cent of the world's total output. The striking development of the Middle East oil industry took place in the nineteen-fifties, with the phenomenal increase in output in the known area and the discovery of new major oil-fields, such as in the Kuwait Neutral Zone in 1953 and in Libya in 1959. About 160 million tons were produced in 1969 in both Saudia Arabia and Iran, closely followed by Kuwait with 130 million, Iraq with 59 million, the Kuwait Neutral Zone with 23·7 million, Abu Dhabi, a small Sheikhdom on the Persian Gulf, where not a drop of oil had been produced as recently as 1961, followed with 29 million. Libyan oil production rose from less than 1 million tons in 1961 to 150 million, and Algerian production during the same period increased from 2 million to 44 million tons. The year 1967 was not a good one for some of the producing countries. Iraq's production fell in comparison with the previous year as the result of a conflict between the Iraq Petroleum Company and the Syrian government, and of the Arab-Israeli war, the Arab boycott, and the closure of the Suez Canal.[19]

Oil has revolutionized the economy of the Middle East. Kuwait has fewer than half a million inhabitants, of whom only 150,000 are Kuwaiti nationals. It has been estimated that its oil revenues are at present of the order of $900 million per year, about $4,000 a year for each Kuwaiti national.[20] Kuwait provides free education and health services; the citizens of Saudi Arabia, whose revenues are of approximately the same order, hardly profited at all from the country's wealth under the reign of King Saud (1953–64); only since then has its oil income been used for the economic development of the country. Most of Middle East oil production is dominated by seven big companies, Royal Dutch Shell, British Petroleum Company, Standard Oil of New Jersey, Gulf Oil Corporation, Texaco, Standard Oil of California, and Socony Mobil Oil – the 'seven sisters'. Other major companies, though not quite in the same league, are the French Compagnie Française des Pétroles and the Italian ENI. These companies have doubled in size during the last decade, but their share of the oil market has shrunk, because total oil production has grown even faster. Various independent companies from all over the world have been operating in the Middle East since the late nineteen-fifties. The production of Iranian oil is in the hands of a consortium of some fourteen oil companies; in Saudi Arabia Aramco, a cartel of four of the five big American companies, is the main producer; in Iraq the Iraq Petroleum Company (IPC) predominates (CFP, Shell, BP and others); in Kuwait the Kuwait Oil Company (an Anglo-American company). In addition, there are a number of local government companies at work, such as NIOC, the Iranian state company which, while cooperating with the consortium, is also competing with it, and the Kuwait National Petroleum Company. The newcomers have received a growing share of the market, among them the (Japanese) Arabian Oil Company operating off the Kuwait Neutral Zone, and ENI (an Italian company), which has been active in Iran and several Arab countries. The whole trend of development in the oil industry has been towards very large units and integrated companies; oil had not only to be produced, but also to be refined, shipped to its destination, and distributed. Consumers have complained about cartel practices and super-profits, whereas the laments of the oil companies and the producer countries have created the impression that cut-throat competition has brought them to the verge of ruin. The enormous revenues earned by the producers show that, despite growing rivalry between companies, competition is still far from complete. Petroleum prices do not necessarily reflect costs,[21] and the days of oligopoly are by no means over. Oil operations in the major producing countries have been on a profit-sharing (50-50) basis; this goes back to a decree by the Saudi government in 1949 demanding 50 per cent of Aramco's income after payment of United States tax. A similar principle had previously been applied in Venezuela, and it meant, in practice, that the governments of the producing countries received roughly 55 per cent – 60 per cent of the profits that were actually made. Since then they have been pressing for a higher share of the profits: the Japanese-owned company in Kuwait splits the profits of its operations in the Neutral Zone 57:43 with the Saudi and Kuwaiti governments. Independent companies and some of the 'seven sisters' have offered the governments concerned not only a higher share in the profits, but also shares in the equity (between 10–30 per cent) in the event of oil being discovered.[22] Operating costs have risen steadily as the result of pressure by the oil-producing countries, lower allowances for marketing expenses, and changes in the royalties-expensing agreements. Spokesmen for the oil companies have argued that 'pressure from the producing governments on costs is something we can learn to live with, provided we are not at the same time denied freedom to move prices in the market, so as to maintain a commercial margin of profit'.[23] The governments have also forced the companies to give up most of the original concession areas in which no drillings had been made. In Kuwait and Qatar newly established companies have taken over the relinquished areas; in Iraq, under General Kassem, the IPC was deprived of 99 per cent of its concessions and permitted to carry on work only in the oilfields actually being worked.

Relations between governments and oil companies varied from country to country. It hardly needs stressing that every government wanted a maximum income from its chief natural asset, but whereas Saudi Arabia and Kuwait, untroubled by the pressure of popular opinion, believed that this could best be achieved by close cooperation with the oil companies, there was a strong belief in Iran, and even more in Iraq, that the country would fare much better if it took over the management of oil operations. Experience with nationalization in Iran had not, however, been encouraging; the main effect of the pressure exerted by successive Iraqi governments on the IPC was that the development of the industry was slowed down and no new exploratory drillings were made. The demand for the nationalization of the oil industry continued nevertheless to grow in the Arab world, while Syria and Egypt claimed that they did not get their due for serving as transit countries. It was Soviet policy to encourage Middle East governments in their demands on the oil companies and to emphasize the advantages of national oil companies free to trade with everyone. The Iraqi government's lack of vigour in its attitude towards the IPC and its alleged failure to engage in an independent oil policy was (to provide but one illustration) the subject of Soviet criticism in 1961–2. It had not passed unnoticed, a Soviet periodical wrote, that the persecution of democratic elements was intensified at the time of the government's negotiations with the oil companies.[24] The 'crimes of the oil companies' remained for many years one of the central themes of Soviet and communist propaganda in the Middle East.

West Europe and Middle East Oil

Since the end of the second world war the consumption of oil and oil products in West Europe has risen more than tenfold, reaching 455 million tons a year in 1967. This figure represents about half of the total energy consumption. Less than 10 per cent of the oil consumed was found in Europe; the rest had to be imported. Almost 80 per cent of these imports came from the Middle East, Libya, and Algeria. Europe has one important indigenous asset to meet its energy requirements, coal, which before the second world war covered almost all domestic energy requirements.[25] Its role has, however, steadily declined ever since, partly on account of the limited reserves and the desire of the European governments to protect and conserve them, but mainly because the price of the cheapest-grade coal in Europe is about $16 a ton, whereas the price of one ton of oil has ranged in recent years from $10 to $12.[26] The real price difference is even greater, since one metric ton of fuel oil has nearly 1·5 times the heat value of a metric ton of coal; furthermore, coal is subsidized to the extent of about $5 a ton. It has been estimated that West Europe would save about $3·5 billion annually if it switched entirely to oil: 'European coal production is no longer an industry, it is only a means of social insurance.'[27]

These calculations take account only of commercial considerations; they ignore not only the technical and social difficulties involved in such a transition, but also the all-important question of security of supply. How vulnerable West Europe's oil supply really is appeared at the time of the Suez war in 1956: with the blocking of the Canal and the cutting of the IPC pipelines (following the destruction of the pumping stations), two thirds of Europe's total supply was cut off. Several potential sources existed to cover European requirements and replace Middle East oil, above all in North America and Venezuela; on a considerably smaller scale, liquid oils could be provided from other sources, such as the coal-gas industry.

In the event, the effect of the Suez crisis on the European economy was less grave than at first had been expected.[28] Arrangements were immediately made to re-route the world tanker fleet and additional supplies from the western hemisphere reached Europe within a short time. The price of oil went up for a while, but not by very much; certain European industries were affected by the supply situation, but the overall industrial production of OECD Europe continued to rise. There was a loss in internal revenue as a result of the fall in the consumption of oil products, especially motor gasoline, and the crisis also had an effect on the balance of payments by reason of the increased purchases of American oil and additional dollar freights. It was estimated that during the most difficult period of the crisis, the additional dollar bill was running at the rate of between $300 million and $400 million a year.[29] The crisis was short-lived, but it served as a warning that the disruption of oil supplies from the Middle East at some future date, perhaps over a longer period, could not be ruled out. In order to reduce their vulnerability in any future emergency, European governments decided to consider a number of measures, such as the accumulation of larger reserves, the diversification of sources of supply, and the further development of flexibility in the means of transport by alternative routes, and in refinery operations. It was obvious that in terms of money and material there could not be complete insurance against a future crisis. The provision of a single day's storage capacity in Europe and the oil to fill it was thought at the time to cost about $20 million; but it was generally believed that appropriate planning could at least reduce the immediate impact of a new crisis.

These measures were put to the test at the time of the Arab-Israeli war in 1967, when West Europe's oil supply was again cut. The Suez Canal was blocked; Kuwait, Saudi Arabia, Libya and Iraq stopped oil production with the outbreak of the war. In Libya and Saudia this was the result of a strike of oil workers, whereas in Kuwait and Iraq the government decided to ban supplies to a number of countries, including the United States and Britain.[30] The Arab foreign ministers' conference in Kuwait decided after the cease-fire to continue the boycott. The non-producing countries and Iraq (which suggested stopping all oil production for three months so as to deplete Europe's reserves) were the most extreme in their demands; the others had misgivings from the very beginning about the effectiveness of the boycott. In the event, their fears proved justified: the Saudi minister of Petroleum Affairs, said that in retrospect it has been a wrong decision taken on the basis of false information: 'It hurt the Arabs more than anyone else.' The non-Arab producers, including Iran, stepped up their production, and the smaller Persian Gulf principalities continued their supplies; Kuwait and Saudi Arabia boycotted only the United States (which does not depend on Middle East oil) and Britain; Libya (under strong pressure from Egypt) also in theory boycotted West Germany, but in fact tolerated exports to that country. The official boycott lasted altogether three months; as a result, Iraq's production fell by 11·5 per cent, while Iran's went up by 23 per cent. The Arab countries lost several hundred million dollars in royalties. No European country went short of oil, despite the fact that the Suez Canal remained closed; at one stage, in early autumn 1967, stocks were down to about ten days' supplies, but after a little while they were back to seasonal level.[31] It had appeared at first that the 1967 stoppage would be far more serious than the Suez crisis, for in 1956 actual oil production had never been suspended.

The quantity of oil shipped from the Middle East to Europe was much greater in 1967 than it had been eleven years earlier, and it was thought that Europe was therefore more dependent on Arab oil. Radical leaders in the Arab world, as well as the communists, had maintained for years that oil was their most effective weapon; to cut it off would very quickly paralyse European industrial production and thus force West Europe to yield to Arab demands. By means of oil, Cairo and Damascus radio had argued, the Arab countries could dictate their conditions to the West.

Between 1956 and 1967 efforts had been made to diversify West Europe's sources of supply, but these had not been altogether successful, for oil production in Nigeria ceased as the result of the civil war, Algeria agreed to supply only France, and Libya, which was not affected by the closure of the Suez Canal, joined the Arab League boycott. Yet, despite these setbacks, there was no real crisis and price increases were relatively small. The oil industry showed great elasticity: it proved only too easy, as in 1956, to increase oil production outside the Arab world and there was sufficient capacity available to move the volume of oil that was needed. The oil companies had certainly learned one lesson from the Suez war: they were not going to be dependent on the Suez Canal. The oil flow through Suez, almost entirely in the south-north direction, had more than doubled in the decade since 1956; it accounted for about 70 per cent of the total traffic through the Canal. But there had been a movement towards larger tankers (of the 150,000–200,000-ton class), which in any case could not pass through the Canal. These super-tankers operated more cheaply on the Cape route, and after the war of 1967 (in the words of one observer) the movement towards super-tankers turned into a stampede. The number on order increased from 70 to 140, and even bigger tankers were already under construction.[32]

The crisis of 1967 had several important side effects: the extra strain on the balance of payments contributed to the devaluation of sterling; certain oil companies dependent chiefly on the Middle East showed losses in their annual balance sheets, while others, mainly American-based, showed substantial gains. But overall the boycott caused few tremors on the European industrial scene. It demonstrated that oil was not, after all, the deadly weapon some had believed. The dependence of the Arab governments on their royalties, their inability to sustain a long-term stoppage or boycott, seemed to show that Europe's oil supply was still secure. The oil insurance introduced after the Suez war – 60–65 days' stocks of normal consumption and 80–90 days' for OECD Europe as a whole – had proved its worth.

But there remained some nagging questions: what if, as the result of political instability in the Middle East, the oil supply should one day be cut off for a longer period, or perhaps even permanently? The additional cost of supplying West Europe had not been insignificant; the United Kingdom had to spend some $200 million, West Germany $90 million, Italy $80 million, France $40 million.[33] What if these extra costs were to continue or even increase in future? The oil companies and their advisers, and above all the West European governments, soon began to consider how to cope with future emergencies. Some, arguing that oil was for the time being irreplaceable, advocated stockpiling on a scale sufficient to provide (at an annual cost of some $870 million)[34] reserves for nine months' oil consumption and for one or two years' electricity supply. Others, looking ahead to the more distant future, pointed to alternative sources of energy that would become available. The discovery of major new oilfields in Europe was thought to be unlikely, and while American reserves may be far greater than is at present thought, it was assumed that the cost of production there would always be considerably higher than in the Eastern hemisphere. Experts pointed to the increasingly important role of natural gas; in the United States it already covers about 30 per cent of the total energy demand; in Europe, too, the consumption of natural gas is likely to grow at a faster rate than oil, even though it is unlikely to catch up with oil in the near future. Within the general framework of the energy balance, electric power has steadily grown in importance, and it has been estimated that around 1980 it will cover almost half of the total energy requirements. After an uncertain start, there has been rapid progress in nuclear technology. It is no longer in doubt that with the advent of the fast-breeder nuclear power is becoming economic, that in the not too distant future it will provide energy at prices competitive with all but the cheapest crudes, and that in the seventies it will be an important source of energy for generating electricity in Europe. Before the Arab-Israeli war it was generally thought that the switch from oil to uranium in generating power would take longer, not because of technological or economic considerations, but because of the innate conservatism of the public utilities. However, the uncertainties of the Middle East oil supply may well embolden them to take the plunge sooner. The main factor so far inhibiting the use of nuclear energy in ways other than generating electricity has been the absence of a rival to the petrol engine and the high cost of small nuclear reactors – those below 500-megawatt capacity. But in this field, too, a technological breakthrough cannot be ruled out. Given the necessary challenge, such as the danger of a breakdown in oil supplies, it may come earlier than now expected.

West Europe's dependence on Middle East oil must be considered in the general context of its future energy requirements. It will remain the natural market for Middle East oil provided that there continues to be a secure supply of cheap oil. The transition towards the wider use of sources of energy other than oil, which in the long run is inevitable anyway, would be accelerated by political instability in the Middle East. It would no doubt for a number of years entail heavy financial investment and major technical problems. But West Europe's energy supplies would seem to be assured (admittedly at high cost) except in the unlikely event of a total Middle East oil embargo, and future technological progress will make it less dependent still.

The Soviet Union and Middle East Oil

The remarkable growth of Soviet oil production has been noted; it is expected to continue, to reach about 450 million tons in 1975 and in 1980 between 600 million and 700 million tons. The original targets were even higher, but have been slightly lowered. A number of reasons have been suggested for these cuts. It is much easier to boost the flow of oil than to increase refining capacity and to expand the petrochemical industry, which requires heavy financial investment. No new major oilfields have been found in the European part of Russia, drilling costs are increasing, transport costs have become higher, and the cost of oil production (on which we have no exact data) probably compares unfavourably with that of the Middle East.[35] Natural gas plays an increasing part in the Soviet energy balance:[36] enormous quantities of gas have been found in Siberia and Sakhalin, but to carry gas fixed installations are needed and the cost/unit of energy is about double that of crude oil: to pump Sakhalin and East Siberian natural gas to Europe does not seem to be a sound economic proposition.

Soviet energy consumption, too, is growing rapidly, at least by 7 per cent annually, possibly even faster. Oil is likely to provide 40 per cent of the total Soviet energy demand, and most observers expect that in 1980 the total demand for oil will be between 600 million and 700 million tons, i.e. somewhat less than the expected production. In particular gasoline consumption in road transport is likely to rise very fast during the next decade, and there will be a much higher demand by industry as production increases.

According to these estimates, the Soviet Union will not have sufficient oil to cover its own needs, let alone a certain surplus for export. Whether Soviet oil exports to West Europe and Japan will continue to grow as in the recent past seems far more doubtful. The Soviet Union has in the past all but monopolized East Europe's oil supplies; of a consumption of about 40 million tons per year (1966) only 15–16 million tons have been produced locally, mainly in Rumania. It has been calculated that by 1980 East European demand will rise to 190 million tons or even more,[37] while local oil production will increase only to about 30 million tons a year. For a number of years the coming oil shortage has been freely discussed by Soviet and East bloc economists. A Polish economist writing in 1966 noted that even at the optimistic figure of only 90 million tons to be imported, the countries of East Europe would be paying out $1·4 billion a year of their scarce foreign currency.[38] As far as oil supplies are concerned, the Soviet Union is not interested in giving East Europe first priority; it wants above all to improve its own terms of trade, either by earning foreign currency or by selling its raw materials to the industrialized non-communist countries in exchange for machinery and equipment.[39] The exportable quantity of Soviet oil is not likely to grow in proportion to the increasing demand in East Europe; on the contrary, the share of it sold to customers outside the bloc is likely to increase. East European economic planners have been given to understand on various occasions that to lessen the pressure on Soviet oil they would be well advised to look for alternative supplies in the third world, mainly in the Middle East. After the Czechoslovak crisis of 1968 higher priority was again given by the Soviet Union to East European needs, but it is too early to say whether this is a temporary palliative or a major policy shift. East Europe thus faces a fuel situation not altogether dissimilar to that of West Europe; its capacity to make massive oil purchases cannot be rated very high in view of its limited foreign-currency earnings. There are several possibilities of dealing with this shortage – namely, the investment of capital in the Soviet oil industry and/or the development of nuclear and other alternative sources of energy. Parts of East Europe are rich in coal, but concentration on the use of coal and lignite would mean a high-cost economy and backwardness in transport; for the next decade nuclear energy will not be available in East Europe in sufficient quantity. Heavy investment in the Soviet oil industry would make East Europe both politically and economically more dependent on Russia, and may for that reason be considered undesirable. It seems most likely therefore that East European states will prefer direct barter agreements with the Middle East producers, such as the deal (already mentioned) between Rumania and Iran in 1966. It has been estimated that if East Europe were to satisfy all its additional requirements for oil in the Middle East, goods worth between $1 and $2 billion would have to be supplied to Iran and the Arab countries.[40] Deliveries of goods on such a scale would be, to put it cautiously, difficult for the recipients to absorb.

The growing need for oil in the Soviet Union and East Europe has gradually brought about a change in the oil policy of the bloc in the Middle East. Before 1966 the Soviet Union did not appear as a buyer of Middle East oil or natural gas, nor did it display any interest in participating in any way in the production of oil. It was mainly in Soviet and communist propaganda that Middle East oil played an important role: oil, it was argued, had for decades enslaved the peoples of the Middle East; was it not high time for them to be liberated from these shackles? Had not the people a better title to the huge revenues than the company shareholders?[41] 'Arab oil for the Arabs', a *Pravda* headline at the time of the Syrian conflict with the Iraq Petroleum Company in 1966–7, introduced an article which quoted with evident satisfaction the slogans seen on the wall of the oil refinery in Homs: 'Oil in the hands of the working people spells a weapon in the fight against imperialism! The battle for oil spells continuation of the struggle for the strengthening of our independence.'[42] The militant policy of the Syrian government was favourably contrasted with the relative moderation of the Iraqi government: 'The popular masses and national forces [in Iraq] look forward to freeing their oil wealth from the grip of the imperialist monopolies, abolishing the unjust conditions in the present concessions, and amending these concessions to serve Iraq's interests.'[43] It is interesting that this appeal of the Communist party of Iraq did not demand outright expropriation of the foreign companies but merely (as first steps) the establishment of a national oil industry, the amendment of current agreements, and an approach to the 'socialist world to secure the necessary equipment and technicians for the National Oil Company'.[44] Countless statements in similar vein appeared in the Soviet and communist press throughout the nineteen-fifties and sixties; the communists concentrated their organizational efforts, not without some success, on oil workers in the Arab world. At the same time Soviet and East European commentators stressed in their writings West Europe's dependence on Arab oil, asserting that, since there was no way to replace it, the obvious political conclusions should be drawn.[45] Up to the middle sixties the Soviet Union's interest in Middle East oil was on the whole negative. It attacked the Western oil companies, but did not itself need any outside supplies. Some Western observers saw in these attacks an exercise in political warfare calculated to deny West Europe its oil supplies, but it is doubtful whether Soviet policy had in fact such a grand design. The position of the oil companies *vis-à-vis* Arab and Iranian public opinion was in any case precarious, and Soviet experts regarded them as a perfectly legitimate target for a propagandist onslaught.

After 1965, with the changing perspective on oil, Soviet interest in Middle East oil became far more active. During and after the war of 1967, Soviet spokesmen continued to reassure the Arabs that they were not seeking to increase their sales of oil in markets which had formerly belonged to the Arabs. (The Soviet Union had supported the Arab oil boycott; but had not joined it, and there were rumours that Moscow had exploited the situation.) The Soviet argument was that its own share in the international oil trade had remained steady at around 4 or 5 per cent;[46] there was no talk (as there had been in 1960) about recapturing the Soviet Union's pre-war position as one of the world's main exporters of oil.

The Soviet deal with Iran in January 1966 for the supply of natural gas was the major turning-point in Soviet oil policy and an indication of its new interest in supplies; a similar, much smaller, contract was signed with Afghanistan. The year before the Russians had entered into a service contract with the Syrian government to develop the Suwaidiyah oilfield, which in March 1968 began production at the rate of a million tons a year. More ambitious was the exploration service contract with Iraq in late 1967, which was to be paid for in crude oil. It was not clear for a while whether this agreement affected the important North Rumailan field which the Iraqis had also promised to France, and the change of government in Baghdad in July 1968 added to the confusion.[47] This had been a political gesture by the Iraqis; the head of the state National Oil Company declared that the agreement was significant because it 'followed the [Soviet] political backing given the Arabs in the Middle East crisis'.[48] The details of the Iraqi deal are of no great significance in this context, for Russia made a similar proposal to assist Iran in the quest for oil, also to be paid for in crude oil. But it did indicate the new general direction of Soviet oil policy; for the first time since the war the Soviet Union began to import Middle East oil.

Some of the underlying reasons for the oil offensive have been discussed; first among them was the wish to secure energy supplies cheaply in order to meet the growing needs of the Soviet Union and its allies. The economic and political implications were less simple. It had been traditional Soviet policy, wherever their teams prospected for oil or built refineries, to appear as agents of the local government, to lend money, but not to invest capital. For this reason some Western oilmen were as afraid of French and Italian as of Soviet competition.[49] The Soviet intention was, no doubt, to avoid arousing the jealousy and ill will that the presence of the Western companies had often aroused. Its agreements did not really clash with Western deals, which offered large revenues to the host country at no outlay, whereas Russian help cost money, barter goods, or oil.[50] Nowhere but in Spitzbergen had the Soviet Union appeared before as an explorer seeking concessions, but this policy was now likely to change because of its own growing needs and the desire of the host governments for joint-venture contracts, with the Soviet Union putting up most or all of the risk money. The Arab governments, needless to say, did not, as some Western observers had suggested,[51] want their oil industry to come under Soviet domination because of the Arab belief that America and Britain had supported Israel. They wanted maximum profits, and they thought the best way to achieve this aim was to diversify their concessions in the same way that West Europe diversified its supplies. It was thought at the time that these new developments in Soviet oil policy in 1966–7 foreshadowed yet another major initiative: the establishment of large marketing organizations which would make the Soviet Union a leading force in the international oil business, thus providing a successful alternative to the 'stranglehold of capitalist monopolies'. This would involve a great outlay of capital, but it had much to recommend it. For political as well as economic reasons, the Soviet Union was vitally interested in continuing to supply oil to both East and West Europe; the plans for the delivery of natural gas to Italy by way of a giant pipeline were indicative of its desire to keep its external markets. If there was not sufficient Soviet oil available for such operations, handsome profits could be reaped from marketing Middle East oil. Whether such a policy would meet with the approval of both producers and consumers, who might prefer to deal directly with each other, was a different question. But, as a major producer with great marketing experience and financial backing, the Soviet Union was potentially in a strong position to act as middleman.

Soviet interest in Middle East oil, it is often argued, has been political rather than economic. Political considerations are, of course, never absent from Soviet economic policy, but a good Soviet case could be made for increasing its trade with the oil-producing countries of the Middle East irrespective of political interests. The growing need for additional oil supplies for East Europe has been mentioned; the cheapness of Middle East oil in comparison with that produced in the Soviet Union is an additional attraction. The purchase of oil from Middle East countries seems a logical way to balance trade relations and to recoup the Soviet credits that have been extended to them. In the past there was marked reluctance in the Soviet Union and East Europe to import oil from non-communist countries, because of the danger that supplies would be cut off at a time of crisis. But this argument has been gradually discarded: Soviet imports would be quite small and for that reason the question of security hardly arises. East Europe is far more vulnerable, but it has been emphasized there of late that the communist bloc countries would not have to depend on Western oil monopolies, but on companies sponsored by governments well disposed towards the communist bloc. Moreover, it would always be possible to obtain Russian oil in case of an emergency, just as in a crisis West Europe could fall back on Western hemisphere oil.

The growing importance of Middle East oil and natural gas for the Soviet Union and the Soviet bloc is undisputed, but it is unlikely that this will be a factor of decisive importance in shaping Soviet policy in the area. From the Arab and Iranian point of view, the outlets offered by the Soviet bloc are (and will remain) small in comparison with the great consumer markets of West Europe and Japan. If the Soviet Union desperately needed

Middle East oil for its industrial development there would no doubt be far greater pressure to bring the enormous reserves of the Middle East under its control. But this is not a question of life and death for the Soviet Union, which has so far been able to afford a policy of autarchy.* The primacy of politics over economics has been one of the unwritten laws in the Soviet code of conduct. This may change one day, but it is unlikely that the Middle East will be the first exception to this rule.

* It ought to be noted however that the trends indicated in this chapter became even more pronounced during 1968/9. Soviet exports of oil to the West fell from 34 million in 1967 to 32 million in 1968. The target for Soviet oil production in 1980 originally (i.e. in 1961) set at about 700 million has now been reduced to 'over 500 million'. Since Soviet oil requirements that year will be in the range of 600 million according to most Western experts it can no longer be taken for granted that the Soviet Union will be able to cover all its domestic needs from internal sources by the late nineteen seventies. At the same time Western oil consumption continued to increase at a much faster rate than oil production. As a result American, West European and Japanese dependence on Middle Eastern and North African oil is likely to rise during the nineteen seventies until alternative sources of energy will be made accessible.

7
Trade and Aid

The impact of Soviet trade and aid on Middle East politics is usually over-rated. Economic relations between the Soviet Union and most Middle East countries have greatly expanded during the last decade, but with a few important exceptions they are still on a substantially smaller scale than Middle East trade with the West. Soviet development aid is still less than one tenth of one percent of the national income of the Communist country. Commercial transactions *per se* have not yielded a marked increase in Soviet influence. The one important exception is the supply of arms, which both in monetary value and in political significance has been the most important Soviet export. From 1954 to 1966 the Soviet Union provided about $2 billion in arms and military equipment to Egypt, Syria, Iraq and the Yemen; between June 1967 and October 1968 deliveries reportedly totalled $2·5 billion. During the same period (1954–1967) credits totalling $2 billion were extended to the Middle East, of which, however, it is thought only between one third and one half has actually been drawn by the recipients. Soviet military aid, in other words, has been from four to five times greater than economic assistance. While a great deal has been written in Russia during the last decade on the theory and practice of Soviet aid, Soviet arms supplies are never discussed and there are no official figures. The following outline deals only with non-military Soviet aid, politically and economically the less important aspect of trade relations.

Trade with the third world is frequently considered by communist spokesmen as a form of aid. True, Khrushchev and other Soviet leaders can be quoted to the opposite effect ('We are not a charitable institution. We give aid on fair commercial principles'[1]). On other occasions Soviet spokesmen have claimed that the Soviet Union is guided in developing trade and extending aid by the desire to accelerate the revival of the countries concerned, and to speed up the development of their productive forces. At the same time it is politically important as a means of helping them to break out of the imperialist system and to advance their transition on to a non-capitalist road of development. Sometimes the official explanations contradict each other. For instance, it is argued that the Soviet Union does not act primarily from considerations of commercial advantage and the profit motive, but 'from the standpoint of humanity and solidarity with all mankind'.[2] But equally often it is maintained that Soviet trade, especially with neighbouring countries, follows a natural and traditional pattern and is based on sound commercial principles. It is always denied that the Soviet Union is guided by tactical political considerations, that there are strings attached to Soviet aid; Soviet motives in extending aid and developing trade are described as absolutely unselfish and disinterested, in contrast to that of non-communist countries.

The real motives, needless to say, are more complex. Not all Soviet trade is politically motivated: Soviet commercial relations with Europe and America have on the whole fewer political implications than those with third-world countries. It is the Soviet intention to demonstrate to the developing countries that they can achieve real progress only by pursuing an economic policy similar to that of the Soviet Union. Within this general scheme, Soviet aid and trade usually concentrate on certain key countries which for political reasons are of particular importance. In the Middle East there has been a marked orientation towards Egypt and Syria, and, to a lesser degree, towards Algeria and Iraq. Up to 1966, when Moscow made substantial pledges in support of India's fourth five-year plan, Egypt, as the recipient of more than $1 billion in credits, was first in the list of countries receiving Soviet aid. Syria, too, has received substantial help ($233 million), more than either the UAR or India on a *per capita* basis. The selection of these two countries makes it clear that political objectives were of paramount importance; Moscow's aid commitments have often fluctuated with the change in the political climate, as trade relations with Syria show. Aid was restricted when the Ba'th took over in Syria in 1963, but restored in 1964 when the Damascus government modified its anti-communist line. During 1965 and after the neo-Ba'th coup of February 1966, there was a further dramatic rise in Soviet grants. The deterioration in relations with Israel, on the other hand, resulted in the cessation of Soviet oil shipments to that country and the cancellation of all other contracts.

Under Stalin the Soviet Union had shown little interest in the development of trade relations with the countries of the Middle East. During the nineteen-thirties and forties trade was actually declining, a trend which was reversed only after 1953. Between 1953 and 1957 some fifty trade-and-payments agreements were concluded between the Soviet Union and the countries of the Middle East, and the value of trade doubled. The Soviet Union has always shown a preference for bilateral trade agreements: it bought Egyptian and Syrian cotton, Iranian animal and fish products, Yemenite coffee, and Israeli citrus fruits in exchange for Soviet-produced capital goods. At the same time, foreign-aid programmes were initiated, partly no doubt under the influence of the success of programmes operated by the United States. But the Soviet programmes were usually far simpler in structure; aid consisted mainly of low interest credits (usually $2\frac{1}{2}$ per cent per annum) repayable over twelve years and tied to the execution of mutually agreed projects. (Western official aid, on the other hand, consisted to a large extent of free grants or long-term loans carrying a repayment period of twenty years or more.) Soviet interest rates were lower than those normally charged by Western lenders and the various international financial agencies.

Economic cooperation between the Soviet Union and Turkey and Iran has grown only in recent years.* In 1965 both Turkey and Iran received substantial Soviet credits ($210 million and $330 million respectively), but this did not cause a radical reorientation of the trade pattern of these two countries. The development of trade relations between the Soviet Union and the

* In 1968 Iran became the third largest recipient of Soviet aid behind India and the UAR.

Arab countries has been more complex and politically more significant. Trade with Egypt grew from $15 million in 1954 to $184 million in 1961; Soviet exports rising from $7 million to $97 million, imports from $8 million to $86 million. By 1966 the volume of trade had reached $314 million, by 1967 $380 million.[3] Trade with Egypt was based on the agreements of 1958, 1960, and 1964, which concerned the Aswan dam and many other projects, including an atomic reactor, industrial plants, and irrigation systems. The 1958 agreement envisaged a five-year industrial expansion plan of $750 million. There were certain difficulties: Egypt paid the Soviet Union mainly with cotton. But Russia produces sufficient cotton for its own consumption in Central Asia, and the Egyptians objected to Soviet reselling of their chief product on the world market, for this was bound to depress the price. It was doubtful from the very beginning whether Egypt would ever be able to repay its loans. Its balance of trade with the Soviet Union became increasingly unfavourable: – $11 million in 1963, – $21 million in 1964, – $45 million in 1965, and it fell steadily behind in its credit repayments, despite the fact that it had drawn only a little over $500 million of the $1,500 million credits extended by the Soviet Union and East Europe. After Nasser's visit to the Soviet Union in 1965 it was reported that the Soviet government had written off some $460 million of the Egyptian debt, and that only some $35–40 million had actually been paid by Cairo. There were further negotiations with Kosygin (in 1966), with Gromyko (in March 1967), and again with Kosygin after the Six Day War, about a further easing of repayment conditions. The Soviet trade figures do not make it clear to what extent its imports from Egypt are in payment for military equipment, how much is in payment for regular credits, and how much constitutes normal sales. Commercial considerations cannot have been uppermost in Soviet minds in the trade with Egypt; over the years they have lost a great deal of money in that country.

Economic relations between the Soviet Union and Syria developed rapidly on the basis of the trade and technical cooperation agreements of 1956 and 1957. After 1958 the volume of trade fell off, but picked up again in the early sixties. By the end of 1964 total Soviet bloc aid to Syria was about $193 million, of which the Soviet Union had provided $50 million. The Soviet commitment made in 1966 to finance the construction of the Euphrates dam was the biggest single item; other projects included power stations, the building of railway lines, and machinery for factories. Economic relations between the Soviet Union and Iraq had been insignificant under Nuri as-Said, but took an upward turn soon after Kassem came to power. The trade agreements of October 1958 and March 1959 covered a loan of $550 million, and envisaged the establishment of metallurgical works and fertilizer plants, and the improvement of the Iraqi railway network. Up to 1965 Soviet aid to Iraq totalled about $184 million. Kassem's fall caused a temporary slow-down in some of these schemes, but a new agreement concluded in March 1965 announced plans for a large dam and a hydro-electric station on the Euphrates.

All these technical aid programmes provided for the dispatch of Soviet and East European specialists. In 1957 it was reported that there were 350 non-military technicians in Egypt, about 180 in Syria, and 55 in the Yemen. Their number rose to about 3,000 in 1968; their salaries were usually charged in full to the credits extended. The Soviet Union also undertook to train local technicians; about 19,000 skilled workers were given instruction in special schools in Egypt between 1959 and 1967; some 11,000 are said to be in training at the present time.[4] About 20,000 students and technical trainees from third-world countries received part of their training in the Soviet Union between 1955 and 1965, but there are indications that their number is now declining.

The Soviet aid programme to the underdeveloped countries has taken an uneven course. The most rapid expansion took place between 1958 and 1961; 1958 was the peak year in the Middle East, with commitments totalling $278 million. There was a sharp decline in 1961, when not a single new credit was extended to any Middle East country, perhaps as a result of the many commitments entered into by the Soviet Union in Africa in 1961–2. In 1963 economic aid to the Middle East began to increase again and reached a new peak in 1964 and 1965 – $530 million and $574 million respectively, most of it to Egypt.[5] Altogether, out of a total of $5 billion in economic credits and grants extended by the Soviet Union between 1954 and 1966 to underdeveloped countries, the Middle East received about 40 per cent, $2 billion; of Soviet exports to developing countries the share of the Middle East was also about one-third of the total, clearly indicating the importance Moscow attached to that trade in comparison with other parts of the world.[6] However, even after this expansion, Soviet bloc trade with the Middle East accounted for only 11–12 per cent of the area's total trade.* The one major exception is Egypt, which has mortgaged a substantial part of its annual cotton crop to the Soviet Union. A considerable part of the burden of the communist economic aid effort has in the past been shouldered by the countries of Eastern Europe. Between 1954 and 1965 they extended credits totalling $725 million to the area. East European exports to the Middle East have been considerably higher than those of the Soviet Union, again excepting Egypt; imports, on the other hand, were considerably smaller. This resulted in a substantial loss for them, and despite Soviet pressure there has been growing reluctance in East Europe to continue to engage in such unprofitable trade.

It is pointless to discuss Soviet economic relations with the Middle East without referring again to the one item of export which has had by far the greatest political impact. The Soviet Union provided the complete equipment for the Egyptian and Syrian armies, and has delivered substantial quantities of weapons to Iraq (estimated at $300 million before the Six Day War), the Yemen, Algeria, and the Sudan. There were small Soviet arms shipments to the Middle East even before the famous deal with Egypt in 1955, when Britain had been the main supplier to the area of tanks and jet aircraft. Since the recipients had to pay for their purchases in hard cash, there were narrow limits to these sales.[7] The Soviet Union, by offering barter deals, broke the Western monopoly, and made possible far larger purchases. It supplied some 2,000–3,000 tanks to the Arab states, as well as missiles, missile-firing vessels, Ilyushin and TU-16 tactical

* The net outflow of Soviet aid has fallen in recent years; it was about $155 million in 1966 and $125 million in 1967. In 1967 Communist aid offers were 45% lower than in 1966; there had been decreases also during the two previous years.

bombers, the most recent MiGs, and other sophisticated equipment. After June 1967 new deliveries were made on a very big scale to replace the material that had been lost or damaged; some 4,000–5,000 Soviet military advisers supervised the re-organization of the Arab armies and the establishment of new munitions industries. By its willingness to deliver modern arms at low cost or even free of charge, the Soviet Union established a special position for itself in the Arab world. The West could match the commercial offers and the aid schemes proposed by the Russians, but no Western government could have become the chief arms supplier to Egypt and Syria, Iraq and the Yemen. All these countries were ruled by military men who, much as they needed financial aid, valued the supply of arms even more highly.

In trying to develop trade with the Middle East (and the third world in general) the Soviet Union laboured under various handi-caps. It is not one of the great trading powers: having recently been overtaken by Japan, it now ranks sixth in the world. Its share in world trade has in fact declined in recent years. According to OECD calculations, Western public development aid disburse-ments up to the middle sixties were ten times as much as that of the Soviet bloc and China. If Western private investment is added, the ratio is even higher. Leaving arms aside, the Soviet bloc aid commitment to the Middle East has been about $2 billion since 1954, of which, as we said, not much more than one third has actually been disbursed. Western official aid in 1960 and 1961, on the other hand, has been almost equal in volume; it is estimated at about $670 million, not counting private invest-ment.[8] Again in 1966 the non-Communist countries provided $10·562 million worth of resources, exceeding in one single year total Communist deliveries over a period of twelve years. The Soviet Union has faced great problems in carrying out its prom-ises: 'For many aid recipients the phase of actual project im-plementation has proved much less glamorous than the initial announcement of large-scale lines of credit.'[9] Very often the signing of an agreement was followed by time-consuming studies and pilot projects; delays and inefficient implementation also had a detrimental effect. Occasionally the goods supplied were not suited to local needs, or they were found deficient in design, quality, and spares. Bulgarian silos built at Latakia in Syria, to give but one example, were found so defective that compensation was asked for. Mention has been made of the resale of raw materials by Soviet and East European buyers; this has concerned Egyptian and Syrian cotton and other produce.

A comparison of trade and aid figures shows that up to 1966 the Soviet effort in the Middle East has been heavily orientated towards Egypt and Syria. This is not to imply that all Soviet trade in the Middle East has been politically motivated; Moscow has shown considerable eagerness to expand its trade wherever this could be done profitably. But the figures also show that it has been willing to lose substantial amounts of money in order to gain political influence. Investments have been made with an eye to long-term gains rather than immediate successes; they have been concentrated on certain strategically chosen projects, such as the Aswan and Euphrates dams, which for obvious reasons were likely to receive far more publicity than food shipments or other, more prosaic, forms of trade or aid. Soviet economic support, furthermore, was always given with an eye to strengthening the State sector of the economy in such a way as to prove the advantages of the Soviet model for the developing countries. The military and technical programmes have been designed to create a new Soviet-trained *élite* on the assumption that those who receive their training in the Soviet bloc will be orientated towards the East in the same way as earlier Western-trained generations were, broadly speaking, pro-Western. It is by no means certain that such assumptions are correct: prolonged exposure to life in the Soviet Union and the other East bloc countries does not necessarily convert foreign residents to communism.

The idea that the development of trade relations and the extension of economic aid makes friends and influences people still has many advocates in both East and West. Yet it is certainly incorrect in the short view, and only partly true in a longer perspective. Economic penetration helps to establish positions of strength, but it also extends the area of friction and creates discontent and resentment. Measured in terms of political influence, the results are usually meagre. Even the smallest and weakest countries are not often entirely swayed by considerations of economic loss and profit when facing important political decisions.

8
The Soviet Military Presence

The presence of a Soviet fleet in the Mediterranean attracted a great deal of publicity during the Arab-Israeli war of 1967, but it had not come into being overnight; its creation was part of an overall policy aimed at strengthening the capability of the Soviet Union for military action in various parts of the world. An appraisal of the role of the Mediterranean fleet should therefore start with a review, however brief, of the general development of Soviet military doctrine and policy over the last decade.

According to classical Marxist-Leninist doctrine, capitalism leads to war as surely as the clouds bring rain; violence is the midwife of history and the future is envisaged as a series of terrible clashes between the Soviet Republic and the *bourgeois* states. The nuclear age, however, introduced a new dimension: the relation between ends and means, between the prospective gains and the effect of the use of the new weapons, rendered the Clausewitz thesis doubtful if not completely obsolete. For the West, with its defensive mentality, the bomb posed the dilemma of relying on it, without wanting to use it, to preserve the *status quo*. The Soviet bloc faced an even more difficult dilemma. It wanted to change the *status quo*, but it gradually came to understand that in the nuclear age revolutionary violence, the midwife of history, could easily become its grave-digger. The Soviet leaders were ideologically committed to revolutionary action, but they also realized that this could trigger off a nuclear chain reaction. The cardinal question then was how to reduce the risk without abandoning revolutionary ideology altogether. This discussion, which has now lasted for several years, has involved the very essence of the communist movement, its destiny and historical justification: how to preserve a revolutionary dynamic despite the danger of world war? 'Just wars' of national liberation have by no means been ruled out, but there is no guarantee that such 'limited wars', even in the remoter parts of the world, will not escalate into something far more threatening. The new situation gave birth to the doctrine and policy of the limited risk, essays in brinkmanship, based on the assumption that the other side, for reasons such as national parochialism, shortsightedness, lack of nerve, internal resistance by unilateralists, and so on, would not be ready to take equal risks.

Since 1953 Soviet leaders have shown from time to time that the basic policy dilemma was quite clear to them. Malenkov announced soon after Stalin's death that a new world war, given the present means of warfare, meant the destruction of world civilization. A leading Soviet military theoretician wrote in 1960 that a global war would probably mean the end of half of mankind, and the more active and cultured half at that.[1] These were isolated statements at the time, and sometimes had to be withdrawn because of their excessive 'defeatism', but it is known that the problem continued increasingly to preoccupy the Soviet leaders. The Chinese, in their dispute with Moscow, maintained that coexistence was untenable because war as a revolutionary solution in the international class war was inevitable. This policy was unacceptable to Moscow, where it was argued that Peking wanted to instigate a nuclear holocaust because it would result in the destruction of both America and Russia and thus open the way to Chinese world domination.

Western students of Soviet military policy during that period were frequently puzzled. They over-rated Soviet strength, miscalculating the number of Soviet ICBMs deployed. The 'missile gap' was exposed as a myth in 1961; up to that date it had been used by the Soviet Union to make political gains and to keep the initiative in international affairs. On the theoretical level, many Western observers failed to understand that for the Soviet leaders 'peaceful coexistence' and 'cold war' were not contradictory policies, but two sides of the same coin. There was a curious air of unreality in Western discussions about strategic calculations and the arms race. The arms-control approach, with its arguments about first strike and second strike, pre-emption and escalation, missile and deterrent gaps, seemed almost completely to ignore the political element. It was an attempt to abstract Soviet military and foreign policy into a strategic formula, in which flesh-and-blood Soviet leaders appeared as mechanical brains, infallible in their reasoning and completely divorced from any psychological, social, or ideological context. To strengthen the surrealist feeling even further, the debate began to look like a game of chess without a chessboard, its mental constructions and strategic anticipations made in a world in which Kafka met Lewis Carroll, in which the employment of nuclear weapons and the avoidance of their use were envisaged at one and the same time, while 'generations' of such weapons were obsolete before they reached the production stage.

Under Stalin no effort had been made to bring the new weapons into the general framework of Soviet foreign and military policy. His successors – Khrushchev in particular – had almost unlimited confidence in nuclear arms: they would not just deter an aggressor; massive nuclear retaliation, the ability to hit the United States, would make it possible to regain the manoeuvrability and political initiative which for several years had been impaired by American nuclear superiority.[2] The hardening of Soviet long-range missile sites (i.e. making them less vulnerable to enemy attack) and progress in anti-missile defence reduced the danger of surprise attack. It also caused a partial shift from the concept of massive retaliation to a more flexible strategy. Politically it had contradictory consequences; Khrushchev embarked on a policy of rising risks, vigorous diplomatic campaigns coupled with nuclear blackmail, committing Soviet policy and prestige to dangerous situations, culminating in the attempt to place offensive missiles in Cuba. At the same time he realized that the Soviet Union was not likely to prevail over the West in a major armaments race. With the massive increase in American missile production the strategic balance swung against the Soviet Union. As late as autumn 1961 its leaders declared that the number of American missiles was offset by the superior quality of Soviet weapons, but America, with better intelligence than previously, was not impressed. The Soviet leaders, unwilling to give up their ambitious economic development projects and to concentrate on a crash programme of missile production, drew the obvious conclusion and began to work for a *détente* with the West. This was, above all, Khrushchev's line, but his successors did not radically reverse the policy, although there was a gradual shift in emphasis. Soviet military spokesmen argued that under Khrushchev the all-round strengthening of the armed forces had been neglected; the military lobby claimed that they had not sufficient money at their disposal to ensure Soviet defence. Brezhnev and Kosygin accepted these arguments and decided upon a reallocation of resources; the military budget went up by 5 per cent in 1966 and by 8 per cent the year after. These were the published figures; the real increases were probably higher. The Soviet leaders justified this by referring to the worsening world situation and to the more aggressive character of 'imperialism'. Some military spokesmen even began to question the thesis, generally accepted during the Khrushchev era, that war in the nuclear age had become obsolete as an instrument of policy. Colonel Rybkin, writing in 1966, argued that the Soviet Union could not accept the doctrine that victory in nuclear war was impossible; to do so would spread fatalism, even defeatism.[3] He and other hard-liners were criticized by some of their colleagues, and the party leaders stressed that such fundamental decisions would in any case be taken by the political leadership, not by the military, in view both of the political objectives of a future war and of the destructive properties of modern weapons. But Brezhnev, Kosygin, and some of their colleagues were clearly impressed by the arguments of the hawks, in particular that a formal rejection of the political utility of nuclear war was bad for morale, quite apart from the fact that it ran counter to certain basic ideological tenets of Leninism. A policy of *détente tout court* was likely to erode the ideological cohesion of the world communist movement and undermine Soviet prestige in the third world. They did not question the necessity of great prudence in their relations with the United States, but they refused to accept the policy of *détente* as a constraint on political or military initiatives in areas presumed to be of less than vital interest to the Americans.[4] Such initiatives were to proceed according to the rules of the game, but these rules were fairly vague, and as far as the Russians were concerned they were bound to change as Soviet military capability continued to grow.

The post-Khrushchev leadership undertook a substantial build-up of Soviet strategic forces. In summer and autumn 1966 an accelerated programme of ICBM construction got under way, and by the beginning of 1967 the number of operational ICBMs was about 400–450, increasing at a rate of more than 100 a year, compared with the total deployment of fewer than 200 ICBM launchers during the entire Khrushchev period.[5] By 1968 it was thought that the number of land-based ICBM launchers had risen to 750, and Russia achieved parity with the American total of just over 1000 in 1969. In numbers of warheads (including obsolete manned bombers) the American advantage was still 3:1 or more in September 1967, but it had been reduced to 2:1 if not less by 1970.[6] In addition, a massive research and development effort was undertaken in the Soviet Union after 1958 to ensure military-technological superiority. This programme, unlike the American, did not aim mainly at improvement and follow-on of existing weapons systems, but stressed the importance of new break-throughs and new weaponry.

While Soviet military leaders discussed Western intentions and the best ways and means to develop Soviet military power, there was a similar discussion about Soviet aims in the capitals of the West, where some observers argued that there was a danger in taking American superiority for granted and in under-rating Soviet ability to push through priority programmes and to produce an effective and flexible scientific-technological military base; while America and its principal NATO allies were under great internal pressure to reduce their military budgets, the Soviet Union was forging ahead. In addition to the build-up of its strategic forces, steps were taken in Moscow to obtain a capability for direct intervention in future third world conflicts. The 1968 Soviet military budget for the first time earmarked special funds for arms deliveries to 'national liberation movements'. To a greater extent than before, Soviet military spokesmen discussed the possibility of non-nuclear warfare, even in Europe.[7] Previously it had been assumed that a new war, especially in Europe, would witness immediate strategic nuclear escalation.

Basically, of course, the debate was political, not military. Those Western observers who were convinced that the Soviet Union had undergone a process of *embourgeoisement*, contended that with the rising standard of living and the increasing destructiveness of the new weapons, the dynamism has gone out of the communist states in East Europe, though perhaps not of the communist movements in the third world; proletarians now had more to lose than their chains, and had, as a result, become far more responsible, i.e. less revolutionary in character. Soviet doctrinal declarations were not taken at face value:

> Although Soviet propaganda continues to give to the Soviet people a distorted picture of the outside world, and some of the Soviet military still propagate the view that 'imperialism' is actively preparing to launch a war against the 'socialist countries', the Soviet government continued to behave throughout 1967 like a great power concerned to optimize its position within the existing system, rather than like a revolutionary regime out to create a new system . . .[8]

It followed that Western policy should promote the spread of these trends by working for a *détente* with the Soviet Union and that the common security interests of the two super-powers should be stressed (as in the non-proliferation treaty). Nothing should be done to provoke the Russians. It did not really matter if they caught up with the West in the output of ICBMs, for once a certain level was reached, 'strategic superiority' lost its meaning. Exponents of this school also argued that the emerging threat to both the super-powers from the more militant Chinese was drawing them together.[9] These views found their reflection in continued American hopes for a real *détente* with the Soviet Union in 1967–8, and in the assumption that Soviet action in Czechoslovakia was only a temporary aberration and that, even if it was not, it should not be permitted to affect the overriding necessity for Soviet-American understanding.

A more pessimistic view of Soviet intentions was also represented; this, while not denying that the Soviet regime had become more conservative and nationalist in character, questioned whether it had necessarily become less aggressive. The quasi-Marxist argument that greater wealth would manifest itself in the Soviet bloc in a genuine desire for peaceful coexistence was not accepted; East Germany, it was pointed out, was the communist country with the highest living standards, but was also the one closest to Stalinism within the bloc. According to this school of thought, it was for a variety of reasons more likely than not that the Soviet Union would pursue a more aggressive policy in the years to come, and it was doubtful therefore whether much importance could be attached to the various American-Soviet treaties for which the doves were willing to make concessions. The Soviet Union was gradually catching up with America in the strategic balance; if it had followed a hard line in the past, on a basis of relative military weakness, was there any reason to doubt that it would assert its interests in various parts of the world with even greater emphasis once it reached parity, let alone superiority? It was irrelevant whether Soviet pressure was interpreted with reference to traditional revolutionary ideology or on the basis of the nationalist-totalitarian character of the regime, in geo-political terms or in terms of big-power policies. All big powers have the tendency to expand, until they encounter resistance. Such expansion can always be explained with reference to defence and security; a glacis, or sphere of influence, is clearly needed to defend the Soviet Union against its enemies. But then the sphere of influence itself has to be defended against enemies, real or, more often, imaginary; the allies of the Soviet Union will be secure only if their neighbours, and preferably their neighbours' neighbours as well, are at least neutralized. It may not always be possible to achieve such optimal security, but it is clearly the long-term political and military aim. The weaker the neighbours, the greater the temptation to extend the sphere of influence, and the greater also the chances of success.

During the last years of Khrushchev's rule a determined effort was made to improve the reach and the mobility of Soviet conventional and general-purpose forces. Much of the emphasis was on the development of the naval forces for both 'blue-water' and amphibious landing operations. At the same time large transport aircraft were built to reinforce Soviet long-range air-lift capability.

This was one of the lessons from the Soviet setback in Cuba in 1962, strengthened by the growing conviction that Soviet involvement in the Middle East, Asia, and Africa made the existence of a long-range task force a matter of vital importance. In pursuance of this policy, the underseas fleet was expanded; together with the naval air arm (a land-based force of some 850 aircraft), it was given the leading place in the build-up of Soviet naval power.[10] Soviet nuclear-powered submarines began to undertake regular patrols in distant oceans, and made a round-the-world cruise in 1966. Aircraft and troop-carrier construction and the building of helicopter carriers was stepped up to make intervention with local landing parties possible.[11]

The decision to station Soviet ships permanently in the Mediterranean, taken in 1963 or early 1964, was also part of this policy. The existence of these units had been known to experts, but it was only after Brezhnev's call for the withdrawal of the American Sixth Fleet in April 1967 and the Arab-Israeli war that the general public began to take note of the presence of the Soviet fleet and to ponder its implications. There was little the Western powers could do about it: the Mediterranean is open to all seafaring nations and the Soviet naval presence there was not unprecedented. There had been Russian naval units in the area during the Napoleonic wars; Paul I had wanted to occupy Malta, but the British had forestalled him; the Russians fought a naval battle near Mount Athos in 1807, and took part in the battle of Navarino in 1827. The Crimean war marked a setback to the Russian fleet, but towards the end of the century, within the framework of the French-Russian alliance, Russian units began again to appear in the Eastern Mediterranean. After the revolution Soviet destroyers and later on whole flotillas visited Italy, calling at Greek and Turkish ports on their way. These regular calls came to an end only in 1935 with the *rapprochement* between Hitler and Mussolini. In the nineteen-fifties Soviet submarines were stationed in Albania, but these bases ceased to function with the break in Soviet-Albanian relations.

In some important respects the Soviet naval presence of the sixties was different: it was permanent, far more substantial, and part of an overall political and military design. In Stalin's days the main role of the navy was to support the army; there had been a big postwar naval construction programme (including aircraft-carriers), but it received low priority and was time and again postponed.[12] Under Khrushchev, too, Soviet admirals faced an uphill struggle in their efforts to convince the political leaders that the navy's activities should not be limited to coastal waters, but that it should be given the capability to engage in independent action on the broad oceans. The access of both the Baltic and the Black Sea fleets to the high seas is by way of straits, not under Soviet control, while the Northern fleet is located far from the political and industrial centres of the Soviet Union. To overcome these geographical handicaps, the admirals suggested greater strategic mobility using techniques which would enable them to keep their ships away from port over long periods.[13] In the early sixties they had no port facilities in the Mediterranean, but employed instead sheltered, shallow coastal waters as permanent holding grounds: near the Greek island of Cythera, in the south-eastern Cyclades, south of Malta, at the Alborran islands east of Gibraltar, and in the Gulf of Hammamet, off Tunisia. There was a steady procession of oil-tankers, repair-ships, ammunition-barges, submarine-tenders, and other naval auxiliaries to and from these holding grounds. But as the Mediterranean fleet grew in size, the floating bases became inadequate and Soviet warships began to call more and more often at Port Said, Alexandria, and Latakia for refuelling and refitting. From 1961 the Soviet naval commander-in-chief, Admiral Gorshkov, visited Egypt regularly almost every year. The Soviet Union received permanent bases in Egypt in all but name; at almost any given time there were Soviet men-of-war in the Egyptian ports or in Latakia. Officially this remained an *ad hoc* arrangement only because any formal pact would have smacked of traditional imperialist practices. It was Soviet policy to run these bases as unobtrusively as possible, and both the Egyptians and the Syrians had their own reasons for not giving undue publicity to these arrangements.

The role and growing importance of the Soviet fleet was described by its commander in a programmatic article in 1963:

Formerly our warships and naval aviation were a junior service concerned mainly with supporting the ground troops. Now . . . we must be prepared through broad offensive operations to deliver crushing strikes against sea and ground targets of the imperialists on any point of the world oceans and adjacent territories.[14]

Four years later, on the occasion of Soviet Navy Day, 1967, Gorshkov wrote that the big imperialist powers had long lost complete supremacy at sea and that sooner or later they would have to realize that they had no supremacy at all. 'The Soviet navy's ensign is now proudly flown in all the seas and oceans.' On another occasion Gorshkov revealed details about the decision taken in the nineteen-fifties to construct an ocean-going navy capable of carrying out offensive tasks of a strategic nature, in response to the expansion of Western sea power in the decade after the Second World War.[15] This decision implied the development of a Soviet task force, including Polaris-type submarines, as well as missile-carrying forces and nuclear weapons capable of engaging in limited war.

Among the Soviet ships regularly deployed in the Mediterranean before the Arab-Israeli war were two cruisers of the *Sverdlov* and *Kirov* class, armed with six-inch guns and guided missiles. There were also *Kynda* and *Kaskin* class guided-missile frigates, with surface-to-surface and surface-to-air missile-launchers. These ships were highly rated by Western observers. An American commentator noted that the *Kyndas* in particular represented an effort by the Soviet navy to close its gun gap, to gain a high level of fire-power, doubly necessary in view of the lack of carrier-based aircraft. The absence of aircraft-carriers has been adduced as proof of the absence of Soviet offensive aims in the Mediterranean. But the building of such carriers would have involved heavy expenditure; the construction of helicopter-carriers represents a compromise. Furthermore, given the growing Soviet influence in Egypt and Syria and the possibility of stationing aircraft in those countries, it was not so certain that the Soviet Union actually needed aircraft-carriers in the area.

The small Soviet Mediterranean fleet, the '*Eskadra*', also included before May 1967 a number of conventional submarines, among them at least one carrying guided missiles, nine destroyers, several intelligence vessels, as well as survey ships, submarine-tenders, etc., altogether about half that of the American Sixth Fleet, which consisted at the outbreak of the war in June of forty-six ships. Later on as many as sixty Soviet ships were counted, including fifteen destroyers, but their number fluctuated from day to day.[16] In September 1968 the new Soviet helicopter-carrier *Moskva* joined the Mediterranean fleet. The Soviet Union had an edge of more than 3:1 over the American fleet in the number of submarines, but the presence of two aircraft-carriers, the *Saratoga* and the *America*, made the US fleet more powerful than a comparison of mere numbers would indicate.[17] Some Western reports about growing Soviet strength in the Mediterranean were alarmist, 'inspired by naval lobbyists and patently exaggerated; missiles with a range of ten miles are equated with those of hundreds, and aged cruisers are presented as fierce new contenders for naval supremacy';[18] inferior in numbers and lacking air cover, the Soviet Mediterranean fleet (it was argued) was no match for the Sixth Fleet; it was a political weapon rather than a war fleet. According to C. Gasteyger, the greatest effect of the build-up was psychological, at least during the early stage. But the strategic position of the West was likely to deteriorate in the years to come, whereas the Soviet Mediterranean fleet was to be increased in strength; the Soviet merchant and oil-tanker fleets are also expanding rapidly. The Eastern Mediterranean was, to a certain extent, hostile waters for the Sixth Fleet; the Soviet missiles had a far greater range than any naval guns, perhaps more than a hundred miles. The British decision in 1968 to retain in the Mediterranean two frigates and a Canberra reconnaissance squadron was not sufficient to restore the former balance. Admiral Griffin, commander-in-chief of Allied Forces, Southern Europe, commented in 1967 that the Soviet fleet could not project military power at a long distance from home into areas 'where it can hurt us seriously', and predicted the building of further helicopter-carriers (similar to the American assault ships) and the build-up of the Soviet Marine Corps.[19] Admiral Rivero, his successor, on the other hand, said he was not convinced that the Soviet fleet would be substantially increased in the future: 'even a stronger Soviet fleet would be threatened by our aircraft'.[20] His optimism may have been connected with the plans to establish an inter-Allied Mediterranean fleet advanced in summer 1968.

The presence of a permanent Soviet Mediterranean fleet gave rise to much speculation about its military and political purpose. It was thought that the actual combat value of a relatively weak naval force was strictly limited. It could act within limits as a deterrent to nuclear strikes from the American aircraft-carriers and Polaris submarines; this was, no doubt, part of the intention behind the Soviet decision to keep a fleet in the Mediterranean.[21] American naval commanders frequently complained about Soviet harassing tactics and extensive surveillance; the Soviet fleet was clearly collecting intelligence on the Sixth Fleet's capability for both nuclear and limited warfare, and the Soviet government must have immediately known in June 1967 that there was no truth in the charges made by President Nasser and King Hussein about the intervention of the Sixth Fleet in the Arab-Israeli war. The military importance of the Soviet presence in the Mediterranean was, however, seriously reduced and Soviet strategic mobility restricted by the closure of the Suez Canal as the result of the war, and it was clearly in the Soviet interest to try to bring pressure on Israel to withdraw from the Canal. Its closure prevented Soviet access to the Persian Gulf and the Indian Ocean, and as a result the Soviet Far Eastern, not the Mediterranean Fleet, was called in to show the flag in such distant places as Basra and Mogadishu.

Although the military purpose behind the build-up of the Soviet Mediterranean fleet should not be under-rated, the over-riding considerations behind the decision were clearly political in character. It reflected the desire to make effective political use of sea power, to strengthen the Soviet position in the Middle East, to give fresh courage to Egypt and Syria, to bring pressure on all other countries in the area. While unable to stand up to the American fleet if it came to war, the Soviet naval presence meant nevertheless that the Western naval monopoly in the Mediterranean had come to an end:

The Russian squadron there does for Russia's Arab friends what the American troops in Germany do for America's allies in Europe: if it gets involved in a fight it could bring Russia's full weight in after it. Its presence will make the Western powers step just that more gingerly in any future crisis.[22]

The Soviet naval presence thus acted as a factor inhibiting any Western military move, even though its main immediate impact was no doubt meant to be psychological. A Soviet naval visit to Egypt four weeks after the defeat in 1967 was intended to reassure President Nasser, but Admiral Molokhov's declaration on that occasion, that the Soviet vessels were ready to cooperate with Egyptian armed forces to repel any aggression,[23] was toned down in the Soviet press. Throughout 1967 and 1968 Soviet cruisers and escort ships showed the flag in the Persian Gulf, in Mogadishu, in Madras, Bombay, and Karachi. These visits gave rise to much speculation about possible Soviet intentions to acquire naval bases in the Indian Ocean (in South Arabia and in the Andaman and Nicobar Islands), following Britain's withdrawal from East of Suez in 1971; they also reflected growing Soviet concern with Chinese intentions in South-East Asia, suggesting their connection with long-term plans rather than immediate policies. For, despite its striking growth, the Soviet navy during the late sixties was clearly not yet in a position to undertake all the military and political tasks which some Western observers thought had been assigned to them.

During the Khrushchev era a Soviet project for an atom-free zone in the Mediterranean had from time to time been mooted. With the build-up of the fleet the idea was dropped on the ground that the presence of Soviet ships was a reassurance to the progressive forces in the area and protected the independence of the small nations. When asked at a press conference in Sofia whether the Soviet plan to turn the area into a 'zone of peace' could be combined with the Soviet naval presence, Gromyko said that Soviet ships in the Mediterranean were serving precisely the interests of European security and peace. As a Black Sea power, the Soviet Union was also a Mediterranean country, and it was therefore only natural that it should be interested in the peace and security of a region close to its southern borders.[24] These views were shared by Egypt and Syria, whose representatives declared repeatedly that they regarded the Soviet fleet as their shield against the aggressive designs of the American Sixth Fleet. Similar opinions were voiced by the majority at a conference of 'progressive movements in the Mediterranean', which took place in Rome in April 1968. Among those present were representatives of the Syrian Ba'th and the Egyptian ASU, the Algerian FLN, the Communist parties of France, Italy, Cyprus, Greece, and Morocco, and the Turkish Labour Party.[25] But there were significant differences in the attitudes of the various parties and countries; the Yugoslavs argued that American Atlantic policy was the main threat to peace and demanded the withdrawal of the Sixth Fleet, which was a 'constant danger to the freedom and independence of the Mediterranean countries'; with its removal the main reason for the presence of the Soviet fleet would disappear.[26] The Yugoslavs thus ultimately wanted both fleets to withdraw, an attitude which, needless to say, did not please Moscow and which, incidentally, prevented the adoption of unanimous resolutions at the Rome conference.[27] Yugoslavia's past experience with Soviet foreign policy had not always been fortunate, and when Admiral Gorshkov, on the occasion of an official visit to Belgrade in April 1967, asked for naval bases (to replace the Albanian base at Valone), the Yugoslav government is said to have rejected the demand on the grounds of its country's neutral policy.[28]

Non-communist countries had even graver misgivings. Italy felt threatened by the presence of the Soviet fleet, although (a fact usually forgotten when comparisons are made between the Soviet fleet and the Sixth Fleet) the Italian navy was superior to the Soviet 'Eskadra' in conventional fire-power. After the occupation of Czechoslovakia, the Italian Communist party, too, opposed the presence of the Soviet fleet in the Mediterranean. Spain had justified the Soviet naval presence in 1965, mainly no doubt because it resented its exclusion from NATO. Moscow had reciprocated on various occasions; in August 1967, during the UN debate on Gibraltar, the Soviet bloc had given full support to the Spanish demands. At the same time the build-up of the Soviet fleet was also used by the Spanish government to ask for greater political and military help from the United States. Castiella, the foreign minister, declared in the

Cortes that the Soviet naval presence had greatly increased the strategic significance of the Spanish coastal areas.[29] In France concern was expressed about the relatively weaker American position and the delivery to Algeria and Egypt of Soviet missile-carriers.[30] But fears about the possible consequences were felt most acutely in the Eastern Mediterranean, in Greece, Turkey, and Israel. A Turkish government newspaper asked: 'What are those Soviet vessels looking for in a sea where they have no coast? The Russians are trying to establish a net throughout the Mediterranean to control the area.'[31] Early in 1968 the Turkish Foreign Ministry published figures showing that during the previous year, 1967, a record number of Soviet warships had passed through the Straits, 107 of them after the Arab-Israeli war. In the Turkish view, there was nothing the country could do to lessen the danger; a revision of the Montreux Convention was certainly out of the question. The age-old Russian dream of getting a firm foothold in the Mediterranean had finally come true not by over-running, but by by-passing Turkey.

Above all, Israel had reason to feel concern. Advanced Soviet missiles had been used in the sinking of the Israeli destroyer *Eilat* in October 1967.[32] After this incident a number of Soviet warships were immediately dispatched to Port Said on the mistaken assumption that Israel intended to take reprisals against that city, and that the presence of Soviet units would deter it. This move, unpublicized in the Soviet press, was in some ways a symbolic act, a classic case (to quote an American observer)

of how a major power with nearby conventional forces may feel obliged to respond when an important state with which it is developing close relations, feels itself in danger. It showed that commitment to a certain regime, an investment of national prestige, could lead towards military protection of that regime and through the presence of conventional forces, towards a higher risk of combat involvement, even though this may not have been the original intention.

The Port Said incident may have foreshadowed in some ways the shape of things to come: what if in future a Soviet warship or aircraft stationed in Egypt were hit in the course of a battle? Would the Soviet forces retaliate by a strike against Israel, and would Israel hesitate to fire back? Would it be possible to halt the escalation? The Israeli military were not overawed by the Soviet presence; they felt that the Soviet Union did not have the capacity to engage in any major action in the near future, and they tried to leave no doubt that any Soviet attack would be resisted. It was the Israeli assumption that while Soviet ships could fire rockets at targets in Israel from some distance, a landing operation was ruled out for years to come. Soviet commentators had admitted that it might be five years before Soviet forces were capable of executing and supporting even a lightly opposed landing in that part of the world.[33] Above all, Israel assumed that the Russians would not want to overstep the line, which could involve them in a dangerous confrontation with the United States.

The long-term perspectives were less clear. Khrushchev's policy in the Cuban missile crisis had been foolish in the eyes of his successors, not because it had been too daring, but because the Soviet Union did not have sufficient strength to back up its initiative when challenged. Brezhnev and Kosygin therefore gave priority to a swift build-up of the strategic missile forces and nuclear-powered missile-launching submarines as the 'principal means of deterring an aggressor and decisively defeating him in war'.[34] The Soviet objective was to achieve parity with the United States in the number of launchers by 1970 or at most a little later, and ultimately superiority.[35] (Whether 'superiority' still made sense in the age of MIRVs and other new weapons, and whether parity had not in fact already been reached, were different questions.)

At the same time great efforts are now being invested in strengthening Soviet non-nuclear long-range strike forces. The construction of helicopter-carriers capable of carrying 30–35 helicopters, and the reactivation of the Soviet Marine Corps, are part of this scheme. The marine force counted only 6,000–8,000 men in 1968 (compared with 280,000 American marines), and it was dispersed over four fleets; there was an airborne force of 50,000 and long-range transport aircraft capable of lifting tanks and artillery and up to three divisions. The supply operation on short notice to Cairo after the Six Day War, to the Yemen in November 1967, and the deployment of Soviet troops in Czechoslovakia in August 1968, showed that the Soviet Union had made progress in mastering the requirements of long-distance military intervention, but so far these forces have not encountered opposition, or have been deployed in countries contiguous to the Soviet Union. In the Middle East the Soviet Union is not in full control of the lines of sea and air support and military intervention would present far greater difficulties. It is unlikely that it would be undertaken with small forces in the hope that the adversary would be too stunned to offer serious resistance. The availability of overwhelming force would be, in Soviet eyes, a pre-condition for success; no one wants to repeat Stalin's mistake in Finland. Such overwhelming force will not be available for long-range intervention for at least a number of years. The Soviet Union will therefore be reluctant to become directly involved in military operations in the Middle East in the near future – certainly not by committing ground-combat units. In the more distant future the Middle East remains for political and strategic reasons the most likely direction in which Moscow's capability in the use of limited military power might be applied.

Long-term Soviet aims in the Middle East cannot, of course, be discussed in isolation from the relations between the two super-powers. Since, at latest, 1963, the date of the test-ban treaty, there has been general agreement between Russia and America about global spheres of influence. While the *détente* gave the world several years of relative peace, its limitations are obvious. It reflected the strategic and political balance of power in 1963, internal developments in Russia and America, as well as the situation in other parts of the world. Any major change affecting one of these factors is bound to upset the balance and thus affect the *détente*. The world situation of 1963 cannot be frozen; there is no good reason to believe that the Soviet leaders regard it as a permanent arrangement. Total war is ruled out but the rules of the game and the division of spheres are considered subject to modification with the growth of Soviet military power and its ability to exploit Western weaknesses and conflicts in the third world.

The place of the Middle East in the West-East *détente* has never been clarified. It had been a British and French sphere of influence until the nineteen-forties. In the fifties and sixties Western influence was greatly reduced, whereas the Soviet Union acquired a dominant position in several Arab countries and succeeded in neutralizing others. Whether Soviet influence will increase now depends on the intensity of internal conflict, domestic developments in the countries of the area, the attitudes of governments, and public opinion. In this struggle for influence, the Soviet Union, like other big powers, is using various means to assert its position, of which the military presence is certainly not the least important. But the future of the Middle East also depends to a large extent on American capability and American intentions, which are less clear than Soviet aims. It depends on the general trend of American policy between the extremes of globalism or isolationism, on the decision as to how high the Middle East ranks in American global priorities and commitments. While Soviet military power is likely to grow within the next decade, and to lead to a higher risk policy, it is by no means certain that, even with Soviet supremacy established, the Middle East would necessarily turn into a Soviet sphere of influence, similar to East Europe. The further growth of American isolationism, a consequence of the Vietnam war and of a latent trend on both the right and the left of the American political spectrum, would make it, of course, much easier for the Soviet Union to achieve its aims. The disappearance of the 'American threat' would open up many possibilities in the area, ranging from mere neutralization (on the Finnish or Afghan pattern) of Middle East countries to satellization or even territorial annexation. An American retreat from the Middle East and the Eastern Mediterranean may not be likely at present, but the possibility, either as a result of a shift in the global balance of power or as the consequence of some major political miscalculation, cannot be altogether dismissed. The prospects for a united Middle East defence effort in the foreseeable future are nil, for internal conflicts run far too deep; the countries of the Middle East, even if united, are in any case too weak to resist a super-power bent on dominating the area.

These are the worst prospects facing the Middle East; there is, needless to say, no certainty that they will come to pass. The

Soviet regime may mellow in time and become more peaceful in character; it may be satisfied with the territorial advances made under Stalin after the Second World War. Its growing capability to intervene in other parts of the world, including the Middle East, must not necessarily lead to further conquests in that undefined no-man's-land between Russia and America. Moscow may have to face more urgent preoccupations, both at home and abroad, during the years to come, and the Middle East may receive a further respite. All these possibilities exist, but a realistic appraisal of the situation has to be based on the probability of limited war in the Middle East. In such a situation, the Soviet decision to intervene, and the extent of its intervention, will depend on the wider risks involved; and on the resolution and the military capability of the countries likely to offer resistance.

9
Communism, Maoism, Arab Socialism

The beginnings of communism in the Middle East can be traced back almost fifty years, but nowhere did it attain any political significance until well after the Second World War. Before that an objectively revolutionary situation (to use Leninist terminology) did not exist, and the sectarian-dogmatic approach of the Stalin era narrowly circumscribed the freedom of action of communist parties. Conditions changed only after 1945, when communism became fashionable among the intelligentsia and occasionally gained influence among the trade unions. The communist parties shed their hostility to Islam, and tried hard to accommodate themselves to Arab, Turkish, and Iranian nationalism. In the early years the ethnic and religious minorities had provided most of their leaders and a high percentage of their rank and file, especially in the Arab world; during the nineteen-fifties this too began to change. The general ferment in the Arab world opened up possibilities for a popular-front policy or even a communist bid for power. But in retrospect the balance sheet has been disappointing; individual communists and fellow-travellers have been members of the government at one time or another in Iraq and Syria, Egypt and the Sudan. But the parties as such have not benefited; they do not even have legal status in any Middle East country other than Israel. In contrast to South-East Asia, in this region communism has not so far succeeded in capturing the leadership of the nationalist movement.

In Turkey and Iran, too, the internal ferment favoured the growth of radical movements. But for these countries Russia was the main foreign threat, and a party so closely identified with the Soviet Union could not have a great appeal. For similar reasons

(Soviet opposition to Zionism), communist prospects in Israel were less than bright. In the Arab world and North Africa the breakdown of traditional social structures and ideologies had opened many opportunities to communism, but there, too, the growth of Soviet power did not necessarily enhance the influence of the local communist parties. The military dictatorships that seized power in these countries were in varying degrees friendly towards the Soviet Union. In Egypt, Syria, and Algeria there was also a growing ideological affinity with communism, but the regimes there did not call in the local communist parties (as Cuba was to do later); they set up their own state parties and the ortho-dox communists found themselves excluded from positions of power. Thus while communist ideas became popular in the Arab world in the nineteen-fifties, the official communist parties were largely by-passed, and, as Soviet strength grew, the Soviet brand of communism lost much of its earlier ideological appeal. With the spread of polycentrism, radicals now looked to China, Yugoslavia, or Cuba for inspiration, or advocated some form of national communism. The Soviet Union no longer exercised monopolistic control of the anti-imperialist and anti-capitalist forces; every self-respecting leader in the Arab world now sub-scribed to these doctrines, but this did not necessarily induce him to join the communist party; he could with equal justification be a member of the neo-Ba'th or a left-wing Nasserist. In this way his *bona fides* as an Arab nationalist remained unsullied, for the official communists, despite their demonstrative patriotism, were always somewhat suspect in view of their close ties with the Soviet Union; he could if necessary outflank the official com-munist parties from the left, for they were bound by certain rules of the game (such as Soviet unwillingness to risk a nuclear war on behalf of the Arab world) and could not compete with the ultra-radical slogans of Maoists and the local equivalent of the Castro-Debrayists. The position of the communist parties was further weakened by the ambiguities of Soviet policy towards the Arab world. It was not easy for a communist in an Egyptian concentra-tion camp to defend the 'objectively progressive character' of Soviet help given to Nasser. It was even more difficult for an Iranian communist to explain to the militant rank and file that it was perfectly legitimate for Soviet leaders to praise the Shah while Tudeh denounced him as a criminal and traitor and preached violent revolution. Such conflict situations existed in most Middle East countries, and they contributed to the internal disunity by which the communist parties have been plagued throughout their recent history. The disputes which affected all these parties resulted in many splits on political as well as on personal grounds, with rival cliques competing for the leadership. It was a dismal picture, but it would be wrong to draw premature conclusions about the final decline of communism in the Middle East, for while the communists failed to make headway, the parties in power were no more successful and an acute (or subacute) revolutionary situation continued to exist in many places. The communist failure was relative, not absolute.

The fortunes of the Iranian (Tudeh) Party (TPI) reflect the dilemma that has faced communism all over the Middle East. The TPI, illegal since 1953, has throughout its recent history been torn between the 'revolutionary path' and the possibility of 'peaceful revolution', between collaboration with the national *bourgeoisie* and 'orientation towards the working class', between ignoring and recognizing the economic advances made in recent years.[1] Some of its members bitterly criticized the Soviet Union for helping to stabilize the Shah's regime, while others attacked the party leadership (stationed in East Germany) for not giving emphatic enough support to the *rapprochement* with the USSR on the state level.[2] Throughout the late fifties and early sixties the party was rent by internal strife, and in 1965 two of the seven members of the party leadership, Ahmed Qasemi and Gholam Hussein Forutan, broke away and, with Abbas Shaqai, formed a pro-Chinese communist party, keeping the name Tudeh Party of Iran. Dr Forutan and Qasemi were Stalinist old-timers who had been involved in a previous inner-party crisis in 1948; Shaqai adhered to the Tudeh line in so far as the condemnation of the 'cult of personality' was concerned. But all three 'entirely accepted the Chinese leaders' position', to quote the resolution that announced their exclusion from the party.[3]

It was not the only such split, as the TPI leadership sadly noted; the party had previously experienced 'many incidents of this nature'. After the attempted assassination of the Shah in 1965, one of the principal accused, Nik-Khah, declared that he, too, thought that a new communist party should be established, since the TPI had in practice lost all its revolutionary potential.[4] The publications of the Persian students in Germany also betrayed strong influences of the European new left rather than orthodox communism.

In Turkey the tradition of nationalist deviation has been engrained right from the earliest days of the communist movement. Kemal Atatürk and his successors suppressed communism, and only after the overthrow of the Menderes regime in 1960 did it for the first time receive opportunities to act in a semi-legal framework. Various socialist study groups and journals came into being, most of them advocating a planned state economy and a return to the progressive principles of Kemalism, which, they argued, had been neglected by his successors. This was a time of great social and intellectual ferment, and some of these radical groups attracted many followers among the intelligentsia, and particularly among the students; among the workers they were on the whole less successful. The most extreme of these groups was the Labour Party of Turkey (*Türkiye Isci Partisi*), founded in 1961 and led by Mehmet Ali Aybar, a Paris-educated Marxist. The TIP was a revolutionary party, but for tactical reasons its programme was social-democratic in character, with heavy emphasis on free parliamentary elections.[5] With all its attachment to Marxism-Leninism, the TIP was by no means uncritical of Soviet policy. These manifestations of independence reached a climax in 1968 when Cetin Alton, one of the TIP leaders, openly criticized Moscow economic aid to the Demirel government. In return for this aid, he argued, the Russians could impose their aims on the Turkish government, but these 'were more to their advantage than to that of the Turkish working class'.[6] Shortly after, Aybar, the leader of the TIP, condemned the Soviet Union for reverting to Stalinism during the Czech crisis. The TIP declared that it had from the beginning of the crisis feared that the Soviet Union might act 'out of big-power mentality'.[7]

Israel

In Israel the Communist party (MAKI) split along national lines
in June 1965. The old leadership under Mikunis had loyally
followed the Soviet party line for many years, but in the end it
reluctantly reached the conclusion that Moscow's policy in the
Arab-Israeli conflict was opportunistic, and despite its Leninist
phraseology based on big-power interests. MAKI realized that
the supreme Soviet aim was not the restoration of peace in the
area, but the strengthening of its position by giving support to
Arab regimes which were often far from progressive. (During the
early period of the split the main bone of contention was osten-
sibly the appraisal of the character of the Arab regimes rather
than Soviet policy *vis-à-vis* Israel.) All Arab members of the
party (including Tawfiq Toubi, Emil Habibi, and the former
'nationalist deviationist', Emil Touma), in collaboration with a
few Jews, split away from MAKI and continued to defend
Nasser and the Soviet line. The leaders of the two rival factions
(MAKI and RAKAH) were summoned to Moscow in 1965
and several attempts were made to heal the breach, but these
were unsuccessful, and two Israeli communist parties had to be
invited to the Twenty-third Congress of the CPSU. The basic
communist principle that there could be only one communist
party in each country was ignored for the next two years. Of the
two communist lists, RAKAH, not surprisingly, emerged as the
stronger during the elections in 1965 to the Israeli parliament
(with 27,000 votes to MAKI's 13,000). Most of the electoral
appeal of the Israeli communists had traditionally been in the
Arab districts, such as Nazareth, where, in the absence of a legal
Nasserist or Arab nationalist opposition to the state of Israel, it
acted as a lightning conductor.

The Six Day War made the split between MAKI and Moscow
absolute. The Soviet leadership announced that the pro-Arab
RAKAH was truly internationalist and therefore the only representative of the Israeli working class. The Sneh-Mikunis group,
on the other hand, had supported Israel's 'aggressive war', thus
betraying the basic principles of the working-class movement.[8]

MAKI accused the Soviet Union of deviating from the policy of non-involvement which it had followed in the conflicts between India and Pakistan and India and China. The Soviet Union had identified itself with the Nasser-Hussein-Arif camp, and 'as for Israel, found nothing to compare it with except Nazi Germany'.[9]

From July 1967 RAKAH was recognized as the official Israeli Communist party by the Soviet bloc and by most major communist parties outside it. MAKI was recognized only by Rumania and several smaller European parties, including those of Holland, Switzerland, and Scandinavia. But there was still some uneasiness among other parties about the unconditional support given by Russia to Arab nationalism, and these misgivings (among the Yugoslav, Italian, French, Austrian, and other parties) increased as, at the time of the Czech crisis, traditional anti-Zionist propaganda gave way to openly anti-semitic attacks in Poland, the Soviet Union, and, to a somewhat lesser degree, in East Germany.

The struggle between MAKI and RAKAH became very bitter indeed after the Six Day War. RAKAH demanded the unconditional surrender of all Israeli-occupied territories, and regarded the MAKI line (against annexation of occupied territories, but demanding a withdrawal only against guarantees) as a 'chauvinist deviation'.[10] But RAKAH, despite its identification with Arab nationalism, had to fight a struggle on two fronts: most Arab 'progressive' parties refused under any circumstances to cooperate, let alone appear in public with, Jews (or Israeli Arabs). The Israeli communists, on the other hand, unlike their comrades in the Arab countries, did not altogether deny the right of existence of Israel. Arab communist leaders (such as Fuad Nassar, the head of the Jordanian party) came out in favour of the Arab guerrilla organizations[11] even before the Six Day War, whereas RAKAH was opposed to 'individual terror' and dissociated itself from the policy of a 'people's war' against Israel. Soviet policy on guerrilla warfare against Israel was ambiguous and RAKAH and the Arab communists could interpret it in different ways.

Iraq

The history of the Iraqi Communist party with its sudden ups and downs during the last decade is an uninterrupted series of splits, of left-wing and right-wing deviations. Communist influence reached its peak under the Kassem government in the spring of 1959, but, as Soviet spokesmen later said, 'serious leftist political errors' were committed, undisciplined elements had resorted to acts of violence, i.e. established a reign of terror.[12] This referred above all to the Kirkuk riots on 14 July 1959, in which communists played a leading role. But soon the tide turned against them. Kassem preferred to establish a local communist party of his own, headed by Daud al Sa'igh, which, though lacking any mass support, made it impossible for the real communist party to be legally recognized.[13] One section of the Iraqi party called for a 'radical revolutionary course' in response, meaning armed struggle, whereas the majority under Soviet guidance condemned this 'dogmatic and sectarian approach'. The communists continued to support Kassem, even though their party remained illegal and was subjected to sporadic persecution.[14] Several party leaders were excluded when they persisted in their deviation and those remaining complained about baleful Chinese influences in their party. When Kassem was overthrown in 1963, Moscow without much success called for an armed uprising against his successors, whereas Peking justified the *coup* carried out by the Ba'th, which it described as progressive in character.[15]

The fall of Kassem was a heavy blow for the Iraqi communists; thousands of members and fellow-travellers were arrested by Arab nationalists thirsting for revenge for the persecution they had suffered under the Kassem regime. The communists who escaped arrest reorganized in an illegal party, but were harassed by police action even after the Ba'th had been overthrown and General Arif seized power.

The conflicts between 'activists' and 'moderates' in the party continued; there were differences of opinion on the Kurdish issue and with regard to the appraisal of the Arif regime and the Bazzaz government. Kurds had always constituted a high percentage of both the party leadership and the rank and file; at the third party conference in 1968 (to give but one illustration), 31 per cent of those present were Kurds and 62 per cent Arabs.[16] The Iraqi party had long insisted that the ultimate goal for the Kurdish nation was self-determination, including the formation of an independent state for the whole of Kurdistan, whereas Moscow suggested that the Kurds should be satisfied with self-government. The Iraqi party leadership believed that the Kurdish problem could be solved only by a National Front government with communist participation. Meanwhile, the continuation of the war in Kurdistan was likely to weaken the Baghdad government, which was the communists' main enemy. Ideological issues quite apart, there was a great deal of internal strife on purely personal grounds. The 'Ramsi-Walid faction' and the 'Nadjm group' were accused in 1967 of having established a 'splitting centre hostile to the party'. They were charged with sectarian opportunism, anti-internationalism, liberalism, and, on top of it all, physical assaults against other party leaders, kidnappings, and an attempt to take over the party leadership by force.[17]* The Iraqi communists supported the Soviet leaders against Peking[18] and welcomed the occupation of Czechoslovakia. But on domestic problems they remained a house divided.

Syria and Lebanon

The Lebanese Communist party split in 1964; the minority faction led by Yussef Mubarak and Mustafa Shaker claimed that the majority had gone too far in support of Nasser. Without identifying itself fully with Maoist policies, it refused to accept the

* There was a 'Central Committee of the ICP' under Amer Abdullah and Bahaeddin Nuri in which Chinese influence was said to be strong. The 'Central Command of the ICP' under Aziz al Haj, a communist journalist domiciled in Prague between 1963 and 1968, was probably nearest to the Soviet line, and in 1968, after the Ba'th *coup*, it expressed willingness to cooperate with the regime. Lastly, there was a smaller faction, the 'Struggle Organisation'. The three groups resorted to violence to gain control of party funds and printing presses (*Al Anwar*, 17 June, 1968; *Information Bulletin*, 10, 1968).

Soviet position in the conflict with China. In its journal, *Ila al Amam*, it accused Khalid Bakdash, the leader of the Syrian communists, of various revisionist deviations, of being insufficiently militant in the struggle against Israel, and of 'having forced many true revolutionaries to resign from the communist party'.[19] This group also claimed that Bakdash's policy of calling for joint action by all Arab countries to eliminate the 'traces of Israeli aggression' was basically 'Pétainist' in character.[20] Israel could be defeated not by an alliance with the reactionary Arab states, but only by means of a people's war as defined at the Havana Tricontinental Conference. If these were Chinese concepts, they were not necessarily anti-Soviet in character, *Ila al Amam* argued. Objective circumstances in the Arab world made it impossible to choose the peaceful road; the Arabs would have to sacrifice 20, 30, 40 million of their 100 million in order to rid themselves of Israel for ever.[21] The best-known convert to this group was the Syrian General Afif al Bizri, a former chief of staff, who was permitted by the neo-Ba'th to return to Syria after the Six Day War and who, much to Bakdash's chagrin, preached 'positive neutralism' in the dispute between Moscow and Peking.[22]

The Syrian party did not have to cope with as many splits in its ranks as the other Arab parties, but on the other hand its relations with the neo-Ba'th were far from satisfactory. Bakdash and Abdel Samad Saker, his second in command, had for years resisted Soviet pressure to cooperate more closely with the neo-Ba'th, which they asserted was unwilling to establish a common progressive front; as a result, cooperation between the communist party and the neo-Ba'th was, as one of their leaders stated on the eve of the Six Day War, 'small and limited'.[23] The basic weakness of the Syrian communists was their failure to infiltrate the army to any large extent. While the mass basis of the neo-Ba'th was exceedingly weak, certainly inferior to that of the communists, its influence among the officer corps made its political position almost unassailable.

Egypt

The ups and downs of communism are more difficult to follow in Egypt than in any other country, for there was never, for any length of time, a central, Moscow-supported, official party. There were a great many *Marxisants* among the intellectuals of Cairo and Alexandria in the nineteen-fifties; most of the young army officers also toyed with communism at one time or another, but they joined at most one of many discussion clubs. A well-disciplined, united party did not come into being until the experts of the Italian Communist party took the initiative in 1957.[24] Following their efforts and long talks between the various factions concerned, a unified Egyptian Communist party was established in January 1958. All but a few dissenters joined this new organization and President Nasser for a while turned a blind eye. Officially communism in Egypt was still illegal, but since the new party promised loyal support to the regime it was not at first harassed. This interlude lasted, however, only a few months; with the merger of Syria and Egypt and the rise of Kassem in Iraq, the Egyptian communists faced a new and complicated political situation. Their Syrian comrades bitterly attacked the enforced union with Egypt, and the Iraqi communists were, if possible, even more hostile. The Egyptian party again split; the majority advocated collaboration with Nasser, the minority bitterly opposed it.[25] Meanwhile Nasser, provoked by communist attacks from Baghdad and Damascus, turned against communism at home without discriminating between sympathizers and enemies in the Egyptian party. Almost all leading party members were arrested or fled abroad. The only organized communist activity in Egypt between 1958 and 1964 took place in prisons and concentration camps.

As relations between Cairo and Moscow improved, discreet Soviet pressure was exerted on behalf of the Egyptian communists; Khrushchev made it known that much as he wanted to visit Egypt it would be most embarrassing for him to do so while so many Egyptian communists were still in prison. Nasser took the hint and the communists were released. Haykal published an article in which he argued that communism in Egypt had failed because of its isolation from the national movement, but at the same time he advocated greater freedom for Egyptian communists on condition 'that their activities do not endanger the principles and basic values in which the overwhelming majority of the society believes'.[26] In view of growing cooperation between Moscow and Nasser's regime, the continued existence of an Egyptian Communist party became a cause of real embarrassment for the Soviet Union. In April 1965, again after intervention by the Italian party, the Egyptian communists announced the voluntary dissolution of their movement. It had in fact led a mere shadow existence after the release of its leading members from prison; strict supervision by Nasser's secret police had made any political action on their part impossible. The former party members were instructed to join the ASU, Egypt's state party, but a small group ignored this order and continued to oppose the government. Its leaders were arrested in November 1965 and brought to trial. *Pravda* washed its hands of these 'political adventurers', whose leader, Hussein Ara, had allegedly acted under Chinese influence.[27]

This was the end of Egyptian communism as an independent force. Under the new policy of licensed infiltration, several dozen party members attained positions of some importance within the state and party apparatus. They gradually took over the ideological secretariat of the Arab Socialist Union, founded the 'Institute of Socialist Studies' and the periodical *Al Tali'a*, and through their friends in the press, the radio, and television exerted a considerable influence on Egyptian domestic propaganda and the ideological training of young cadres. Lotfi el-Kholy, editor of *Al Tali'a*, organized an ideological seminar in Cairo in collaboration with leading communist experts from abroad. With Nasser's blessing, they propagated 'scientific socialism' (i.e. a mixture of Leninism and Nasserism), as distinct from 'Arab socialism', which Nasser himself said was a mere invention of the newspapers. But there remained differences of opinion as to the interpretation of 'scientific socialism', especially with regard to such questions as the dictatorship of the proletariat, the class struggle, and Islam. *Al Tali'a* performed a fascinating but awkward tightrope act between the doctrines emanating from Cairo and Moscow, Peking and Havana. The Nasserist left showed itself receptive to the ideas of the European new left and Che Guevara, partly no doubt because Soviet ideological orthodoxy had become so much less fashionable. The romantic figure of an authentic revolutionary had a far greater appeal to young Egyptians than the time-honoured Leninist texts. After the Six Day War the *Al Tali'a* faction was the first to suggest giving military bases in Egypt to the Russians and establishing joint arms factories.[28] It also demanded the further promotion of the 'revolution' in Egypt, meaning above all the promotion of its own members to positions of greater influence. This they achieved to a certain extent in the course of the reorganization of the ASU in 1968. But while *Al Tali'a* enjoyed Soviet sympathy, there were indictations that it did not have its full trust and that, above all, it was not considered strong and influential enough to be a serious contender for political power. In the struggle for power that unfolded after the war of 1967, Soviet support was clearly for men like Ali Sabry and the 'centrists' in the ASU (as represented by the periodical *Al Kateb*) who were pro-Soviet in their foreign political orientation, but, unlike the *Tali'a* group, had no pronounced ideological interests and commitments. But this group, too, was to come to grief soon after Nasser's death.

Sudan

The achievements of Sudanese communism in recent years have remained largely unnoticed by most outside observers. Sudan, unlike Egypt or Algeria, is not a key country and not much attention has been devoted to its domestic affairs. The communists played an important part in the *coup d'état* of 1964, and dominated the 'Front of Professional Organizations', including the influential Sudanese Lawyers Association. In the provisional government that took power the communists held over a quarter of the portfolios, a share out of proportion to their real strength in the country, but they continued to harass the government from within, asking for an even greater share of power for themselves and their various front organizations (such as the Gezira Tenants Association). In a government reshuffle the communists lost all their posts but one, and when the SCP refused to accept this, they found themselves excluded from the government coalition altogether.[29] In December 1965 the SCP was banned, but it almost immediately reappeared as the Sudanese Socialist party and continued its activities through an elaborate network of front organizations. At the same time the Communist party insisted on its legal rights and brought an action in the courts to compel the government to recognize it. The Sudanese government countered by arresting some of the party leaders on such charges as possession of arms. Increased communist activity in recent years made the non-communist parties in the Sudan more aware of its real aims, and it thus became more difficult for the communists to infiltrate other political and professional groups and to apply the united front technique. Abd al-Halik Madjub, the party leader, pondering the reasons for the 1965 defeat, declared that his party should have been more aware of the importance and the delicacy of the religious factor in the political and social struggle; it should have made use of religious belief, as the Algerian comrades had done with some success.[30] This referred to Bechir Hadj Ali, the secretary-general of the Algerian party, who in a series of articles had maintained that there was no contradiction between socialism (as a political aim) and Islam as a state religion, that religion had a considerable revolutionary potential, and that philosophical discussions which would only result in dissension among the progressive national forces should be eschewed: 'The Algerian masses will advance towards communism with the Koran in one hand and *Das Kapital* in the other.'[31]

In May 1969 following yet another military coup a dictatorial regime was set up in which the Communists were prominently represented. The established political parties were dissolved and their leaders arrested.[32] Subsequently the Communist party split and some of its leaders were arrested having turned against the ruling military junta.

The Role of the Party

Among the many problems facing communists in the Middle East during the fifties and sixties, the one over-riding in importance all others was the question whether the party was still necessary, or whether in the higher interests of the cause they ought to renounce independent party propaganda and to present themselves as advisers and assistants of the nationalist leaders, but not as their rivals. Suggestions on these lines were made with increasing frequency in the Soviet Union. This strategy of 'licensed infiltration' by individual communists into the leadership of mass parties in one-party states was nothing less than the 'deliberate renunciation of independent communist parties publicly acting as such'. It certainly was an innovation in Soviet policy and the world communist movement.[33]

The beginning of this new strategy can be traced back to the years after Stalin's death, the time of the Bandung Conference and the Khrushchev-Bulganin trip to India in 1955. It was then that the new Soviet leadership first realized that the national liberation movement in the third world opened up new prospects for communism and that it could substantially change the global balance of power. While the 'national *bourgeois* leadership' in the underdeveloped countries had been ridiculed and attacked during the Stalin era, emphasis was now put on the progressive nature of their movements, even if their ideology was often 'petty *bourgeois*' or 'utopian' in character.[34] From 1954 onwards the Soviet Union began to give massive support to countries of the third world – economic aid and arms as well as political assistance. There was no attempt yet to work out a systematic approach to the problems of the third world, apart from a few propositions which were applied indiscriminately to national liberation movements in general without taking account of the great dissimilarities between them. Only after 1959, under the impression of Castro's victory in Cuba and the rise of Kassem in Iraq, but also of the persecution of communists in Egypt and in Kerala, did a new approach find favour in the Kremlin. It was realized then that aid alone was not sufficient to influence the general trend of political development in the third world, and that it would have to be coordinated with greater communist pressure from inside these countries.[35] In the 1960 declaration of the eighty-one communist parties and, more specifically, in the 1961 Draft Programme of the Communist Party of the Soviet Union, the new concept of the 'independent state of national democracy' was formulated. This was the first systematic attempt to shape doctrine to catch up with the facts and to coordinate Soviet and Chinese views on the subject.[36] Above all, it was a more activist approach than the classical communist thesis that ex-colonial countries would all have to go through a *bourgeois* revolution, and that the best policy for communists was to work through various popular and national fronts. But since there was only, at best, a small industrial proletariat in most of these countries, and since the number of communists was even smaller, the old approach had usually condemned the small communist parties to inaction. According to the new line, the state of national democracy ('based upon a strong peasant-proletarian alliance with petty-*bourgeois* support') was able in certain conditions to prepare the road to non-capitalist development, provided that certain preconditions existed. The new regimes would have to be anti-imperialist in character, well disposed towards the Soviet Union, and ready to implement radical social and economic reforms and to give local communist parties full freedom of political action.[37] The new approach justified economic and political support for the new nations, but ideological endorsement at the expense of the local communists was withheld.

This ingenious new formula was, however, soon found wanting. Only in Indonesia did a national-democratic front develop as foreseen in the Soviet concept, a coalition of nationalists and communists initially under nationalist leadership, but with growing communist influence. Cuba omitted the national democratic stage altogether; Castro declared his regime 'socialist' under the leadership of a Marxist-Leninist party. All other Asian and African countries in which the Soviet experts had detected left-wing trends turned into one-party states in which no communist competition was tolerated.[38] After the communist party had been banned even in Algeria (1962), a country on which Moscow had put such high hopes, a revision of the whole strategy became clearly necessary.

The reconsideration of the situation in the third world and its implications for the world communist movement played an important part in the Sino-Soviet dispute, and was the subject of a great many articles, speeches, exchanges, and seminars throughout 1963–6. According to the official Soviet view, cooperation with the third world was to continue in so far as it was 'objectively progressive'. Some of the third-world leaders might establish reactionary political regimes and subject communists to persecution, but such regimes were likely to be short-lived. The Chinese stated that they were willing to collaborate even with kings, princes, and aristocrats, but only if the communists were able to retain their independence; these must always insist on retaining the leadership of the revolution; on no account must they become the 'tail of the landlords and the *bourgeoisie*'. But the Chinese line was impractical because it shirked the most important political issue facing the communists: should they turn against non-capitalist regimes which were carrying out far-reaching social and economic reforms because these were unwilling to give full political freedom to the local communists and come gradually to accept their leadership?

Some Soviet observers began to advocate a new approach. G. Mirsky wrote in 1964 that the national liberation movement could immediately break out of the framework of *bourgeois* revolution and begin the transition to socialist revolution: 'If the conditions for proletarian leadership have not yet matured, the historic mission of breaking with capitalism can be carried out by elements close to the working class. Nature does not suffer a vacuum.'[39] Such unorthodox opinions were at first subjected to criticism, but within a year most experts had come to subscribe to these views, and, more important, Khrushchev himself declared that Egypt had 'embarked on the road to socialist development', an unprecedented compliment that meant breaking with all previous doctrine. According to this analysis, the actions of the new leaders in the third world mattered far more than their words; the ideologies of the developing states were not the most important factor in evaluating their progressive nature.[40] Another writer noted that 'social and economic reforms in these countries were often deeper and more radical than the theories elucidating them'.[41] The young officers, the students, and the lower ranks of the bureaucracy in the new countries were now described as essentially progressive elements, whose often quaint and contradictory ideological pronouncements should not be given excessive weight, for even *bourgeois* leaders would gradually go over from nationalism to the positions of socialism and the working class.[42] If so, the role of the communist parties was bound to be downgraded. 'Life demands the formation of a bloc of left forces, in which the most consistent and best trained Marxist-Leninist elements should play the role of friend and assistant of the national democrats, ideological beacon of socialism and vanguard fighter.'[43] This was a substantial retreat from the doctrine of national democracy and it encountered resistance from the Chinese (who argued that belief in the possibility of a non-capitalist way of development in the third world was meaningless talk), from part of the Soviet apparatus (especially among the guardians of doctrinal orthodoxy), and, not surprisingly, from among the Afro-Asian communists directly concerned.

After Khrushchev's fall the brakes were applied. Economists and ideologists continued their disputes about the class character of the new countries, the bureaucratic *élites*, their self-styled socialism, their foreign policies.[44] Could the dangers of *bourgeois* nationalism be ignored? Would not the ideological initiative be lost if the downgrading of the communist parties went too far? Under Khruschev's successors there was a general shift of priorities away from the national liberation movement towards communist construction in the USSR.[45] It was not a radical break; the first indications had already been detected during the last months of Khrushchev's rule; the change was caused *inter alia* by the growing strain on the Soviet economy of the many commitments to the new nations. The setbacks suffered by many 'national democratic' regimes (Indonesia, Ghana, Algeria) also contributed to the general disappointment, and as a result the national liberation movement was given a low rating in Soviet world strategy. Some new ideological modifications were made: the non-capitalist path of development was defined as not synonymous with the socialist path, but merely a stage towards it. The concept of the 'state of national democracy' was supplemented by the new formula of 'revolutionary democracy' which was to apply above all to Algeria and Egypt, where communist parties were enjoined to infiltrate state parties and the government in order to bring them over gradually to the communist position.[46]

Many leading Arab communists were indignant about the lowly role assigned to them by Moscow, arguing that the possibility of the restoration of capitalism in Egypt was by no means excluded, that a one-man dictatorship and a bureaucratic state machine was no guarantee for the gradual transition towards socialism. It could not be taken for granted, they said, that the 'Arab socialists' would gradually become adherents of 'scientific socialism'. Concessions to the nationalist *bourgeois* leaders would weaken the proletarian basis of the communist parties and limit their influence. No other social group, certainly no individual, could take over the historical mission of the working class and the communist party. 'Arab socialism' was a mere conglomeration of scientific and utopian socialism, petty-*bourgeois* ideas, narrow nationalism, religious prejudices, and subjective idealism; it did not aim at abolishing the exploitation of man by man.[47] This, in brief, was the line taken by the Syrians and their leader, Khalid Bakdash. Fuad Nassar, the head of the Jordanian party, was closer to the Soviet view. He believed that it was a mistake to regard the national liberation movement merely as a reserve or an auxiliary of the socialist revolution; any attempt to limit its role to the anti-colonial and anti-feudal struggle could only harm the movement and weaken its alliance with the world socialist system. If the national liberation movement was given sufficient support it would turn against capitalism even before the proletariat took a leading role in it. A communist *rapprochement* with this movement involved no dilution of Marxist-Leninist ideology; ideological contradictions and disagreement would continue to exist, but these could be resolved peacefully.[48] Nikola Shawi, the leader of the Lebanese party, took a position in between the two extremes in this dispute. He did not agree with the view held by some of his allies (presumably the pro-Nasser party in Moscow) that it was necessary immediately to merge the socialist parties and organizations into one political movement. On the other hand, he agreed with the Russians that some countries could develop from colonial and semi-colonial regimes to socialism as the non-proletarian strata of the population were joining the struggle against capitalism and setting themselves socialist aims.[49] The Iraqi party in principle supported the idea of a united front, but stressed that it would be difficult, if not impossible, to pursue such a policy wherever the non-communist leaders of the national movement insisted on a one-party system.[50] All Arab communists agreed that the seizure of power by their parties remained the final goal; disagreements concerned the period of transition, and no one could know how long this would last.

The dispute lasted for several years; eventually each party devised its own tactics, adjusting itself to the different conditions prevailing in its own country. In Egypt, where State power was strong and communism relatively weak, the Communist party was dissolved; in Iraq the party remained in isolation; in Syria there was limited cooperation with the neo-Ba'th. Fairly close contacts were established between the CPSU and the Egyptian ASU and the Syrian neo-Ba'th, whereas relations between Moscow and the Algerian FLN remained more formal and distant. In a series of meetings between leaders of the Arab communist parties in Prague, Vienna, and elsewhere between 1964 and autumn 1967, an attempt was made to work out a common platform with regard to current problems.[51] The parties agreed to support Moscow in its dispute with the Chinese, and in 1968 they gave their blessing to the Soviet occupation of Czechoslovakia. (The Moroccan party was the only one to strike a note of dissent.) There was unanimity with regard to Israel: the struggle against imperialism and Zionism had to be intensified, but, according to a communiqué published in 1968, it was wrong to rely entirely on guerrilla war against Israel 'such as suggested by the Mao Tse-tung clique'. The same communiqué emphasized the necessity to step up the campaign against the rightist trend in the Arab national movement, according to which nationalization and other socialist measures had not worked and should not be continued. Lastly, the dangers of closer cooperation with 'French monopoly capitalism' were stressed.[52]

The attitude of the Arab communist parties with regard to the Arab-Israeli conflict did not substantially differ from that of Nasser and other 'revolutionary democrats'. This made their position in the Arab world much easier than in 1948, when they had the unpopular task of defending the Soviet stand in favour of the partition of Palestine. Now they were swimming with the current. But this raised again the question of the very *raison d'être* of the parties: if they agreed with the 'progressive leadership' of the national movement on all essential points during the transitional period, how was the continued separate existence of the communist parties to be justified?

From the Soviet point of view, the Arab communist parties are of limited use. True, Moscow can rely more on them than on Nasser and the neo-Ba'th, but this is a question of degree, not an issue of principle. Proletarian internationalism has given way to loyalty to the Soviet Union, *tout court*. The Czechoslovak crisis, and before that the dispute with China, have shown the Soviet leaders that they can no longer take the loyalty of many communist parties for granted, whereas non-communist regimes like Egypt and Syria have given them full support. 'Material interest' and political dependence make far more reliable allies than ideological conviction – this is the lesson of the last decade as regards relations between the Soviet Union and outside regimes and parties. With the transition from Bolshevism to a nationalist-socialist policy, the Soviet Union can invoke 'proletarian solidarity' less and less frequently with any hope of success, whereas there are no such problems in its relations with its clients. The links with Arab communism will not be cut, but wherever the respective party is not a factor of major political importance and whenever its existence constitutes an obstacle to Soviet policy in the Middle East, it is bound to come out second best in this conflict of interests.

The Arab communists can have no illusions about their prospects in the years to come. Popular opinion groping for radical solutions to the crisis in the Arab world does not on the whole favour the Soviet brand of communism. The communist parties have to resist growing pressure on the left as well as on the right. They have to cope with the growing disillusion in Russia and communism that has been spreading in the Middle East, and to compete with various other radical ideologies. They still have their faithful cadres and, though a minority, it is not impossible that they may come to power in one or two Arab countries within the framework of a national front. But past experience has shown that these are not likely to be lasting successes: the communists have no chance of becoming popular mass parties in the Middle East unless they adjust themselves to a much greater degree than in the past to the specific conditions in the Arab world. For an independent radical part of the left there are good prospects in the Middle East, but the communists are not yet an independent party and they would have to pay more than lip-service to Islam, to disavow dialectical materialism, and to give up any idea of nationalizing the land. In other words, it would involve their ceasing to be communists and turning into a national-socialist party. This is by no means impossible; they have already gone a long way towards it. Perhaps this is the road on which they may one day succeed, provided, of course, that they prevail over the many competitors who have already staked their claims in this promising field.

10
Conclusion

The Soviet position in the Middle East is stronger today than it was ten years ago. This was not the result of invasion, nor of infiltration by stealth: the Soviet Union became a Middle East power by invitation. It has seized no military bases, but was offered the facilities it wanted by the governments of Egypt and Syria, Algeria and the Yemen, of their own free will. Soviet progress has been gradual, unlike its advance into Eastern Europe after 1944. Not one country has been taken over, no attempt has been made to impose from above the communist political and social system. There have been changes in some countries, but they were the outcome of internal ferment, not outside pressure. Soviet influence has grown not because of the spread of communist ideology, but as the result of efforts made on different levels to make friends and influence people: loans, arms supplies, political assistance, support of the Arab countries against the West and Israel. It has always been Soviet policy to stress that this assistance, in contrast to imperialist aid, is selfless and free of ulterior motives; neither bases nor oil nor political conformity are expected in return. The Soviet Union has been willing to cooperate with kings and sheikhs as well as ultra-radical revolutionaries. The fact that some of these leaders were militantly anti-communist was no obstacle; it complicated relations in some cases, but on the whole Moscow showed great moderation and patience in the face of Egyptian tantrums (in 1959–61), and turned a blind eye to the suppression of communism in Turkey and Iran. Israel was the only exception, but in this instance, too, the reasons for Soviet hostility were not primarily ideological. Having to choose between the Arab states and

Israel, Moscow opted for the bigger battalions, which it thought were also the stronger battalions. The anti-Jewish prejudices of the Soviet leadership should not be under-rated, but what in the last resort prevented a *rapprochement* between Moscow and Jerusalem was not anti-semitism, but the simple fact that Israel was so small. Size has always been of great significance in shaping Soviet attitudes to other countries; more than once this has been the source of political mistakes.

Soviet objectives in the Middle East are easily defined: to remove Western influence in the area and to strengthen the Soviet position there as much as possible. Turkey and Iran have been to some extent neutralized; with the *détente* in world politics, the conviction grew in Ankara and Tehran that the military danger from the north had passed and that the Soviet Union had given up its old annexationist aims. Soviet policy impressed on both countries the benefits that would accrue from closer economic relations. Suspicion of the powerful neighbour did not fade away completely; it emerged again with the appearance of the Soviet fleet in the Mediterranean and Soviet intervention in East-Central Europe in 1968. The change in Turkey's and Iran's foreign policy was not caused by resentment of the West, though this motive was not altogether absent; it was largely due to the shift in the global balance of power and the proximity of these countries to the Soviet Union.

In Syria and Egypt the Soviet Union found more fertile ground, providing scope for closer political collaboration. Anti-Western feeling was, and is, for historical reasons more intense in these Arab countries, the inclination towards extreme political solutions more pronounced. Ideological affinity played a certain role; Western support for the 'reactionary' Arab states was an aggravating factor, and Moscow's hostility to Israel was greatly appreciated in the Arab world. While the emphasis in relations with Turkey and Iran was mainly on economic collaboration, Soviet political and military help was the great attraction for the Arab world. What started in the nineteen-fifties as a 'strictly business transaction' later became a fairly close political alliance. Following the deterioration of the Egyptian economic situation and the Arab defeat in 1967, the dependence of the 'progressive'

Arab countries on the Soviet Union markedly increased. Radical Arab leaders were firmly convinced during the nineteen-fifties that while the West and Israel constituted a mortal threat to Arabism, the Soviet Union for a variety of reasons did not. By the middle sixties they were so deeply immersed in the fight against Israel (and in the struggle for their own political survival) that they had little time or energy to ponder the long-range perspectives, an inability compounded by their capacity for self-delusion and their lack of political experience. While not unaware of their weakness, they felt almost unlimited self-confidence: once having coped with the threat of Zionism, they would successfully defend their independence against all comers.

Soviet successes in the Arab world were striking, but not without their problems. Much money and great efforts were invested in Egypt and Syria, yet the loans and the arms have been used in ways that were not always to Moscow's liking. Egypt and Syria became client states, but not satellites; even after the Six Day War Russia was unable to exert full control in Egypt. It had accepted responsibility, albeit reluctantly, without being always able to impose its will. Soviet help had been provided to make the radical Arab regimes showcases for the superiority of socialism, but their economic achievements were certainly no more striking than those of the 'conservative' countries. The weakness of the radical regimes had some indirect advantage, for it strengthened their dependence on the Soviet Union, but it was hardly a good advertisement for the efficiency of communism.

When the Western powers were the dominating force in the Middle East, they had the monopoly of committing mistakes, whereas the Soviet Union, not being involved in Middle East affairs, enjoyed a great deal of prestige precisely because of its apparent position as a dispassionate, seemingly remote onlooker without any specific interests in the area. But as it became involved in Middle East politics, it had to make choices: it could no longer please everyone, and the aura of disinterested altruism began to disappear. It was Soviet policy to extend its influence without provoking a frontal clash with the United States. Frequently this proved only too easy; there was nothing the United States could do about the internal politics of Syria and Egypt, or a *coup* by radical forces in other Arab countries. Time and circumstances seemed to be working for the Soviet Union in the Middle East, but not always. Whenever the Soviet protégés ran into trouble, direct Soviet intervention became necessary, and this naturally involved risks. Notwithstanding Soviet reservations about its client states, a major setback suffered by any one of them was almost automatically interpreted as a Soviet defeat, and reluctance to come to the help of the 'progressives' was regarded as an admission of weakness. The establishment of client states had a logic and a momentum of its own. It is difficult to get out of obligations and cut losses; having gained footholds in the Middle East, the Soviet Union became increasingly involved in crisis situations it could not fully control; having provided considerable economic assistance to Egypt for more than a decade, Moscow could not discontinue its aid, however costly the venture and however unpromising the long-term prospects. In the past, a substantial part of this burden had been borne by the other East European countries, but they were increasingly reluctant to shoulder this load indefinitely. The complications arising from the supply of arms are even more serious. Arms deals were from the Soviet point of view the most effective way of undermining the Western position in the Middle East and winning friends in the Arab world. But the arms were not delivered as a straightforward business transaction; they gave the Soviet Union a vested interest in the fortunes of Egypt and Syria, the Yemen and Algeria, and it became identified with them. The Arab defeat in 1967 thus adversely affected Soviet prestige. The re-equipment of the Arab armies became necessary, regardless of cost, and has thus involved Soviet prestige even more than in the past. Yet another Arab defeat by Israel must appear well-nigh intolerable in Soviet eyes, but since it has no full control over the armies of the UAR and Syria, and since its capacity to intervene in a war is probably still limited, the Soviet position is not without hazards.

The build-up of a Soviet Mediterranean fleet entails similar problems. The absence of a striking force has served in the past as a plausible reason for refraining from direct if limited military intervention, comparable to the landing of American troops in the Lebanon in 1958. With a substantial fleet in the Mediterranean, the Soviet Union can make its presence felt more directly by showing the flag not only in the Mediterranean, but eventually in the Persian Gulf and the Indian Ocean as well. It has raised Soviet prestige and forced all Mediterranean and Middle East countries to recognize the growing Soviet strength in the area. At the same time it enhances the risks: in the event of a conflict, Soviet policy-makers face the choice of backing down or of escalating a local conflict into a much wider confrontation.

There are other problems, some of them caused by the uneven advance of Soviet influence in the Middle East. The very fact that Syria at one stage moved far towards a radical system frightened Syria's neighbours, and made them more aware of the dangers involved. The Soviet Union would have preferred to encourage Syria without antagonizing its neighbours, but this was not possible. The decision would have been less painful had it been a straightforward choice between 'rising' and 'declining' forces. But in reality the state of affairs is far more intricate: the basis of the national-socialist regimes in Syria, Egypt, and Algeria, not to mention the Yemen, continues to be fragile; their overthrow from within is by no means excluded. National rivalries further complicate the situation: the Soviet Union wants to be on good terms with Greece and Turkey, with Turkey and Syria, with Iran and Iraq, despite the conflicts between these respective pairs. It would like to support Tudeh and the Shah, the Turkish communists and their enemies, the Iraqi opposition and government. The list of policy dilemmas is long, covering every Middle East country, both on the domestic level and in its relations with other states. In most cases a choice has to be made, and this usually implies antagonizing someone.

There is also the eternal problem of priorities. The Soviet Union has had to pay for its new status as a Middle East power $6–8 billion in military aid alone. In a war the cost in terms of money is hardly ever counted, let alone disputed. In peacetime, on the other hand, the cost of economic and military assistance is open to scrutiny and comparison. Few questions are likely to be asked while the going is good, but when there are setbacks the value of the investment is liable to come up for debate: would the cause of socialism not have been better served by using the billions of rubles given to Egypt for domestic economic purposes? The Soviet Union is a big country, but can it go on providing for a growing number of destitute client states? Financial considerations rarely figure in the discussion of decisive political issues, but there are priorities, and the place of the Middle East in the scale of Soviet political aims is likely to be re-examined from time to time in terms of loss and gain, especially if there should be unforeseen difficulties.

What, then, are the short-term Soviet aims in the area? The rapid transformation of the radical-nationalist regimes into fully fledged satellites is certainly not among them. It would give the Soviet Union few benefits it does not already possess. Further nationalization in the 'progressive' countries would not necessarily bring them more securely into the Soviet orbit, whatever the ideologists may claim. It would be desirable from the Soviet point of view if power in the radical Arab countries came to rest in the hands of a disciplined and ideologically trained *élite*, but this is unlikely to happen in the near future. The present *élites* are on the whole pro-Soviet; Oriental communism is unlikely to be affected by the liberal and democratic deviations of Western communism. The danger of national communism, on the other hand, is equally strong in East and West, and no cure has so far been found for it. There is also the constant temptation for communists in the third world to play Peking against Moscow and vice versa. These are real problems and the Soviet Union will have to live with them for a long time.

The present state of affairs has many advantages for Moscow, and its perpetuation seems to be the aim of Soviet policy in the Middle East. Important positions have been gained during the last decade and it seems wiser to consolidate them than to press for full satellization of the pro-Soviet regimes. Whether the Soviet Union will have things all its own way is less certain, for Middle East politics have a life of their own; sooner or later outside powers find themselves confronted with situations they did not envisage in their political planning.

The Soviet Union owes its successes in the Middle East in the final analysis to a number of happy coincidences. It did not have to work very hard to realize its aims. The key to success was not a 'correct Marxist-Leninist' appraisal, nor the triumph of the local communist parties; not loans or credits, nor very cunning diplomacy. Moscow did not gate-crash; it was invited to become a major Middle East power by Egypt and Syria. In many respects the Soviet Union was an ideal ally for the radical Arab leaders – powerful, but not so wealthy as to provoke feelings of envy. Ideologically it was far better suited to the radical mood prevailing in the Arab world than Western democracy or liberalism. The Soviet Union became a leading Middle East power because it was militarily strong and geographically close, and it is therefore idle to speculate whether its advance could have been prevented. With the West in retreat, the Middle East became a power vacuum, bound to be filled by the most powerful neighbour. Arab enmity towards Israel was certainly important, but it was an aggravating circumstance, not the decisive factor. The inroads Moscow has made in the Yemen and Algeria, in the Sudan and Somalia, show that it has improved its position even in countries where Israel was not a major issue. But was not the Arab decision to tie their fortunes to the Soviet Union extremely shortsighted? What if victory over Israel could be achieved only at a formidable price – namely, growing dependence on Russia? In a long-term view, the Arab leaders need the West more than the West needs them, simply because nature has placed them in the vicinity of the super-power with the greater appetite and the fewer scruples. Their chances of remaining independent without the support of an outside power cannot be rated very high. Many Arabs are uneasily aware of the grave problems they face, but their leaders reassure them: the Soviet Union is totally different from the Western imperialists, asks for nothing in return, nor does it aspire to dominate the area. All fears are therefore misplaced.

What direction is Soviet policy likely to take in the years to come, and how are the Middle East countries likely to react? There are no certainties, only trends and possibilities, and about these, too, it is now more difficult to speculate than before. The Middle East political scene is forever changing; it cannot be analysed in isolation from all other major political and military problems in the contemporary world.

Seen from the present, the future of the Middle East depends above all on internal developments in the Soviet Union and, to a lesser extent, on the United States. Essentially, the Soviet Union has become a conservative society with a superstructure of revolutionary ideological phraseology; its appeal as the home of communism scarcely extends beyond its own borders; the idea of world revolution was abandoned long ago. But the Soviet leaders still feel they have to expand their sphere of influence, their own *cordon sanitaire*. Once a sphere of influence is established there is a temptation to look for yet another beyond it, to make it quite secure: empire-building is a self-generating business. They know that, as a Russian eighteenth-century statesman said, 'that which stops growing begins to decay'. As the Soviet Union reaches strategic parity with the United States, there is greater readiness to follow a high-risk policy in areas thought to be non-vital to America. It has entered a stage of transformation, but not, as was widely assumed after Stalin's death, into a more liberal and democratic system. The Soviet leaders cannot dissociate themselves altogether from the old beliefs because this would undermine the legitimacy of their rule. In competition with China for leadership over the camp, if for no other reason, they are under strong pressure to keep up the revolutionary posture and to pursue a militant foreign policy.

The paradox of Soviet development is that while militarily the country has become so much stronger during the last twenty years, politically it is far weaker than under Stalin, when no opposition was tolerated inside Russia or the Soviet bloc. Power has passed into the hands of bureaucrats, men without any marked interest in ideas or theories. They have no clear concept of the future, but take the existing order of things for granted and want to prevent any major change. The political weakness, the many conflicts inside the Soviet bloc and within the Soviet Union itself, are not necessarily conducive to a policy of *détente*; there is many a historical precedent for escape into activism.

At the present time Soviet foreign policy seems closer to that of Ivan Kalita and Ivan the Terrible than to that of Lenin. The emergence of one supreme leader is a distinct possibility, but there are a great many others besides. While orthodox Marxism-Leninism was the guiding principle, it was not too difficult to understand and sometimes to predict Soviet attitudes, despite the distortions of the 'cult of the individual'. It was relatively easy to imagine how a well-disciplined Marxist-Leninist would behave in a given situation, but it is becoming more difficult each year to anticipate the reactions of the latter-day Bolshevik, whose ideology is a mixture of many strange elements, and whose attitude fluctuates unpredictably between extreme caution and surprising recklessness. During the sixties there was an understanding with the United States about spheres of influence, and certain rules of the game are still observed. But with strategic parity the question of the rules of the game and of a re-division of spheres of influence is bound to be reopened. The Soviet Union has pursued a foreign policy that even from a position of relative weakness did not lack drive or self-confidence; how far will it go in a position of strength? The Middle East is in geopolitical terms Russia's back garden; this at any rate is how Soviet leaders see it. They seem to believe that an area so close to their borders should become their sphere of influence.

The stability of the sixties and the rules of the games were based on the credibility of the American deterrent. As strategic parity is reached, some American commitments are bound to re-examined in the light of a new world situation. It will be asked to what extent American national interest is involved in the defence of the Middle East. Less, no doubt, than Russia's; much less than Europe's. The Middle East has long ceased to be geographically important; there are no cross-roads in the air age. Military bases in the area are desirable, but by no means essential; the ICBM has changed all that. The United States is not a major importer of oil; less than 3 per cent of the oil consumed in America comes from the Middle East. True, the production cost of Middle East oil is among the lowest in the world; but this concerns above all the oil companies. As far as American national interest is concerned, Middle East oil is not a decisive factor at this stage. There are ties of friendship between the United States and some Middle East nations: Turkey, a NATO member, Israel, and a few others. Neoisolationists will no doubt argue that their fate is not a matter of life and death for America. Yet the fate of the area as a whole will remain a matter of supreme concern to all American policy-makers, for if it were to become an exclusive Soviet sphere of interest the repercussions on the world situation would be immediate and far-reaching. It would decisively shift the balance of power and would have incalculable consequences all over the world.

It was generally believed in Washington during the sixties that, given a strong military presence in the Middle East, the Soviet Union would not deliberately enter on a course of action that would bring about an escalation of the conflict on to the global scale. Despite the traditional Russian interest in the Middle East, the Soviet Union has no vital economic stake in the region, nor does the Middle East constitute a military threat. The Soviet drive to the south is basically a forward political-prestige operation, potentially rewarding, but not essential. Hence there is a good chance in Washington's view that due caution is likely to be exercised in Moscow with regard to the risks involved. But there remain several major question-marks. Centrifugal forces have been at work for a long period in both West and East, but the process has not been symmetrical: whereas in the Soviet Union the feeling of political weakness may well lead into an escape into action, it is strengthening neo-isolationism in the United States. As the Soviet leaders realize that it is becoming more and more difficult to hold the empire built by Stalin, their methods are likely to become more repressive rather than more tolerant. There is not the slightest doubt that they want to keep what they have, and this can be achieved only by extending their spheres of influence. The feeling of weakness adds urgency to this belief.

In America, on the other hand, the Vietnam war has strengthened latent isolationist feelings, to which is added the fear of overcommitment and a growing belief, not only among the pacifists and the New Left, that America should attend to its domestic problems and stop playing the world's policeman. Since the White House, the State Department, and even the Pentagon do not take their decisions in a vacuum, but are influenced by public opinion, it will depend in the last resort on domestic developments whether and how vigorously America will defend its interests in the Middle East.

As the Soviet pressure grows, the call for a more active American policy is likely to emanate from Europe, Asia, and the Middle East. In the view of many Europeans and Asians, American interventionism and the cold-war mentality used to be the main threat; in future they may come to regard American isolationism as the main danger. Soviet foreign policy is likely to concentrate on the areas adjacent to the Soviet Union in Europe, on the Middle East and Asia. As a result, Americans now feel less concerned about Soviet policies than those geographically nearer to the Soviet Union who have begun to realize that the roles are about to be reversed and that an immediate threat will affect them far more than the Americans.

The inability of West Europe to overcome its internal divisions, to develop a political will and a policy of its own, and its political and military impotence, is the great tragedy of the post-war period. West Europe still has far more vital interests in the Middle East than America, but it has found itself totally incapable of asserting its influence and pursuing an active European policy in the area. Twenty years after the end of the war, West Europe has abdicated in the Middle East, and this despite the fact that it is economically stronger than the Soviet Union and in most other respects potentially its equal. The resistance to European unity, first by the British, later by de Gaulle, has virtually reduced Europe's influence to nil; and nowhere is the decline more palpable than in the Middle East.

A small country, however stable internally, is not normally able to resist prolonged and determined pressure by a superior power; Czechoslovakia in 1938 and again in 1968 is an obvious illustration. The advent of the atomic bomb changed this, at least for a while, creating a unique constellation from which the small countries benefited. The global equilibrium and the overriding threat of nuclear war tied the hands of the big powers and made it possible even for small countries to retain their independence, sometimes in open defiance of their much stronger neighbours. But it is by no means certain that this particular constellation will last forever. It is already argued that real independence has become impossible in the long run without a nuclear capacity. The smaller countries are likely to become vulnerable once more; they will be able to resist a super-power which is firmly resolved to impose its political will and has the power to do so only if they are united and internally stable. On both these counts the Middle East scores very low. Its internal problems are immense. Peace and stability seem to be as far away as ever, and further violent upheavals appear almost inevitable in the Arab world. There will be more revolutions and quasi-revolutions, but the experience of two decades has created scepticism about the effects of revolutionary action: so far it has produced no achievements which arouse marked enthusiasm. Economic progress and the rate of modernization in Iran has been impressive, and substantial advances have been made by Turkey during the last decade. But the starting-point was abysmally low in both countries, and the time needed to catch up has to be measured in decades rather than years. Economic progress by itself will not, moreover, solve the political problems; on the contrary, it will probably aggravate them and precipitate social change, non-violent or violent. It is doubtful whether the Middle East monarchies will survive for very long; they are too much out of tune with the *Zeitgeist*, although they are not necessarily less efficient or more corrupt than the radical *élites*; the transition from monarchy to military dictatorship will not by itself resolve many problems. No Middle East junta has been strikingly successful so far. Only Turkey and Israel have democratically elected governments. So, within limits, has the Lebanon. Whether the multi-party system will be able to weather the coming storms in these countries is a question that cannot be answered with confidence.

No solution is in sight for the crisis of the Arab world. The conflict with Israel overshadows at present its deeper problems. There is growing bitterness and frustration, and as the destruction of Israel does not seem near, the Arab masses are likely to turn sooner or later against the Arab governments of the day which have been unable to fulfil most of their promises. The economic prospects of some Arab countries are not as unpromising as Egypt's, but most of their energies are sapped and their resources squandered on the military build-up. Egypt's long-term economic prospects would no doubt improve if it gained control over the oilfields of Libya (having so far failed to do so on the Arabian peninsula). But in view of the heavy emotional involvement in the Israeli issue, it is not at all certain how public opinion would react to such a deflection from a war of revenge. Even an Arab victory over Israel would immediately create new problems. It might lessen Arab dependence on the Soviet Union, but the struggle for domination in the Arab world would become more intense; there are many candidates for ruling Palestine and Jordan. The fight between 'radicals' and 'conservatives' (and among the radicals themselves), submerged at the present time, would immediately enter a new and more bitter phase. Since no one leader and no one country is strong enough to unite the Arab world, all indications point to a long period of internal strife. Future wars between the Arab states and Israel seem almost inevitable, but a total Arab victory is unlikely. Meanwhile, the drift towards anarchy in the Arab world seems to be continuing. All immediate political problems apart, there is a deep-seated malaise throughout the area, dissatisfaction with established ideologies and institutions, with governments and society, 'conservative' and 'radical' alike. Among the intelligentsia both Islam and communism are losing ground, democracy is unattainable, planned economy has not worked, military dictatorships have been strong on propaganda, but on little else besides. Nor is Arab nationalism much of a guide to the perplexed. This breakdown of old, established beliefs and values, and the absence of new ones to replace them, is producing a crisis deeper and more intractable than the transient political problems now plaguing these countries, and the growing sense of despair leads them to seek ultra-radical solutions, resulting in incessant changes of government, stagnation, and decline. Perhaps one day the vicious circle will be broken by a new idea or a new leader or movement of national and social renaissance. Today no such saviour is in sight. This drift towards anarchy may not cause undue concern among the Russians. For Israel it would remove the immediate danger; whether it would be a blessing in the long term is more doubtful. It would mean that Israel would not be able to talk to anyone in authority in the Arab world. But negotiate at some future date they must. The only alternative is a permanent struggle in which they cannot afford to lose a single battle and cannot gain a lasting, decisive victory. Zionism had two basic aims: to restore dignity to the Jewish people and to give it security. It has succeeded in the first part of its programme, but security is as far away as ever. Immigration remains the cardinal problem, but a mass influx of American or Soviet Jewry, the two great remaining reservoirs, is highly unlikely in the foreseeable future. That being so, the historical mission of Zionism has changed its character and the state of Israel will have to come to terms with its new function, not on the basis of some ultimate goal, but in its present shape and prospects.

The Arab-Israeli conflict has all but monopolized public interest in Middle East tensions. But there is also the Yemen and the struggle for South Arabia, the Persian Gulf, the unsolved problem of Cyprus, and a great many other equally explosive issues. Nowhere are the problems of the area near a solution, and the internal weakness of the Middle East is bound to make it an easy prey. But as the Soviet military presence becomes more palpable, and its political implications more obvious, America (and the West) may find itself in greater demand than at present as a counterforce to Soviet pressure. The Soviet Union was welcomed in the fifties and sixties as a counterforce against 'Western imperialism'. Since then the political scene has radically changed, and it is gradually coming to be understood that the domination of the Middle East by one great power is not in the best interests of any country in the area. In some capitals it will no doubt take a little time to grasp and digest this, and no radical change in attitude can be expected in a few months or years. But there is a good chance that self-interest and the instinct of survival will eventually make most, though perhaps not all, of these countries recognize these basic facts and act accordingly. If this analysis is correct, the political (in contrast to the military) problems facing the West in the Middle East will ease in the years to come.

Meanwhile, there is the constant danger of local military conflicts escalating into a wider conflagration. Lasting agreement between the two super-powers seems a distant possibility despite the temporary meeting of minds in the talks in New York in 1969 about the Arab-Israeli deadlock. The drive to the south is one of the traditional directions of Russian foreign policy; with the retreat of the West the Middle East has become a power vacuum, and the emergence of China as a great power, hostile to the Soviet Union, has given additional impetus to Soviet activities there and in the Indian subcontinent. Yet it is unlikely that the Soviet Union will be in physical control of the area in the foreseeable future, and there remains a strong element of uncertainty in all these calculations. Moscow may be drawn more deeply than it wants into the problems of the area, whose objective importance is limited. It has been said about Vietnam that it became important mainly because the Americans decided to send an army there. The same applies to the Middle East: the Soviet advance now gives it a significance it would not otherwise have. It is an unfortunate by-product of this advance that it aggravates most of the internal problems of the Middle East. Montesquieu once said: 'Happy the nations whose annals of history are boring to read.' The boring years in the Middle East were always the happy ones. It would be a great contribution to peace in the area if the world's attention was not permanently focused on it. There may be no cure for its sicknesses, but it would alleviate them if the problems were reduced to their real size: Middle East conflicts flourish in the limelight and begin to wither when ignored. Unfortunately, the Middle East is unlikely to be ignored in the years to come; it will probably get more than its share of attention. There are no certainties: the Soviet Union may be deflected from its pre-occupation with the Middle East by increasing unrest in Eastern Europe, by the growing menace of China, or by internal problems that cannot even be foreseen. The struggle for power among the Soviet leaders may sooner or later again enter an acute phase. But all this will rather contribute to instability than to peace. The permanent Middle East crisis will in all probability be further aggravated, and the whole area could be one of the main zones of conflict in the turbulent years that seem to lie ahead.

Notes

Notes

Chapter 3

1. On recent developments in Turkey and Turkish-Soviet relations: Gasratyan, M. A., *Turtsiya v 1960–63 godakh*, Moscow, 1965; Mango, Andrew, 'Turkey in the Middle East', *Journal of Contemporary History* (July 1968); Kannapin, Hans Eckhardt, '*Die türkisch-Sowjetischen Beziehungen seit 1960*', Osteuropa (1967), 2; Fernau, F. W., '*Nachbarschaft am Schwarzen Meer*', Europa Archiv (1967), 17; Eren, Nuri, '*Die türkisch-sowjetischen Beziehungen*', ibid. (1965), 9; a series of eight articles in *Yeni Gazete* (December 19, 1966 et seq.); Vdovichenko, D. I., *Borba politicheskikh partii v Turtsii,* Moscow, 1967; Rozaliev, Yu. N., *Klassy i Klassovaia borba v Turtsii*, Moscow, 1966.

2. *Izvestia*, 30 December 1953.

3. *Cumhuriyet* (Ankara), 5–15 December 1961.

4. *Krasnaia Zvezda*, 14 and 28 December 1961.

5. Kannapin, loc. cit., p. 119.

6. *Yeni Istanbul*, 12 March 1963.

7. For subsequent appeals of similar character see *Sosyal Adalet*, December 1965; Kannapin, loc. cit., p. 124. On the Soviet appraisal of socialist and pseudo-socialist forces in Turkey, Gasanova, E. Yu., in *Narody Azii i Afriki* (1965), 1, (1968), 3.

8. Including *Vatan Milliyet*, and *Cumhuriyet*. See also Kannapin, loc. cit., p. 121.

9. *Pravda*, 10 December 1964.

10. Kannapin, loc. cit., p. 123.

11. Our Radio (broadcasting station in Eastern Europe of the Turkish Communist party), 25 June 1966.

12. Our Radio, 4 February 1967.

13. ibid.

14. Statement of the Central Committee of the Turkish Communist party dated 25 February 1967, broadcast over Our Radio, 13 March 1967.

15. Our Radio, 17 March 1967.

16. Tass International Service, 19 December 1966.

17. Reuter, 3 March 1964.

18. *Izvestia*, 25 January 1965.

19. *Novoe Vremia*, 19 August 1966.

20. Moscow Radio, 19 December 1966.

21. *Neue Zürcher Zeitung*, 22 and 23 December 1966.

22. *Izvestia*, 24 December 1966.

23. ibid.

24. *Akis*, 27 June 1966.

25. Tass, 27 December 1966.

26. Ugolkov in *Pravda*, 5 April 1967.

27. Our Radio, 7 April 1967.

28. Tass, 29 September 1967.

29. *New York Times*, 11 October 1967.

30. loc. cit.

31. *Sovetskaia Rossiya*, 19 September 1967.

32. Tanju, Sadun, in *Ulus*, 5 October 1967.

33. *New Times*, 17 April 1968; *Izvestia*, 1 June 1968; *Za Rubezhom*, 30 May 1968.

34. Orkunt, Sezai, in *Cumhuriyet*, 9 November 1967.

35. *Krasnaia Zvezda*, 3 September 1966.

36. Ulman, Haluk, in *Cumhuriyet*, 20 December 1966.

37. Quoted in *Christian Science Monitor*, 27 May 1968.

38. OECD: *Turkey* (Paris, July 1967), p. 29.

39. *Neue Zürcher Zeitung*, 10 February 1967.

40. *New York Times*, 9 June 1968.

41. Laqueur, W., *The Soviet Union and the Middle East*, London, 1959, pp. 207–8; on Soviet-Iranian relations in the nineteen-fifties; Alekseev, L., *Sovetskii Soyuz i Iran*, Moscow, 1963; Agakhi, A., *Rasprostranenie idei Marksizma-Leninizma v Irane*, Baku, 1961; Ivanov, M. S., *Noveishaia Istoriia Irana*, Moscow, 1965.

42. *Pravda*, 2 July 1954, 16 March 1955.

43. *Middle East Record*, 1960, p. 65.

44. ibid.

45. *Pravda*, 16 September 1962.

46. Kasatkin in *International Affairs* (Moscow) (April 1968); Tuganova, O. E., in *Mezhdunarodnie otnosheniya na blizhnem i srednem Vostoke*, Moscow, 1967, 268.

47. Avery, Peter, in *The World Today*, July 1965.

48. Konstantinov, G., in *Aziia i Afrika Sevodnia*, June 1962, 58.

49. *Izvestia*, 16 September 1962.

50. Volodarsky, M. I., in *Narody Azii i Afriki* (1966) 3, 154.

51. Ivanov, M. S., op. cit., p. 246.

52. Shatalov, I., in *International Affairs*, May 1968.

53. *Mizan Newsletter* (September 1966), 214–15.

54. National Voice of Iran (Communist broadcasting station in Eastern Europe), 24 January 1967.

55. ibid., 23 January 1967.

56. Statement of the CC, People's Party of Iran, in *Information Bulletin* (31 March 1966).

57. Eskandari, Iraj, in *World Marxist Review* (May 1965), 45–54.

58. Radmanesh, Reza, in *World Marxist Review* (November 1967), 21.

59. Paklin, N., in *Izvestia*, 21 September 1966.

60. Meyer-Ranke, Peter, '*Iran's neue Rolle: Ordnungsmacht in Mittelost*', *Aussenpolitik* (May 1968), 300.

61. *Pravda*, 4 March 1968.

62. For a recent Soviet analysis of Iran's economic development, see Ivanov, M., '*Tendentsii razvitiia Ekonomiki Irana*' in *Mirovaia Ekonomika i Mezhdunarodnie Otnosheniya* (December 1967). See also Kasatkin, loc. cit.

63. *New York Times*, 15 March 1968.

64. Hartshorn, J. E., *Oil Companies and Governments*, London, 1967, 324–5.

65. *Christian Science Monitor*, 15 March 1968.

66. *Petroleum Press Service* (April 1968), p. 127.

67. Rachkov, Boris, in *International Affairs* (April 1966), 15.

68. Kasatkin, D., in *International Affairs* (January 1967), 94; Soskin, B., in *Bakinskii Rabochii*, 8 December 1966.

69. Radio Peyk-e Iran, 18 January 1967, and other broadcasts in December 1966 and January 1967.

70. Arabadzhian, A. Z., in *Narody Azii i Afriki*, (1968), 2.

71. Moscow Radio, 17 February 1968.

72. Spandarian, V., in *New Times*, 29 March 1968.

73. Arabadzhian, loc. cit.; see also *New York Times*, 15 March 1968.

74. ibid., 14 July 1966.

75. ibid., 19 September 1966.

76. Radio Peyk-e Iran, 4 March 1967.

77. *Christian Science Monitor*, 8 December 1967; *New York Times*, 22 May 1968.

78. Radio Peyk-e Iran 16 December 1965; National Voice of Iran, 16 December 1965.

Chapter 4

1. See Ivanov, K., and Scheinis, Z., *Gosudarstvo Izrail, evo Polozhenie i Politika*, 2nd ed., Moscow, 1959; Leonidov, A., *Za Kulisami izrailskoi politiki*, Moscow, 1959. Almost all articles in Soviet newspapers and periodicals on Jewish topics and Israel have been reprinted in *Evrei i evreiski Narod* (1959–in progress) and (selectively) in *Jews in Eastern Europe* (1959–in progress).

2. Kichko, T. K., *Iudaizm bez Prikraz*, Moscow, 1964.

3. *Komsomolskaia Pravda*, 4 October 1967.

4. For the war scare of May 1966: *Al Ba'th* (Damascus), 1–5 May 1966; *Izvestia*, 7 May 1966; *Arab World*, 9 May, 1966; *Pravda*, 21 May 1966; Tass statement, 27 May 1966; Moscow Radio interview with Ibrahim Makhus, Syrian Foreign Minister 29 May 1966; *Jewish Observer*, 3 June 1966; *Washington Post*, 28 May 1966.

5. *New York Times*, 3 March 1968, referring to the trial of Shams al Badran, Egyptian minister of war during the crisis.

6. The various possibilities are discussed in some detail in my *The Road to War*, London 1968, Chapter 3.

7. *Izvestia*, 30 May 1967; Mayevsky in *Pravda*, 1 June, 1967.

8. *Izvestia*, 20 May 1967.

9. Mayevsky in *Pravda*, 21 May 1967.

10. *Pravda*, 1 June 1967.

11. *Izvestia*, 3 and 4 June 1967.

12. *Pravda*, 24 May 1967.

13. Laqueur, *The Road to War*, 138–9.

14. *Pravda*, 10 June 1968.

15. Tanjug, 15 June 1968.

16. Radio Moscow, 16 June 1968.

17. *Izvestia*, 15 June 1968.

18. *Sovetskaia Rossiya*, 23 June 1968.

19. *Krashaia Zvezda*, 17 June; *Pravda Ukrainy*, 18 June 1967.

20. *Trud*, 23 June; *Krasnaia Zvezda*, 4 July 1967.

21. *Krokodil*, 19 June 1967.

22. *Komsomolskaia Pravda*, 8 August 1967.

23. Primakov in *Pravda*, 13 and 14 June 1967.

24. In a series of six articles in *Pravda* between 27 July and 9 August 1967. See also Astakhov, K., in *International Affairs* (October 1967).

25. Ivanov, K., In *Mezhdunarodnaia Zhizn* (June 1968), 16.

26. Volsky, D., in *Mirovaia Ekonomika i Mezhdunarodnie Otnosheniya* (August 1967), 24.

27. Beliaev in *Pravda*, 3 July 1968.

28. Beliaev and Primakov in *Za Rubezhom*, 22 September 1967.

29. Mirsky, G., in *New Times*, 5 June 1968.

30. ibid.

31. ibid.

32. *Nedelya* (Moscow), 18 June 1967.

33. '*Obozrevatel*' in *Pravda*, 13 April 1968.

34. Such as the resolution adopted by the Warsaw meeting of the East European Foreign Ministers. *Soviet News*, 2 January 1968.

35. Ivanov, K., loc. cit., 18–19.

36. For instance, Davico, O., in *Komunist* (Belgrade), 28 March 1968.

37. Soviet books about Israel and the Six Day War include Beliaev and Primakov, *Golub spushchen*, Moscow, 1967, and Demchenko, P., *Arabskii Vostok v chas ispitanii*, Moscow, 1967.

Chapter 5

1. *Egyptian Gazette*, 26 April, 11 June 1960.

2. Laqueur, W., *The Soviet Union and the Middle East*, London, 1959, *passim*.

3. Haykal, Muhamad Hasanain, in *Al Ahram*, 22 January 1965.

4. On the Soviet-Egyptian crisis of 1959 see Smolanski, Oles M., 'Moscow-Cairo Crisis 1959' in *Slavic Review* (1963), 713–26; John H. Burnett's dissertation, Chapter 5.

5. Nasser's speech on 23 December 1958, in *Al Gumhuriya*, 24 December 1958. See also his speeches in Damascus on 11, 12, 13, 15, 20, 22 March and at the Officers Club, Cairo, 25 April 1959, translated in Khalil, Muhammad (ed.), *The Arab States and the Arab League*, Beirut, 1965, 946–82.

6. Hafid, Karim, in *World Marxist Review*, June 1960.   See also the editorial in *World Marxist Review*, August 1960, and Mahmud, Faruq, ibid., March 1960.

7. *Pravda*, 17 March 1959; *Al Gumhuriya*, 23 and 31 March 1959; *New York Times*, 20 March 1959.

8. ibid., 23 March 1959.

9. *Pravda*, 30 March 1959.

10. *Mideast Mirror* (Beirut), 5 April 1959.

11. *New York Times*, 22 February 1959.

12. *Pravda*, 30 March 1959.

13. *New York Times*, 21 May 1959.

14. *Al Ahram* (Cairo), 9 May 1960.

15. ibid., 19 and 20 May 1960.

16. *New York Times*, 22 January 1960.

17. Cairo Radio, 12 October 1960.

18. On the Douglas amendment and the 'Cleopatra' incident: *New York Times*, 22 April – 1 May 1960; *Jerusalem Post*, 21 April – 6 May 1960; *Al Gumhuriya*, 18 April – 10 May 1960.

19. *Mirovaia Ekonomika i Mezhdunarodnie Otnosheniya*, June 1964, p. 75.

20. Beliaev and Cheprakov in *Kommunist*, June 1964.

21. Mayevsky in *Pravda*, 24 August 1961.

22. Mayevsky in *Mezhdunarodnaia Zhizn*, July 1966.

23. '*Obozrevatel*' in *Pravda*, 31 May 1961.

24. *Al Gumhuriya*, 5 and 6 June 1961.

25. *New York Times*, 8 June 1961.

26. *Pravda*, 2 May 1962.

27. Mirsky, G., in *New Times*, 1962, 4.

28. Mirsky, G., in *Mirovaia Ekonomika i Mezhdunarodnie Otnosheniia* February 1964, 22.

29. Ra'anan, Uri, 'Moscow and the Third World' in *Problems of Communism*, January 1965.

30. Nassar, Fuad, 'On Arab Unity', *World Marxist Review*, February 1964, p. 22.

31. Beliaev, I., *Pravda*, 27 March 1964.

32. Khrushchev's speeches in Cairo (10 May 1964); Aswan (16 May 1964); Cairo (20 May 1964); and Moscow (27 May 1964).

33. *Pravda*, 24 May 1964.

34. Khrushchev at the banquet on 18 May 1964. In the Radio Moscow version this became 'should it become necessary to repel the schemes of the aggressor'.

35. *Mideast Mirror*, 26 September 1964; Tass, 23 September 1964; *Al Akhbar*, 23 September 1964; Cairo Radio, 29 September 1964.

36. *New York Times*, 5 September 1964.

37. *World Marxist Review*, November 1964, 71–80; *Pravda*, 11 December 1964; Tiagunenko in *Krasnaia Zvezda*, 11 October 1964.

38. *Al Ahram*, 29 May 1964.

39. ibid., 23 October 1964.

40. *Pravda*, 11 December 1964.

41. Simoniia, N. A., in *Narody Azii i Afriki*, 1966, 6.

42. On Malik's mission see Middle East News Agency (MENA), Cairo, 13 November 1964.

43. On Shelepin's visit see *Mideast Mirror*, 2 January 1965.

44. *Al Ahram*, 6 November 1964; Tass, 11 November 1964.

45. Mikoyan's and Nasser's speeches, Radio Moscow, 31 August 1965; joint communiqué, MENA, 1 September 1965; see also *Arab World*, 31 August, 2, 3 September 1965.

46. *Al Ahram*, 3 September 1965.

47. *Arab World*, 6 September 1965.

48. *Pravda*, 18 May 1966.

49. ibid., 19 May 1966.

50. ibid., 20 May 1966.

51. Tanjug in English, 29 March 1967, quoted by Kimche, D., and Bawly, D., *The Sandstorm*, London, 1968, 51.

52. *Ekonomicheskaia Gazeta*, 1967, 21, 45.

53. Smetanin, N., in *International Affairs*, July 1965, 39.

54. Primakov in *Pravda*, 8 August 1966; Beliaev in *Pravda*, 23 July 1966.

55. Beliaev and Primakov in *Pravda*, 29 October 1966.

56. *Jewish Observer and Middle East Review*, 31 December 1965, 11 March 1966; Smith, Hedrick, in *New York Times*, 5 April 1966; Hottinger, Arnold, in *Neue Zürcher Zeitung*, 2 May 1967.

57. Grishechkin, K. I., in Goncharov, L. V. (ed.), *Ekonomika Afriki*, Moscow, 1965; Garshin, I. I., in Zhukov, Y. M. (ed.), *Sovremennie Teorii Sotsializma*, Moscow, 1967; Kiselev, V., in *Mirovaia Ekonomika i Mezhdunarodnie Otnosheniia* (1963), 10. These discussions have been conveniently summarized in *Mizan Newsletter*, April 1964, 'Differing Views on the UAR', March 1966, 'The UAR and Proletarian Dictatorship', and January 1968, 'UAR and USSR: The Dialogue of Socialism'.

58. On the Cairo Seminar, October 1966, on 'National and Social Revolution in Africa' see *Problems of Peace and Socialism*, December 1966, *International Affairs*, January 1967, and *Mizan Newsletter*, March 1967.

59. Repin, A., in *Novoe Vremia*, 5 July 1968, 5.

60. Beliaev and Primakov, *Pravda* 31 July 1967.

61. ibid.

62. *New Times*, 1967, 26, 7.

63. *Za Rubezhom*, 1967, 27, 7–8.

64. Moscow Radio (in Arabic), 8 July 1967.

65. Primakov, Tass, 26 and 28 April 1968.

66. Quoted in *The Guardian*, 1 March 1968.

67. Primakov in *Novoe Vremia*, 16 February 1968.

68. In a cable to Brezhnev, Kosygin, and Podgorny, United Press report, 26 July 1968.

69. *Look* interview, *New York Times*, 12 March 1968.

70. Nasser's speech at the ASU National Congress, Cairo Radio 23 July 1968.

71. ibid.

72. On Nasser's visit to Moscow in July 1968, the official communiqué in *Pravda*, 11 July 1968; see also *Daily Telegraph*, 2 July 1968, *Neue Zürcher Zeitung*, 8 July 1968.

73. On the Yugoslav attitude to the presence of the American and Soviet fleets in the Mediterranean see *Za Rubezhom*, 1968, 5, quoting *Vjesnik; Le Monde*, 13 April 1968; *Cumhuriyet*, 18 April 1968; *Guardian*, 25 July 1968.

74. *Guardian*, 5 July 1968.

75. Laqueur, W., *The Road to War*, 183.

76. Vera Ketlinskaia in *Znamia*, March 1968.

77. *New York Times*, 16 May 1968.

78. *The Times*, 25 April 1968; *New York Times*, 22 October 1968.

79. For instance, Repin, A., in *Novoe Vremia*, 5 July 1968.

80. Laqueur, W., *The Soviet Union and the Middle East*, New York, 1959, 247–8.

81. Plishevsky, I., in *World Marxist Review*, July 1961; also *Noveishaia Istoriya Stran Azii i Afriki* (Moscow, 1965), 399, 441; a summary of Soviet attitudes to the union in *Mizan Newsletter*, January 1966, 29 et seq.

82. *Izvestia*, 10 October 1961.

83. Mirsky, G. I., *Arabskie Narody prodolzhaiut Borbu*, Moscow, 1965, 74 et seq.

84. On the history of the Ba'th see *Nidal al Ba'th*, Beirut, 1963–5; Jaber, Kamel S. Abu, *The Arab Ba'th Socialist Party*, New York, 1966; Saab, Edouard, *La Syrie ou la révolution dans la rancoeur*, Paris, 1968; Torrey, Gordon H., *Syrian Politics and Military*, Columbus, Ohio, 1964; Ben-Tzur, Avraham, 'The Neo-Ba'th Party of Syria' in *Journal of Contemporary History*, July 1968.

85. Mirsky, G., in *New Times*, 1963, 34.

86. *Pravda*, 12 March 1963; Vishnevski in *Izvestia*, 7 June, 20 July 1963.

87. Moscow Radio, 11 April 1963.

88. Primakov in *Pravda*, 14 November 1965; *Pravda*, 26 February 1965; Demchenko in *Pravda*, 28 January 1965.

89. Muliukov, Seiful, Moscow Radio, 26 February 1965.

90. *Izvestia*, 20 February 1965.

91. as-Samadin, Zahir Abd, in *World Marxist Review*, July 1964.

92. Shimmel, N., in *New Times*, 1966, 6.

93. Vishnevetsky in *Izvestia*, 14 March 1966; Primakov in *Pravda* 18 March 1966.

94. *Nidal: Al Shaab*, early April 1966, quoted in *Information Bulletin*, 8 July, 1966; *Al Akhbar*, 17 January 1967; see also Bakdash, K., in *World Marxist Review*, December 1965.

95. *Al Anwar*, 5 February 1965; *Al Jaridah*, 20 February 1965; *Al Hayah*, 20 February 1965.

96. *Al Nahar*, 13 April 1966; *New York Times*, 14 April 1966; Novosti news agency quoted in *Al Anwar*, 21 April 1966; *Al Hayah*, 23 April 1966.

97. *Al Hayat*, 29 May 1966, quoted in *Arab World*, 30 May 1966.

98. Beliaev and Primakov in *Pravda*, 2 June 1966; Medvedko, L., in *International Life* (Moscow), July 1966; Demchenko, P., in *New Times*, 30, 1966.

99. *Al Thawra* (Damascus), 30 October 1964.

100. *Al Hayat*, 1 June 1966.

101. On Zu'ayin's trip to Moscow and the Euphrates dam project: *Arab World*, 19, 25, 26, 27 April 1966; Moscow Radio, 19, 25 April 1966; joint communiqué, Tass, 20, 23, April 1966; *Al Thawra*, 24, 26 April 1966; *Al Ba'th*, 23, 25, 26 April; *Mideast Mirror*, 23, 30 April 1966; Damascus Radio, 30 April 1966.

102. *The Arab World*, 30 May 1966.

103. ibid., 29 April 1966.

104. Tuganova, O., in *Izvestia*, 3 September 1966; *Le Monde*, quoted in *Atlas*, September 1966, 43–4.

105. *Al Ahrar* (Beirut), 23 April 1966.

106. *Pravda*, 21 January, 12 February 1967.

107. Moscow Radio, 27 May 1966.

108. See Laqueur, *The Road to War*, 71–108.

109. *Izvestia*, 28 March 1968.

110. Medvedko in *Pravda*, 16 April 1968.

111. Quoted in *International Affairs*, May 1967, 115.

112. On communism in Iraq, 1958–61, see *Middle East Record*, 1960, 239–44; 1961, 266–76.

113. Aziz el Haj in *World Marxist Review*, November 1963, 36 et seq.

114. Including *Ittihad al Sha'ab, Sawt al Ahrar, Al Shabibah, Al Insaniyah, Al Hadara, Al Siyasi al Jedid, Al Thabat*, and others. Some of them were temporarily closed down even before October 1960; a few continued sporadically during the first half of 1961.

115. On the purge of the Journalists Union see *Iraq Times*, 3 March, 2 June 1961 and *Al Zaman*, 2 and 4 June 1961.

116. *Pravda*, 25 October 1961.

117. *Iraq Times*, 23 December 1960; *Al Fajr al Jadid*, 22 December 1960.

118. Grishin press conference, Baghdad Radio, 14 March 1960.

119. *New York Times*, 8 May 1960.

120. Moscow Radio, 14 July 1960.

121. *Izvestia*, 16 April 1960.

122. *Al Bilad*, 1 April 1960.

123. Donskoy, P., in *Aziia i Afrika sevodnia*, July 1961.

124. ibid., March 1961; Andreev, Y., in *Voprosy Vostokovedeniia*, January 1961.

125. For Soviet views on the Kurdish campaigns and the Kurdish problem in general, Demchenko, P., *Irakskii Kurdistan v ogne*, Moscow, 1963; Kamel, M. A., *Natsionalno-osvobozhditelnoe dvizhenie v Irakskom Kurdistane*, Baku, 1967.

126. *Middle East Review*, 21 October 1961.

127. *World Marxist Review*, 21 October 1961.

128. Radio Peyk-e Iran, 21 October 1961.

129. Jabar, Ali, in *Al Waqt*, 1962, 8, quoted in *Neue Zürcher Zeitung*, 10 January 1962.

130. Demchenko, Pavel, *Irakskii Kurdistan v ogne*, 3–5.

131. ibid., 60.

132. Demchenko, P., in *New Times*, 1966, 7, 18.

133. Primakov, E., in *Pravda*, 18 January 1967.

134. Pogodina, I., ibid., 6 July 1966; Potomov, Yu., ibid., 2 February 1966.

135. Seiful-Mulyukov, F., in *New Times*, 1966, 28, 20.

136. Voice of the Iraqi People, 20 September 1966, quoting *Regay-e Kurdistan*, July, 1966.

137. Voice of the Iraqi People, 23 March 1967.

138. See, for instance, *Regay-e Kurdistan*, July 1966; *Tariq al Shab*, February 1967; quoted in Voice of the Iraqi People, 24 February 1967.

139. *Pravda*, 25 February 1963.

140. *Neue Zürcher Zeitung*, 12 April 1963.

141. *Al Jamahir*, 21 February 1963.

142. *Pravda*, 21 December 1963.

143. ibid., 18 July 1964.

144. Primakov in ibid., 13 July 1964.

145. Voice of the Iraqi People, 21 June, 6 July 1966.

146. Resolution of the Central Committee of the Iraqi Communist party (August 1966), Voice of the Iraqi People, 29 September 1966.

147. ibid.

148. Stupak, A., in *Izvestia*, 13 July 1968.

149. *Problemy Mira i Sotsializma*, July 1968, 93.

150. *Neues Deutschland*, 23 April 1967.

151. Voice of the Iraqi People, 24 and 26 February 1968.

152. Demchenko, P., in *Izvestia*, 3 August 1968.

153. Sultanov, A. F. (ed.), *Sovetsko-Arabskie Druzhestvennie otnosheniia*, Moscow, 1961, 114–17.

154. *Middle East Record*, 1961, p. 694.

155. Radio Baku, 1 November 1963.

156. Primakov in *Pravda*, 2 February 1966; Volsky in *Novoe Vremia*, 12 May, 1967.

157. *Nouvel Observateur*, 26 April, 3 May 1967.

158. *Pravda*, 19 January 1967.

159. Tass, 2 January 1968.

160. Smith, Hedrick, in *New York Times*, 15 December 1967.

161. *Economist*, 14 September 1968; for other Soviet comments on developments in the Yemen in 1967: Medvedko, L., in *Mezhdunarodnaia Zhizn*, 1968, 2; Demchenko, P., in *Aziia i Afrika Sevodnia*, 1968, 2; Volsky, D., in *Novoe Vremia*, 28 April 1967, and in *New Times*, 27 March 1968.

162. *Arab World*, 24 March, 11 April 1968; *Neue Zürcher Zeitung*, 24 February, 10 May, 8 June 1968; *New York Times*, 16 April 1968.

163. *Economist*, 27 April 1968.

164. *Pravda*, 29 November 1967.

165. Radio Peace and Progress (Moscow), 17 November 1967.

166. *Al Hayat*, 24 January 1968.

167. Radio Peace and Progress, 24 April 1968.

168. *Izvestia*, 28 March 1959.

169. *US News*, 26 December 1966; *Izvestia*, 24 December 1966.

170. *Pravda*, 3 October 1967.

171. *Taqadum* (organ of the Jordanian Communist party), February 1968, quoted in *Al Ittihad*, 8 March 1966.

172. Sontag, R. J., and Beddie, J. S. (eds.), *Nazi-Soviet Relations 1939–1941*, Washington 1948, 259.

173. Langer, W. L., *The Diplomacy of Imperialism*, New York, 1956, 752.

174. Curzon, G. N., *Persia and the Persian Question*, London, 1892, II, 456.

175. I have drawn in this section on a number of papers on the situation in the Persian Gulf submitted to conferences in England in June and September 1968, under the sponsorship of the Institute for Strategic Studies (London) and the Institute for Strategic Studies (Washington) respectively, especially those by Mr D. A. Schmidt,

Brigadier W. F. K. Thompson, Professor B. Lewis, Mr C. Tugendhat, Mr T. Stauffer, Major General J. L. Moulton, Professor P. J. Vatikiotis, and Mr Desmond Wettern.

176. Leonidov, A., in *Sovremennii Vostok*, October 1958; see also *New Times*, 1958, 43; a survey of Soviet literature on the Gulf States before 1959, in *Mizan Newsletter*, January 1959.

177. Andreasyan, Y., in *Vokrug Sveta*, April 1953.

178. Cairo Radio, 20 May 1964.

179. *Mirovaia Ekonomika i Mezhdunarodnie Otnosheniia*, February 1965, 137–8.

180. *New Times*, 1968, 11, (editorial).

181. *Novy Vostok*, Vol. 20/21, 400.

182. *Izvestia*, 29 November 1964; *Pravda*, 4 November 1964.

183. ibid., 27 May 1966.

184. *International Affairs*, March 1968, p. 44; see also Ivanov, K., in *New Times*, 1968, 8, 18.

185. Tass statement, 3 March 1968; see also *International Affairs*, March 1968, 75–6.

186. Medvedko, L., in *New Times*, 20 March 1968, 16.

187. Schmidt, loc. cit., note 173, 48.

Chapter 6

1. A Soviet writer in *International Affairs* (July 1960), quoted in *The World Today*, July 1964, 313.

2. Hartshorn, J. E., *Oil Companies and Governments*, 2nd ed., London, 1967, provides a general introduction.

3. Ebel, Robert E., *The Petroleum Industry in the Soviet Union*, Washington, 1961; Judy, Richard, *Die Bedeutung der Sowjetunion für die Weltölwirtschaft von 1960 bis 1975*, Hamburg, 1963.

4. National Petroleum Council, *Impact of Oil Exports from the Soviet Bloc*, Washington, 1962; Lubell, Harold, *The Soviet Oil Offensive and Inter-Bloc Economic Competition*, Rand Corporation paper RM 2182–PR, December 1961; Hoskins, Halford L., and Herman, Leon, *Soviet Oil in the Cold War*, Washington, 1961; Hoskins, Halford L., *Problems raised by the Soviet Oil Offensive*, Washington, 1962; *Soviet Oil in East-West Trade*, US Senate 86868, 3 July 1962, Washington, 1962; Saylor, John P., in *Congressional Record*, 18 February 1963; Dirksen, E., in ibid., 11 April 1963.

5. Huttlinger, Joseph P., in *World Petroleum*, November 1962, 52–5.

6. Hoskins and Herman, op. cit., 9.

7. Adelman, M. A. Clawson, Marion (ed.) in *Natural Resources and International Development*, Baltimore, 1964, 96.

8. *Petroleum Press Service*, November 1960.

9. Gurov, Y., in *Ekonomischeskaia Gazeta*, September 1967; *Financial Times*, 6 June 1966.

10. *Middle East Mirror*, 1 October 1960.

11. *Petroleum Press Service*, September 1960.

12. Getty, G. F., in *Washington Post*, 31 March 1963.

13. *Platt's Oilgram News Service*, 15, 28 February 1963.

14. Gurov, loc. cit.

15. *Petroleum Press Service*, June 1968.

16. *Neue Zürcher Zeitung*, 19 April 1968.

17. *Prace*, 17 May 1968.

18. Bogomolov, in *Voprosy Ekonomiki*, February 1966.

19. *Petroleum Press Service*, January 1968.

20. Hartshorn, op. cit., p. 321.

21. The literature on oil-pricing is vast and bewildering. See, for instance, Ovens, David, *Crude Oil Prices*, London, 1958; Leemen, Wayne A., *The Price of Middle Eastern Oil*, Ithaca, 1962; Issawi, Charles, and Yeganeh, M., *The Economics of Middle Eastern Oil*, New York, 1962; Frank, Helmut J., *Crude Oil Prices in the Middle East*, New York, 1966.

22. On oil concessions see Mikdashi, Zuhayr, *A Financial Analysis of Middle East Oil Concessions 1901–1950*, New York, 1965; 'Oil in the Persian Gulf', in *The World Today*, July 1964.

23. Barran, D. H., in *Petroleum Press Service*, July 1964.

24. Andreev, Yu. N., in *Problemy Vostokovedeniia*, January 1961.

25. 'Problems and Objectives of Energy Policy', in *OECD Observer*, October 1966.

26. European Coal and Steel Community, *Annual Report, 1967*, Statistical Appendix, Table 13.

27. Adelman, M. A., *Security of Eastern Hemisphere Fuel Supply*, MIT Working Paper 6, Department of Economics, December 1967.

28. *Europe's Need for Oil*, OEEC Publication, Document C (57) 234, January 1958, 39.

29. ibid., 42.

30. *Neue Zürcher Zeitung*, 19 August 1967.

31. Hartshorn, J. E., 'Oil and the Middle East War' in *The World Today*, April 1968, 155.

32. Tugendhat, Christopher, in an unpublished paper on 'Oil in the Persian Gulf', July 1968.

33. OECD estimates, *Petroleum Press Service*, March 1968, 83.

34. Adelman, M. A., loc. cit., 7; see also *Petroleum Press Service*, January 1968, 3.

35. ibid., November 1967.

36. ibid., May 1968.

37. Wasowski, Stanislaw, *The Fuel Situation in Eastern Europe*, Research Paper 366 (September 1967), Institute of Defense Analysis (Washington, 1967), 18–24.

38. Albinowski, Stanislaw, in *Polityka* (Warsaw), 24 September 1966; see also *Independent Petroleum Monthly*, February 1967, and B. Rachkov, in *The New Middle East*, May 1969.

39. Wasowski, loc. cit., 34; see also Dudinsky, I., in *Voprosy Ekonomiki*, May 1966.

40. Wasowski, loc. cit., 49.

41. El Salloum, Abdel Wahab, *The Problems of Oil in Iraq*, published by the Permanent Secretariat of the Organization for Afro-Asian Peoples Solidarity, Cairo, n.d.

42. Medvedko, L., in *Pravda*, 6 March 1967.

43. Voice of the Iraqi people, 13 April 1967.

44. ibid.

45. See, for instance, Ascher, Konstantin, in *Deutsche Aussenpolitik* (East Berlin), June 1968.

46. Gurov, Y., in *Ekonomicheskaia Gazeta*; quoted in *Soviet News* (London), October 10, 1967.

47. *Petroleum Press Service*, February 1968.

48. *New York Times*, 31 December 1967.

49. ibid., 5 May 1968, 31 December 1967.

50. *Petroleum Press Service*, February 1968.

51. *New York Times*, 8 January 1968.

Chapter 7

1. Quoted in Kocharian, in *Sovremennii Vostok*, July 1959, 4. For Soviet trade and aid to underdeveloped countries see Berliner, Joseph S., *Soviet Economic Aid*, New York, 1958; *The Sino-Soviet Economic Offensive in the Less Developed Countries*, Department of State Publications 6632, May 1958; Goldman, Marshall I., *Soviet Foreign Aid*, New York, 1967; Müller, Kurt, *Über Kalkutta nach Paris?*, Hanover, 1965; US Congress Joint Economic Committee, *New Directions in the Soviet Economy*, Part IV; 'The World Outside: Soviet Foreign Aid to the Less Developed Countries', by Leon Tansky, Washington, 1966.

2. Rymalov, V., in *International Affairs*, September 1959, 24.

3. Merkulov, V., in *Vneshnaia Torgovlia*, April 1968.

4. Smirnov, V., and Matiuchin, I., in *Vneshnaia Torgovlia*, January 1968.

5. Tansky, loc.cit., 951–3.

6. Department of State Research Memorandum RSB-80, 21 July 1967; *Communist Governments and Developing Nations: Economic Aid and Trade*.

7. Sutton, John L., and Kemp, G., *Arms to Developing Countries*, Institute for Strategic Studies Paper No. 28, October 1966.

8. OECD, *The Flow of Financial Resources to Developing Countries in 1961*, Paris, 1963.

9. Tansky, loc. cit., 969.

Chapter 8

1. Laqueur, W., and Labedz, L., 'On Thermonuclear Coexistence', *Survey*, October 1961. The best introduction to the subject is Wolfe, Thomas W., *Soviet Strategy at the Crossroads*, Cambridge, Mass., 1964.

2. Gasteyger, Curt, 'Modern Warfare and Soviet Strategy' in *Survey*, October 1965, 46.

3. Kolkowicz, Roman, *The Dilemma of Superpower; Soviet Policy and Strategy in Transition*, IDA Research Paper P-383, Washington, 1967; see also Wolfe, Thomas W., *The Soviet Military Scene: Institutional and Defense Policy Consideration*, Rand Corporation Paper RM-4913-PR, 1966.

4. Kolkowicz, op. cit., 12–13.

5. Wolfe, Thomas W., 'Soviet Military Policy' in *Current History*, October 1967, quoted from *Survival*, January 1968, 4.

6. *The Economist*, 6 July 1968.

7. Jonas, Ann M., in *Air Force Magazine*, January 1968.

8. *Strategic Survey 1967*, published by the Institute for Strategic Studies, London, 1968, 25.

9. 'Additional Dimensions of Soviet Strategy', in *Air Force Magazine*, February 1968.

10. Gorshkov, Admiral, quoted in Wolfe, Thomas W., *The Soviet Quest for More Globally Mobile Military Power*, Rand Corporation Memorandum RM-5554-PR, December 1967, 8.

11. ibid.

12. Herrick, Robert Waring, *Soviet Naval Strategy*, Annapolis, 1968, chapter 4.

13. Murphy, F. M., 'The Soviet Navy in the Mediterranean', in *US Naval Institute Proceedings*, March 1967, 39–44; see also Mason, Ph.,

and Couhat, J. Labayle, '*La Présence Navale Sovietique en Méditerranée*' in *Revue de Défense Nationale*, May 1968, 858–73.

14. In *Kommunist Vooruzhonikh Sil*, July 1963.

15. Gorshkov's article in *Morskoi Sbornik*, Moscow, 1967.

16. Cleveland, Harlan speech at the National Press Club, Washington, DC, on 23 August 1967, 'The Resurrection of NATO'.

17. Kelly, Orr, in *Evening Star* (Washington), 22 June 1967.

18. Martin, Laurence, in *Spectator* (London), 10 May 1968 and 4 October 1968.

19. *US News and World Report*, 11 December 1967.

20. *Der Spiegel*, 1968, 20.

21. Herrick, R. W., op. cit. pp. 154–55; on the Soviet Mediterranean '*Eskadra*' see also Gasteyger, Curt in *Foreign Affairs*, July 1968; Griswold, L. (ed.), *Background for Tomorrow*, 21 August 1967; *Jane's Fighting Ships, 1967–8*, introd.

22. *The Economist*, 18 May 1968.

23. *Christian Science Monitor*, 12 July 1967.

24. *Borba*, 17 February 1968.

25. *Unità*, 21 May 1968.

26. *Internationale Politik* (Belgrade), 5 April 1968.

27. ibid., 5 March 1968.

28. *Le Monde*, 6 June 1967.

29. Welles, Benjamin, in *New York Times*, 17 April 1968.

30. *Revue de Défense Nationale*, January 1968.

31. *Christian Science Monitor*, 27 May 1968.

32. Ferron, James, in *New York Times*, 23 October 1967.

33. Mackintosh, Malcolm, in *The World Today*, April 1968, 150.

34. *Kommunist*, January 1968.

35. McNamara's statement to Senate Armed Services Committee, 1 February 1968: *Strategic Survey*, 1967, 22; Long, John, *The Soviet Armed Forces in the 1970s: Daily Information Bulletin* (Radio Liberty), 2 May 1968.

Chapter 9

1. For the history of the TPI in the nineteen-fifties see *The Evolution of Communism in Iran*, Tehran, 1959.

2. Eskandari, Iradig, in *World Marxist Review*, May 1965, 54–5.

3. Radio Iran Courier, 3 January 1966; see also 'Statement of the CC People's Party of Iran on the activities of the splinter group', December 1965, in *Information Bulletin*, 31 March 1966.

4. *Kayhan International* (Tehran), 24 June 1965.

5. Karpat, Kemal H., 'Socialism and the Labour Party of Turkey' in *Middle East Journal*, spring 1967.

6. Article in *Aksam* quoted in *The Times*, 12 July 1968.

7. Ankara Radio, 21 August 1968.

8. *Kommunist*, No. 11, July 1967; *Pravda* 8 August 1967.

9. Sneh, Moshe, in *Kol Ha'am*, 25 June 1967; see also *Information Bulletin* of both Maki and Rakah, 1966–7; *Kol Ha'am*, 12 November 1967.

10. *Rakah Information Bulletin*, August 1967; *Maki Information Bulletin*, December 1967; *Al Ittihad*, 27 October 1967.

11. Nassar, Fuad, in *Voprosy Istorii KPSS*, 1967, 2, 23.

12. *Kommunist*, 1959, 12; *Iraqi Review*, 6 September 1958.

13. Uri Dann's book, *Iraq under Kassem* (New York, 1969), provides the fullest analysis of this subject.

14. Shevliagin, in *Sovetskaia Rossiia*, 10 June 1960.

15. Muliukov, Seiful, in *Trud*, 26 September 1963.

16. Voice of the Iraqi People, 6 January 1968.

17. ibid., 30 September 1967; *World Marxist Review*, April 1968, 41.

18. *Tariq al Sha'b*, February 1967.

19. *Ila al Amam* (Beirut), 10 September 1967; also Marjan, Badr, and Nimr, Nasib, ibid., 3 September 1967.

20. This is part of a polemic against a report by Bakdash on the August 1967 conference of the Central Committee of the Syrian party, published in *Nidal al Sha'b*.

21. Nimr, Nasib, in *Ila al Amam*, 10 September 1967.

22. *Al Siad* (Beirut), 12 December 1967.

23. *Al Nahar*, 5 April 1967; *Al Hayat*, 7 April 1967; Faysal, Yusuf, at the SED Congress, Voice of the Iraqi People, 6 May 1967.

24. Spano, V., in *Unità*, 5 December 1967; Berner, Wolfgang, *Die KP Italiens und die aegyptischen Kommunisten 1956–58* (*Berichte des Bundesinstituts für ostwissenschaftliche und internationale Studien*, No. 28, 1967); Berner, Wolfgang, '*Nasser und die Kommunisten*' in *Europa Archiv*, 1965, 15; Malek, Anwar Abdel, *Egypte, Société Militaire*, Paris, 1962.

25. Barat, M., in *France Observateur*, 8 January 1959.

26. *Al Ahram*, 29 January 1965.

27. *Al Gumhuriya*, 10 January 1966.

28. See *Al Tali'a*, August, November, December 1967, *passim*.

29. A communist account of the events of 1965 is provided by Abdallah, H., in *World Marxist Review*, February 1966.

30. Tanjug, 11 March 1965.

31. *Unità*, 30 June 1964.

32. *Economist*, 1 June 1969.

33. Lowenthal, R., in *Survey*, January 1966, 46–7.

34. For accounts of the changes in Soviet attitudes on this subject see Ra'anan, U., in *Problems of Communism*, January 1965; Lowenthal, R., in *Survey*, April 1963; Kanet, Roger E., in *Russian Review*, January 1968; Yellon, R. A., in *Mizan*, March and July 1967.

35. Lowenthal, R. (ed.), in *Entwicklungsländer zwischen nationaler und kommunistischer Revolution*, Hanover, 1965, 16–17.

36. Ra'anan, U., loc. cit., 23.

37. ibid.

38. Lowenthal, R., *Entwicklungsländer* . . . p. 17.

39. Mirsky, G., in *New Times*, 1964, 18.

40. Ivanov, K., 'National Liberation Movement', *International Affairs*, 1965, 5, 65.

41. Tiagunenko, V., in *Mirovaia ekonomika i mezhdunarodnie otnosheniia*, 1965, 8, 85.

42. See the contribution by Avakov, R., in the discussion on 'Socialism, Capitalism and the Underdeveloped Countries', in *Mirovaia Ekonomika i mezhdunarodnie otnosheniia*, 1964, 4 and 6; English abridged version – special issue of *Mizan Newsletter*, November 1964.

43. Ulianovsky, R., in *Kommunist*, 1966, 1.

44. Brutents, K., in *Kommunist*, 1964, 17; 'At the Cairo Seminar', *World Marxist Review*, 1967; see also note 42 and the literature quoted in Ra'anan, Yellon and Kanet, loc. cit.

45. 'The Ebb Tide?' in *Mizan*, September 1966.

46. Mirsky, G., in *Pravda*, 31 January 1965; Ulianovsky, R., ibid., 15 April 1966; Yellon, loc. cit., 168.

47. Bakdash, Khalid, in *World Marxist Review*, July 1964 and December 1965; Sawaja, in ibid., February 1964.

48. Nassar, Fuad, in *World Marxist Review*, September 1966.

49. Shawi, Nicola, in ibid., July 1966.

50. Voice of the Iraqi People, 5 July 1966.

51. Reports on these meetings were published in *Foreign Report*, 14 January and 24 June 1965; Voice of the Iraqi People, 1 June 1967, and *Al Nahar*, 21 November 1967. The authenticity of these reports cannot always be taken for granted.

52. *Al Akhbar*, quoted in *The Arab World*, 8 August 1968.

Bibliography

Bibliography

The most important single source used is the *Mizan Newsletter*. Since its publication in 1959 under the editorship of Colonel Geoffrey Wheeler and later of David Morison, it has been invaluable to all students of the Middle East and of Soviet policies in that part of the world.

Unpublished Sources

I have read with profit the doctoral dissertations of John H. Burnett and Oles Smolanski on Soviet policy in the Middle East in the nineteen-fifties; Mr John Baker's substantial and stimulating paper on Soviet policies in the Middle East (Harvard, 1968); Professor John Armstrong's essay on the same topic; Professor Uri Ra'anan on the background and the wider implications of the arms deal of 1955; Professor Adelman, Dr St Wasowski, and C. Tugendhat on oil policy; Thomas Wolfe and Roman Kolkowicz on strategic problems; Hans Bräker on Islam and Communism; Wolfgang Berner on communism in Egypt; Joseph G. Whelan on The Soviet Union and the Middle East; Messrs Desmond Wettern, Standish, Brigadier W. F. K. Thompson, Professor Vatikiotis, Major-General J. L. Moulton, and Mr D. A. Schmidt on the Persian Gulf.

Books

The essential literature used in the writing of the present study is quoted in the notes (pp. 228–45). The following list includes books that were referred to only on one or two occasions or not at all, but are nevertheless of relevance for the study of the subject.

Al Aqqad, Abbas Mahmud, *Ash Shuyu'iya wa'l Islam*, Cairo, 1959.
Al Fakiki, Abd Al Hadi, *Ash Shuyu'iya wa'l qaumiya al Arabiya*, Beirut, 1963.

Al Gundi, Anam, *Ila aina yasir ash Shuyu'iya bi'l Iraq?*, Beirut, 1959.

Al Munajjid, Salah, *La Bolchevisation de l'Islam chez les Marxistes et les Socialistes Arabes*, Beirut, 1967.

Alekseev, L., *Sovetski Soiuz i Iran*, Moscow, 1963.

Alitovsky, S. N., *Agrarny vopros v sovremennom Irake*, Moscow, 1966.

Andreasian, R. N., and Elyanov, A. Y., *Blizhnii Vostok; Neft i nezavisimost*, Moscow, 1961.

Ash Shuyu'iya al yaum wa radan, Cairo, n.d.

Badi, S. M., *Rabochiy Klass Irana*, Moscow, 1965.

—*Agrarniye otnosheniia v sovremennom Irane*, Moscow, 1959.

Baskin, V. S., *Neftianie monopolii na Blizhnem i Srednem Vostoke*, Moscow, 1957.

Beliaev, I. P., *Amerikanskii imperializm v Saudovskoi Arabii*, Moscow, 1957.

Binder, Leonard, *The Ideological Revolution in the Middle East*, New York, 1964.

Black, Cyril E., and Thornton, Thomas P. (eds.), *Communism and Revolution: the Strategic uses of Violence*, Princeton, 1964.

Bolton, A., *Soviet Middle East Studies* (annotated bibliography), London: Central Asian Research Centre for the Royal Institute of International Affairs, 1959.

Cremeans, Charles D., *The Arabs and the World*, New York, 1963.

Dantsig, B. M., *Irak v proshlom i nastoiashchem*, Moscow, 1960.

Demchenko, P. Y., *Kurdistan v ogne*, Moscow, 1963.

Druza, Al Hukm, *Ash Shuyu'iya al mahalliya wa maraka al Arab. al qaumiya*, Beirut, 1963.

Ellis, Harry B., *Challenge in the Middle East: Communist Influence and American Policy*, New York, 1960.

Fisher, S. N., *The Military in the Middle East and Problems in Society and Government*, Ohio State University Press, 1963.

Gasratian, M. A., *Turtsia v 1960–1963 godakh: ocherk vnutrennei politiki*, Moscow, 1965.

—and Moiseev, P., *Turtsia zhdiot peremien*, Moscow, 1963.

Gataullin, M. F., *Ekonomika O A R na novom puti*, Moscow, 1963.

Imhoff, Christoph von, *Duell im Mittelmeer, Moskau greift nach dem Nahen und Mittleren Osten*, Freiburg, 1967.

Issawi, Charles, *Egypt in Revolution, an Economic Analysis*, London, 1963.

Jaber, Kamel S. Abu, *The Arab Ba'th Socialist Party, History, Ideology, and Organization*, Syracuse, 1966.

Kotlov, L. N., *Iordania v noveisheie vremia*, Moscow, 1962.

Labib, Fahri, and Mustaqawi, Mahmud Al, *Al Itihad al Suvyati wa Misr al Mustaqilla*, Cairo, 1957.

Laqueur, Walter, *Communism and Nationalism in the Middle East*, London, 1956.

—*The Soviet Union and the Middle East*, London, 1959.

Lebedev, Ye. A. (ed.), *Sovremennaia Iordania (Spravochnik)*, Moscow, 1964.

Malek, Anwar Abdel, *Egypte, Société Militaire*, Paris, 1962.

Maliukovsky, M. V., and others (ed.), *Sovremennyi Irak (Spravochnik)*, Moscow, 1966.

Marqas, Ilyas, *Tarikh al ahzab ash Shuyu'i al Arabi*, Beirut, 1964.

—*Al Marksiya fi asrina*, Beirut, 1965.

Meyer-Ranke, Peter, *Der Rote Pharao*, Hamburg, 1964.

'The Middle East and the Arab World', Adelphi Paper No. 20, London: Institute for Strategic Studies, July 1965.

Miovanov, I. V., and Seiful-Muliukov, F. M., *Irak vchera i sevodnia*, Moscow, 1959.

Muhsin, Mahdi, *Die geistigen und sozialen Wandlungen im Nahen Osten*, Freiburg, 1967.

Nasim, Mahir, *Ash Shuyu'iya wa'l Sahyuniya*, Cairo, 1959.

Paliukaitis, I. I., *Ekonomicheskoe razvitie Irana*, Moscow, 1965.

Pegov, S. S., and Alitovsky, S. N., *Irak* ,Moscow, 1966.

Proshin, N. I., *Saudovskaya Aravia (Istoriko-ekonomicheskii ocherk)*, Moscow, 1964.

Qalugi, Qadir, *Tagriba arabi fi'l Hizb Ash Shuyu'i*, Beirut, 1960.

Ruindezh, D. B., *Borba Irakskovo naroda protiv Bagdadskovo pakta (1954–1959)*, Baku, 1966.

Sager, Peter, *Kairo und Moskau in Arabien*, Berne, 1967.

Said, Zaki Hairi, *Al Mitaq al watani wa'n nizam ad dahili li'l Hizb Ash Shuyu'i al Iraqi*, Baghdad, 1960.

Saint-Marie, François de, *Irak Rouge? Kassem entre Moscou et le Caire*, Paris, 1960.

Seiful-Muliukov, F. M., *Irak v borbe za nezavisimost i progress*, Moscow, 1959.

Shamsutdinov, A. M., (ed.), *Problemy sovremennoy Turtsii*, Moscow, 1963.

SSSR i Arabskie Strani (published by the Soviet Ministry of Foreign Affairs, Moscow, 1960).

Sultanov, A. F. (ed.), *Sovetsko-Arabskie druzhestvennie ostnosheniia*, Moscow, 1961.

Tuganova, O. E., *Mezhdunarodnie Otnosheniia na blizhnem i srednem Vostoke*, Moscow, 1967.

Ule, Wolfgang, *Bibliographie zu Fragen des Arabischen Sozialismus, des Nationalismus und des Kommunismus unter dem Gesichtspunkt des Islams*, Hamburg, 1967.

Vatikiotis, P. J., *The Egyptian Army in Politics: Pattern for new Nations*, Bloomington, 1961.

Vatolina, L. N., *Ekonomika obedinionnoi Arabskoi Respubliki*, Moscow, 1962.

Vdovichenko, D. I., *Natsionalnaya burzhuazia Turtsii*, Moscow, 1962.

Vernier, Bernard, *L'Irak d'aujourd'hui*, Paris, 1963.

Vocke, Harald, *Das Schwert und die Sterne. Ein Ritt durch den Jemen*, Stuttgart, 1965.

La voie Egyptienne vers le socialisme, Cairo, 1966.

Westen, Klaus, *Der Staat der nationalen Demokratie: Ein kommunistisches Modell für Entwicklungsländer*, Cologne, 1964.

Zvereva, L. S., *Kuwait*, Moscow, 1964.

Index

Index

More about Penguins
and Pelicans

Penguinews, which appears every month, contains details of all the new books issued by Penguins as they are published. From time to time it is supplemented by *Penguins in Print*, which is a complete list of all available books published by Penguins. (There are well over three thousand of these.)

A specimen copy of *Penguinews* will be sent to you free on request, and you can become a subscriber for the price of the postage. For a year's issues (including the complete lists) please send 30p if you live in the United Kingdom, or 60p if you live elsewhere. Just write to Dept EP, Penguin Books Ltd, Harmondsworth, Middlesex, enclosing a cheque or postal order, and your name will be added to the mailing list.

Note: *Penguinews* and *Penguins in Print* are not available in the U.S.A. or Canada

Also by Walter Laqueur

The Road to War

This is a well-documented account of the main milestones on
the road that led to the Six Day War – and beyond. Walter
Laqueur concentrates on those weeks of mounting tension and
feverish diplomacy which preceded the outbreak of war, but he
also analyses the underlying cause of the war – the clash of
rival and irreconcilable nationalisms. He paints a surprising
picture of the Middle East and world opinion: of the Arab
nations torn by internal dissension and whipped into a
war-frenzy by decades of irresponsible propaganda – yet
stumbling unprepared into the long-awaited conflict; of an
Israeli government which was unready and confused; and, on
the sidelines, of Russia and America, two impotent
super-powers outpaced by events and unable to restrain their
protégés. And in a chapter written specially for this Pelican
edition he brings the story of Middle-Eastern conflict
up to date.

Europe since Hitler

'There were parades, laughter and dancing in the streets all over Europe on Victory Day, but on the morning after, Europeans began to take stock of the consequences of the war.'

Thus Professor Laqueur sets the scene for his masterly survey of the history of our times – the first of its kind. He traces the political developments, the economic and social trends and the cultural movements in Europe since the end of the Second World War, ending his narrative with the Czech crisis of 1968.

This is a history which demonstrates in authoritative detail that, far from 'dying in convulsions' (as Sartre and others predicted), post-war Europe has found a new vigour which has astonished friends and foes alike.

'The author's range is impressive, he writes well and his views are sensible' – *Economist*

'Professor Laqueur, like General de Gaulle, sees his Europe as stretching from the Atlantic to the Urals, and gives as much attention to the affairs of the Soviet bloc as to those of the countries west and south of the iron curtain' – Max Beloff in the *Spectator*